The Anxiety Cure

An Eight-Step Program for Getting Well

Robert L. DuPont, M.D.

Elizabeth DuPont Spencer, M.S.W.

Caroline M. DuPont, M.D.

John Wiley & Sons, Inc.

New York · Chichester · Weinheim · Brisbane · Singapore · Toronto

This book is dedicated to our spouses,
Helen, Spence, and Paul.
You are our strongest allies,
our unfailing supporters,
and our best friends.

The information contained in this book is not intended to serve as a replacement for professional medical advice. Any use of the information in this book is at the reader's discretion. The author and publisher specifically disclaim any and all liability arising directly or indirectly from the use or application of any information contained in this book. A health care professional should be consulted regarding your specific situation.

Library of Congress Cataloging-in-Publication Data:
DuPont, Robert L.
    The anxiety cure : an eight-step program for getting well / Robert
L. DuPont, Elizabeth DuPont Spencer, Caroline M. DuPont.
      p. cm.
    Includes bibliographical references.
    ISBN 0-471-24701-4 (paper : alk. paper)
    1. Anxiety—Treatment.   2. Anxiety—Popular Works.   I. Spencer,
Elizabeth DuPont.   II. DuPont, Caroline M.
III. Title.
RC531.D87   1998
616.85'2230651—dc21   97-44043

Printed in the United States of America
10 9 8 7 6 5 4 3 2 1

CONTENTS

PART THREE: Helping the Anxious Person

PART FOUR: The Anxiety Cure: Eight Steps to Getting Well

CONTENTS

PART ONE: What Is the Anxiety Cure?

PART TWO: The Basics of Anxiety

PART FIVE: Anxiety and Your Daily Life

PART SIX: Anxiety over the Life Span

PART SEVEN: Maintenance

FOREWORD

Welcome to *The Anxiety Cure*, a warm, wise, and thoroughly wonderful book for people with anxiety disorders and for everyone who cares about them. As a clinician, educator, and patient advocate, and having overcome my own debilitating height phobia, I know firsthand the importance of offering those who suffer from an anxiety disorder accurate, up-to-date, and inspirational information. This book clearly accomplishes this while also outlining roles for family members and welcoming them into the healing process, should they care to participate. Friends and family members involved with someone who is actively seeking treatment for an anxiety disorder, as well as one who is reluctant to try to get better, will find help in this book.

This is a book about which I care a great deal. Its warm tone, caring message of hope, and its clear path to getting well will bring lifesaving help to individuals and families in all parts of the country. This book will help you make the best use of modern medicines and of the new nonpharmacological treatments for anxiety disorders. Using the eight steps detailed in this book you will cover all the important paths to finding your road to recovery. Among other things, you will learn ways to cope with anxiety, evaluate your need for medication and therapy, and recruit your own support person to help you on your journey to win your own "anxiety cure."

Let me introduce the team of authors: a father and his two daughters, each a mental health professional specializing in the treatment of anxiety disorders. Bob and Caroline are psychiatrists and Elizabeth is a clinical social worker. This book is the culmination of a dream of sharing their family story and their new treatment techniques for anxiety. They work together in Rockville, Maryland, as researchers and treatment providers. While not listed as an author, the fourth member of this family team, Bob's wife and Caroline and Elizabeth's mother, Helen, is an important part of this story, too, since she runs the family and also manages their practice and their research.

The authors came to this work through their own family's confrontation with anxiety. Their initial recognition of the problem and their determined efforts to find effective ways to overcome handicapping anxiety are the driving force behind *The Anxiety Cure*. The authors share their own and other anxiety sufferers' hard-won knowledge as they show you both the pains of the anxiety disorders and the joys of release. They make anxiety understandable and ultimately manageable by characterizing panic as a "dragon." They show you how the dragon gets his influence over you so that you can tame him, rather than cowering from his terrifying displays of power.

Bob and I met when we teamed up to create the Phobia Program of Washington in 1978. Over the next five years the Phobia Program grew to have active treatment centers in six East Coast cities, treating in that brief time over ten thousand patients suffering from an anxiety disorder. We also teamed up to found the Phobia Society of America (PSA) in 1980. Bob served as its first president. Later, PSA became the Anxiety Disorders Association of America (ADAA), of which I have served as president for more than a decade.

I first met Caroline and Elizabeth when they were in elementary school, and as a family friend and Bob's professional alter ego, I shared their growing up and their educations. I experienced with them Caroline's early anxiety problems and her eventual mastery of her anxiety. I came to have a special relationship with her as we traveled together speaking about anxiety disorders in children, a serious and largely untreated problem that is still underappreciated by most anxiety experts and by parents, teachers, and pediatricians. Caroline has a fabulous gift not only for telling her story but also for bringing others, including children, to an understanding of the problem of clinically significant anxiety and what to do about it, a skill that she has carried into her professional career. Elizabeth brings with her a practical, optimistic, can-do approach with an incredible amount of empathy for those suffering from anxiety disorders. These are special young women who have great gifts as therapists, teachers, and writers.

As you work toward overcoming your anxiety problem, I hope you will turn to ADAA and to other local and national organizations that are devoted to helping people with anxiety disorders. These organizations, which are listed at the end of this book, can provide you with additional information and resources, as well as helpful networking opportunities.

Get ready for an adventure with these three to guide your travels through this book. It is an unforgettable trip with a priceless reward at the end: freedom from the prison of anxiety.

—JERILYN ROSS, M.A., L.I.C.S.W.

PREFACE

We want you to be comfortable with this book and the help it offers you, whether you have an anxiety disorder yourself or are concerned about someone else who suffers from one of these common, painful, and sometimes crippling problems.

Take your time reading this book. If you get too anxious, put the book down for a while and pick it up later. You can also share the book with someone you care about. The reading may be easier when it can be shared and you can discuss your concerns.

This is a book with new ideas based on the experience of hundreds of therapists and physicians over thirty years who have developed and used these ideas.

We the authors have helped thousands of people with anxiety disorders get well. We want you to know, right at the beginning, that you can regain control of your life. Fan that spark of hope of recovery you may have thought went out, perhaps years ago.

We are mental health professionals who treat anxious people, as well as their friends and family, in our clinical practices. This book begins with our family story of anxiety.

The stories we tell usually have happy endings. For some people, it may be easier to read the stories than to read the text when you are feeling anxious. Come back when you're feeling calmer. Do whatever is easiest for you to manage. There is no wrong way to use this book.

We would enjoy hearing about your reactions to *The Anxiety Cure*. You can reach us at our private psychiatric practice in Rockville, Maryland.

DuPont Associates, P.A.
6191 Executive Boulevard
Rockville, MD 20852
301-231-9010

ACKNOWLEDGMENTS

We would not have been able to write this book without the generous help of our colleagues, friends, and family. They continued to motivate us and inspire us with their confidence and enthusiasm throughout the five years it took to write this book.

We especially want to thank our editor, Thomas Miller. Without his hard work and vision, this book would not exist. We also thank Patricia Carson, our administrative helper, who gracefully struggled through the edits of three authors.

For help with editing, we thank Benjamin Hamilton, Shelly Perron, Kathryn McKay, Jill Carlson, William Spink, Paul Carroll, and Helen DuPont. Thanks to Michele Barrett and Kimberly Hans for help with charts and tables. Thanks to Janice Carroll for the fierce dragon illustration.

Thanks to the kids, Robert and David, for knowing when we could not play because we were working, and for playing with us when we were available.

We acknowledge our reliance on the pioneers who created the modern treatments for anxiety disorders. Over the past thirty years we have worked with thousands of professional colleagues, each of whom has contributed to our understanding of these cunning, baffling, and powerful diseases. While we cannot here name all of these experts upon whose strong shoulders we now stand as we look to a future when all who suffer from an anxiety disorder can learn what is wrong with them and what to do about it, we call your attention to seven early leaders who created the modern "phobia clinic," a professional organization dedicated to helping people crippled by anxiety regain control of their lives. Manuel Zane, M.D., and Doreen Powell developed the White Plains Phobia Program while Arthur Hardy, M.D., and Nancy Flaxman built the TERRAP program in California, which later spread thought the nation. Martin Seif, Ph.D., from the Roosevelt Hospital Phobia Program, also had an early and sustained influence on our work. R. Reid Wilson, Ph.D., was another early leader in this rapidly developing field. In the late 1970s, when new hope emerged for the successful treatment of anxiety disorders, everyone in this field gratefully acknowledged their indebtedness to Claire Weekes, D.Sc., the Australian general practitioner who gave so much to therapists and patients alike through her brilliant, unique, and effective books.

These early leaders all focused on what is now called the cognitive-behavioral approach to the treatment of anxiety disorders. In the 1980s a whole new movement was created on the solid foundations laid in the 1960s and 1970s by Donald F. Klein, M.D., the creative psychiatrist who showed the way using medicines to block panic attacks and other anxiety symptoms. He was later joined by Gerald Klerman, M.D., James C. Ballenger, M.D., Bruce Lydiard, Ph.D., M.D., and what ultimately became an army of physicians who brought new hope to people with anxiety disorders through medical treatments. In the early 1990s the National Institute of Mental Health (NIMH), under the wise leadership of Fredrick K. Goodwin, M.D., began to nationally disseminate new important information about treating anxiety disorders both through the cognitive-behavioral approach and through medication. We gratefully acknowledge our debts to these few named leaders and to countless other professional colleagues who have helped us to learn about anxiety disorders and to find better ways to help cure them.

Most of all, we want to thank our patients. You are our teachers and our inspiration as we watch with respect the hard work you do every day to live your lives fully, without restrictions from your anxiety. It is a privilege to be your therapists.

Valuable Lessons

The first time I learned about what I now know to be anxiety disorders was when I was about ten. A favorite aunt was afraid of snakes. At the time, I was fascinated by snakes, so this fear of what fascinated me was incomprehensible. Once when my aunt visited, I caught a snake—something I often did for fun. I brought the snake back and, as my aunt was leaning down, I whipped the snake out from behind my back to show her my treasure. She screamed so loudly that she scared me and I dropped it. My aunt ran away horrified. I was shocked and mystified.

Later, my grandfather developed claustrophobia after he had a retinal detachment and lost some of his peripheral vision. He could no longer sit in the backseat of a two-door car, and he often had to drive with the window open when he sat on the passenger side of the front seat.

I noticed even later that my mother was frightened when one of her children got near an edge that she took to be dangerous. She later admitted to a height phobia. She surely never got on a ladder.

When I was a resident in psychiatry at Harvard Medical School in the early 1960s I treated a female graduate student with a fear of bridges. She was admitted to our psychiatric hospital. All my teachers were psychoanalysts, and I was taught that fears were repressed sexual impulses. I asked this patient about her sexual thoughts about bridges and crossing them. She checked out of the hospital figuring that the doctors there were even crazier than the patients.

When I started my own private practice, a patient who was an elementary school teacher came to see me because of her inability to drive to and from work. I figured her problem was regression and that she was inappropriately dependent on her husband to drive her back and forth to work because her needs as a child had not been met. We talked about these ideas twice a week for three years. She got less dependent and did well in many ways, but she still did not drive.

One day she brought in an article from *Glamour* magazine about a new treatment for a disorder called "agoraphobia." I read the article and set it aside, returning to my previous approach to helping her, which I was sure was just what she needed. She was not satisfied with this approach, and after a few weeks of encouraging me to take the article seriously, she told me she had found the telephone number of the psychiatrist who was quoted in the article as an expert in this new form of treatment. She gave me his name and phone number. It took me a while to overcome my unreasonable confidence in my own unsuccessful approach, but finally I called Manuel Zane, M.D., at the White Plains Phobia Clinic outside New York City. He took my call and patiently explained to me that this new approach involved going with the patient into the situation that produced the phobic fear and helping the patient manage the overwhelming and terrifying feelings that arose in that situation. Never in all of my training as a psychiatrist had I been advised to go anywhere with a patient, most surely not to go driving with them.

I discussed this conversation with my patient, who told me the school year was ending and she had relatives in White Plains. She proposed that we both go to the White Plains Phobia Clinic and see what they had to offer us. After I talked with her husband about this idea and with Dr. Zane, with whom I had developed a relationship by phone, they booked a flight to New York. My patient stayed with her family while I took a hotel room near the hospital. I practically moved in with Dr. Zane and his wife as I worked with him and the wonderful program he founded. I learned about Claire Weekes, M.D., the Australian general practitioner who had written about phobias and anxiety.

In learning about anxiety and its treatment, I felt like a blind person who discovered sight as an adult. My new colleagues and the programs they had founded were my teachers and my role models.

My agoraphobic patient stayed in New York for the summer of 1977 while I returned home. Dr. Zane began to refer patients to me, since he had no one else to send patients to in the Washington metropolitan area for this new way to treat agoraphobia and other anxiety disorders. I felt inadequate to the task as I tried to interest some of the largest clinics and hospitals in the Washington, D.C., area in this new form of treatment. To my surprise, no one was interested. They had not been to the White

Plains Phobia Clinic, and they had no idea how inadequate current treatment was and how much better it could be. When I tried to explain it to them, they acted as if I had fallen under the spell of a cult. In desperation I started to put together groups of phobic people much like the groups that Dr. Zane and Dr. Hardy were running. Since Dr. Zane ran groups at his home, I did the same at my home.

Then a young woman named Jerilyn Ross called, saying she had been a high school teacher in New York. Her friends at the Roosevelt Hospital Phobia Clinic told her that I was starting a similar program in Washington, where she had decided to move. She had worked hard to overcome her own phobia and understood the new techniques, based on her work dealing with her own anxiety disorder. She also proved to be the most gifted anxiety disorders therapist with whom I ever worked.

This group of pioneers was a team. I had never had so much fun as a doctor. My family's home in suburban Maryland was bursting at the seams with phobia groups night and day, six days a week. Our neighbors never complained as the patients' cars filled the streets, but normal life at home became so difficult that in 1979 my wife, Helen, helped me to find an office in Bethesda, Maryland. We moved the Phobia Program of Washington out of our basement.

Later Jerilyn and I traveled to the annual White Plains Phobia Program meeting. I proposed that we create an organization to advocate for the needs of patients and therapists as well as to educate them and the public about the new forms of treatment for anxiety disorders. Manuel Zane, M.D., Arthur Hardy, M.D., Martin Seif, Ph.D., Doreen Powell, and Nancy Flaxman, along with Jerilyn Ross and me, founded the Phobia Society of America (PSA). I was the organization's president. We focused on the word *phobia* rather than on the word *anxiety*, since we were providing treatment that helped people overcome their fears of particular activities, such as the agoraphobic's fear of driving, which had gotten me into this new world in the first place. Later the group extended to an interest in using medications to help anxious people. A wider group of leaders was recruited, including the academic leaders, most of whom were committed to using medications to help anxious patients. Reflecting this new, broader focus, the organization was renamed the Anxiety Disorders Association of America (ADAA), and Jerilyn took over as president.

Over the years I have lost track of the patient with whom I traveled to White Plains in 1977. But that trip changed my life at least as much as it changed hers. After a decade of immersion in the problems of addiction to alcohol and other drugs, I began a new life in the world of anxiety disorders.

In 1983 I met Dr. Claire Weekes at a meeting of the Phobia Society of America. I spent most of two days with her. At one point when I was talking alone to Dr. Weekes, I asked her if she'd ever had a panic disorder. She said, "Yes, I have had what you call panic attacks. In fact, I still have them. Sometimes they wake me at night." I told her I was sorry to hear that. She looked at me with shock: "Save your sympathy for someone else. I don't need it or want it. What you call a panic attack is merely a few normal chemicals that are temporarily out of place in my brain. It is of no significance whatsoever to me!"

I was amazed by that response. This remarkable eighty-year-old pioneer was showing me the ultimate in the cognitive restructuring of panic attacks. Dr. Weekes, using the techniques she teaches others through her inspired books, had taken the menacing meaning entirely away from the panic attack. She gave those attacks no power whatsoever, simply letting them pass and getting on with her life. Few sufferers from terribly painful panic attacks ever reach the heights of cognitive restructuring reached by Dr. Weekes, but her message was clear, and it was accessible to all people who would make the effort to learn it: *the bonus people receive for recovering control of their lives from an anxiety disorder is that the techniques learned to overcome panic disorder have a broad application in all of life's other difficult problems.*

These professional developments, however, do not explain my deep and personal interest in this field from the start. Why was I so fascinated by the patient's driving phobia, and why was I so excited by the new treatment I discovered in White Plains? To understand that you have to know that I have two daughters, my coauthors on this book. When Elizabeth was about five and Caroline about three, the girls were locked in a closet for about fifteen minutes. While Elizabeth showed no ill effects of the experience, Caroline developed a claustrophobia over the following few years. When she started school at age six, she had a terrible time with separation. She would cry and cling when her mother or I took her to school. Helen handled the problem by firmly telling Caroline that everyone in the family had a job and that her job was to go to school. Helen explained that she would be back to pick up Caroline at the end of the school day and that in the meantime her teacher would take good care of her. Then Helen turned Caroline over to her teacher and walked out, despite Caroline's sad tears of entreaties to stay with her.

My approach was different. I sat down and talked with Caroline about her fears. But as we talked, it became clear that Caroline had no idea what she was afraid of and that the longer we talked, the more scared she became.

Once in school, Caroline had another anxiety problem. She was terrified of having a door closed, such as the door to her classroom or the door to a toilet stall. In preschool, her teachers accepted this and left the classroom door ajar, which felt safe to Caroline. At this time, I was not involved in the treatment of anxiety disorders, so I did not label her problem clearly as a psychiatric disorder. What I did see was Caroline's claustrophobia in elevators. When it came time to get into an elevator, she cried and pleaded with us to take the stairs instead, no matter how high we had to go in the building. I tried demanding that she go in the elevator, and she sometimes would, but her distress was so real and so obviously severe that it was a terrible experience for both of us.

When Caroline was nine, I went to White Plains to learn a new way to understand anxiety and its treatment. I had a new way to think about Caroline's problem with elevators and closed doors and a new way to help her: I told Caroline that her fears were understandable and painful but that she could get over them with practice, just as she was then practicing her strokes as a member of the neighborhood swim team. That meant she and I needed to spend time together riding in elevators and closing doors in a gradual way while she was in full control of the exposure.

In the spring of 1978, when Caroline was ten, she proudly announced at my birthday party that she had a special gift for me: she would go with me to a tall building and take the elevator alone to the top and back down again while I waited for her on the ground floor. I could not wait but went that day to the tallest building I could find (which in Washington was about ten stories), and I stood outside that elevator as Caroline pushed the "up" button with a big smile on her face. She had to wait a while to get in an empty elevator, since going on an elevator alone was harder for her than going with other people. Finally a door opened, and there was an empty elevator. Caroline got on, waved good-bye, and disappeared behind the closing doors. It was a long time as I watched the indicator over the elevator record her progress to the top and then back down. At long last the door opened, and my proud and happy ten-year-old daughter leapt into my arms. That was the best birthday present I ever received.

Over the next few years, as I treated more than seven thousand clinically anxious people, many of our family conversations dealt with anxiety in its many disguises. As a family we often went to the local county fair in August. In 1979 I noticed something new: I had a smoldering nameless terror when we got on the Ferris wheel and it stopped at the top of its cycle with our little carriage seemingly swinging wildly in the wind as I looked out over the fair below. I told my daughters that I seemed to have developed a height phobia late in my life or, if I had had it before, I had not noticed it. Starting that year and extending to the present, the girls took turns helping me with my phobia practice as they took me up on the Ferris wheel over and over. I still have twinges when I do it, but I never fail to get on that Ferris wheel each year.

Facing your fears, with the help of those who love you, has become a family coping strategy that goes far beyond just dealing with anxiety. Rather than hide our fears or weaknesses, we have found that talking about them and, even more important, practicing them, is a source of both pride and pleasure for us all. We have learned to turn our problems in life into opportunities and our setbacks into springboards. We learned this valuable lesson from our exposures to Caroline's anxiety. For that gift we are all grateful.

As great a gift as that lesson has been, however, it was not the most recent gift from that dragon. Not only did anxiety give my career a new life and direction, but now with the writing of this book, I have fulfilled my dream of working with my now-grown daughters on a project we all care about with deep passion. This book, and the loving work we are putting into it together, is another gift from the anxiety that for so many years terrorized our family.

ROBERT L. DuPont, M.D.

PART ONE

What Is the Anxiety Cure?

CHAPTER 1

Caroline's Story

Anxiety Is My Companion

Anxiety is my companion. In some ways, I might even say it is my friend. It was not always that way. In fact, for many years we were mortal enemies set on destroying each other. I don't remember when my relationship with anxiety began, but the family story is that when I was around three, I was locked in a dark closet with my older sister, Elizabeth, while playing hide-and-seek. We were not locked in for long, and my sister suffered no ill effects. However, in me it apparently was the trigger for the development of claustrophobia, which is an overwhelming fear of being trapped in a closed space.

By the time I started first grade, I was terrified of being in a room with the door closed. My teacher was a wonderful woman with traditional ways. She believed that the classroom door should be closed when class was in session; she would not change her ways for me, a phobic child. I was terrified. It was the terror that comes from a life-threatening situation, not from a closed classroom door.

One morning my teacher outlined The Plan. Those two words—The Plan—will always be capitalized in my mind. In her no-nonsense way, she explained that the day in her classroom was always the same. She would close the door at the beginning of each class day and open it at the end. I never had to worry that she would close it one day and not open it again. This directly addressed my fears and gave me a way to reassure myself when anxiety hit. From then on, I could cope better with school, and I made it through first grade with few difficulties. The words The Plan became a mantra in our home. "Caroline, today this is The Plan," my mother would say as she outlined my activities for the day. The Plan was comforting and reassuring. As long as I understood The Plan, I could cope. The Plan allowed me to know ahead of time what was going to happen on a given day and took away the constant anticipatory anxiety that I would unexpectedly be forced into a fearful situation.

Identifying the problem was only the beginning of my long road to peace and acceptance. For six long years I suffered. My friends and family suffered along with me.

Although I was a happy and outgoing child with family and friends, I was shy at school. I had low self-esteem. I could not spend the night at my best friend's house because she might sleep with her door closed. I could not go places without my mother because I might be trapped by my fear. I was not trapped physically, but I was unable to go where my friends went, so I was trapped by my own fear and I was left behind. I also worried about my family. Every time we were separated, I would think about all of the horrible things that might happen to them. My fears were hard on my family, and I often felt ashamed of the scenes that I caused and the things we all had to miss because of my anxiety and avoidance.

Any closed-in space was a problem for me, but elevators were the worst. I felt that elevators were almost evil. The doors would stay open too long or close too quickly. The elevator would make strange sounds, or the elevator would be stopped too long before the doors slowly opened. In my imagination, any deviation from the expected was the sign that *this* elevator on *this* ride was going to malfunction.

How could I explain that the fear really did not go beyond the terrible feeling of being trapped? I really did not worry about anything beyond that. Nothing, in my mind, could be worse than that. How could I explain that I never felt trapped in a car when the door was closed? It took longer to get out of a car than to get out of an elevator on the next floor. One scared me, the other never did. I learned that panic is not rational. That just makes it more disturbing and far harder to explain to yourself or to anyone else.

Systematic Desensitization

Around the age of ten, the disparity between my usual, happy outgoing self and the shy, frightened inner self became more obvious to me and to my family. But what could we do? Over the years, my father had become involved in treating several patients with phobias. He learned of a new technique called systematic desensitization. In this process, the phobic person is gradually exposed to the fearful activity until the fear and the activity are no longer matched together. For me, the process involved gradually working up the courage to ride on an elevator alone.

Dad and I started the process of systematic desensitization by sitting at home and talking about elevators. For people who do not have anxiety, it can be difficult to understand that simply talking about the anxious situation can cause terrible feelings of panic. After I became comfortable discussing elevators, we moved up to driving to a building that had an elevator in it and sitting in the parking lot. We sat in the car and talked about the elevator and my fears. During these early stages we also researched the history of elevators and learned how they worked. Eventually, we started going into the building and watching the elevators, then getting in but not letting the door close, then going one floor and walking back down in a stairwell. The big hurdle, which seemed impossible until the very end, was riding in the elevator without my father. Together we came to talk of my fears as a dragon that descended on me. My phobic dragon used fear to cage me. I learned that I had to face and to accept that dragon to regain control of my life.

There was a fairly long gap between the time I was able to ride in an elevator with my father or another trusted adult and the time that I rode in one alone. My hesitation to try this last hurdle must have frustrated and disappointed my father. Finally, I made my decision and did it.

So I rode the elevator by myself and was cured forever, right? Wrong. But the tables had turned on that dragon. I had found the key to conquer my fears. It was many years before I rode in elevators without a second thought, but I never avoided an elevator again. I entered high school with confidence. I began to realize that the lessons I learned were useful and valuable to other people. I began working with my father and his colleague Jerilyn Ross to help other children with anxiety. I spoke on several television programs about my phobia and how I had overcome my fear. The confidence I gained more than made up for the confidence I had lost in the early years.

The lesson I learned not only cured my claustrophobia, it also taught me about life. Many problems in life appear terrifying and unmanageable, but they can be solved by following the same principles that got me on that elevator. Identify the problem, break it down into little steps, take one step at a time, be proud of your successes (even little ones), keep your eye on the goal, and keep moving toward that goal.

Some people ask me if I am still afraid of elevators. I can say with all honesty I am not. The moment I knew that for sure came when I was a resident in psychiatry at Johns Hopkins Hospital. I had been riding elevators without thinking about it for years, but nothing had ever tested my fear of really being trapped. One night I was the doctor on call for the entire psychiatric hospital. *On call* means that besides my normal daily responsibilities, it was my turn to stay the night and take care of any psychiatric patients who required admission or had other problems during the night. I stepped onto the elevator at about 4 A.M. to go down to the emergency room to treat a new patient. I was very tired, and it was clear that I would get no sleep that night. The doors closed, and the elevator began to move. Then it stopped. At first I was calm and pushed the "door open" button. Then I pushed other buttons. Absolutely nothing happened. I began to get scared, my heart pounded, and I felt dizzy. I was trapped! Then it dawned on me: if I was trapped, I could not see the patient in the ER. It was comforting to think that there were other doctors to care for him, so it was not necessary for me to reach the ER right away.

If I was trapped in the elevator at 4 A.M., then nobody would blame me if I lay down on the floor of the elevator and slept a little! Just then, the elevator began to move again, and soon I was busily working in the ER. The significance of finally being trapped in an elevator—my very worst childhood fear—did not strike me until several nights later. I was again stepping onto that same elevator in the middle of the night, and as the doors slid shut, I thought, Oh, I hope the elevator gets stuck for a little while. I would love a rest! When I realized what I had wished for, I laughed out loud.

The Goal of the Anxiety Cure

Live a full, normal life without restrictions because of anxiety disorders.

The realistic goal of treatment is not the elimination of the painful, anxious thoughts and feelings. Getting well from an anxiety disorder means letting go of the wish not to have the uncomfortable feelings of panic and anxiety. Getting well means accepting that the symptoms can come back at any time.

When I started this chapter, I said that "anxiety *is* my companion," not that it *was* my companion. I have learned that anxiety can take many forms and that it can go away completely and then return in another form. But I am not discouraged. Sure, I wish at times that I was not hardwired as an anxious person, but anxiety, though sometimes seriously unpleasant, is not a major factor in my life. Anxiety does not control or limit me. The same skills that I learned in order to conquer my claustrophobia I have used to keep anxiety as only a minor player in my life. I have had people ask how I managed to accomplish some difficult task such as speaking in front of a large group. "You did not look nervous at all!" Nervous? Sure I was nervous, but it's been a long time since being nervous has stopped me from doing what I want to do. I have had a lot of experience living my life while I feel nervous, even very nervous, which now gives me a lot of confidence that I can do whatever I want to do, with or without anxiety.

CHAPTER 2

The Anxiety Cure Program

*You cannot stop the birds of worry from flying over your head. But
you can stop them from building nests in your mind.*
—PROVERB

Welcome to the Anxiety Cure. Now that you have read our family story of anxiety, you have an idea about who we are and how we think about the anxiety disorders. We will outline the Anxiety Cure program and introduce you to most of the basic tools you will need to get on with the joy of your recovery. This new program builds on two decades of experience helping thousands of clinically anxious people, as well as their friends and families, to live full lives without being limited by anxiety disorders. The Anxiety Cure is an active, high-impact, goal-oriented treatment program to get you on the road to recovery, a program that can be tailored to the needs of each anxious person. The book is written to be used on your own, or in conjunction with individual therapy, or with a group program.

One in four Americans will suffer from one of the six anxiety disorders during his or her lifetime:

- *Agoraphobia/panic disorder (PD)*
- *Specific phobia*
- *Social phobia*
- *Generalized anxiety disorder (GAD)*
- *Obsessive-compulsive disorder (OCD)*
- *Posttraumatic stress disorder (PTSD)*

These illnesses create a greater economic burden than any other group of mental disorders, even depression, schizophrenia, and the addictions. Nationally, the economic costs of anxiety disorders were calculated to be $65

14

billion in 1994, the most recent year for which estimates are available. Anxiety disorders are intensely painful and humiliating because the sufferers know they are irrational, but they are unable to free themselves from their grip. It is like putting your hand into a pocketful of fishhooks: the more you struggle, the more hooked you get. Hooked by fear.

This book is written from a family perspective and directly addresses the needs of friends and family members. Anxiety disorders affect not only the lives of the people who have the symptoms but also the anxious person's friends, family, coworkers, supervisors, neighbors, clergy—in short, everyone who comes in contact with the anxious person. When we refer to friends and family, we mean all those who care about an anxious person, whether they live close or far away, whether they are old friends or new acquaintances, and whether they are related or not. The key is being in a caring relationship.

Some anxious people might worry about this book's emphasis on friends and family because they have few such relationships to call on to do the work that we are proposing. Especially if you have social phobia, you may feel that it will be impossible to find people to help you with your problem. Many people with anxiety have weakened their social contacts over time as the anxiety behaviors drive away people who would like to get close to you. If this is the case for you, you will be exploring other ways of connecting to people, and it is likely that increased social contact will be one of the goals that you move toward in your recovery program.

People who care about a person who has an anxiety disorder are frequently unsure about what to do to help. They realize that what they do about the anxiety has an impact on the anxious person, but often no solution seems possible. In *The Anxiety Cure* we outline important roles for caring friends and family, and you will find references to what friends and family can do throughout this book. See especially "Friends, Family, and Anxiety," and the Tips for Friends and Family highlighted at the end of each of the eight steps in Part Four, The Anxiety Cure: Eight Steps to Getting Well.

What Does *Cure* Mean?

This book boldly uses the word *cure* in its title. *The Anxiety Cure* offers you a way to get well, to live a full and normal life without restriction from an anxiety disorder. This is possible—sometimes with and sometimes without medicines—despite the fact that the *anxiety disorders cannot be eliminated by any form of treatment.* A cure is keeping the dragons of worry from building nests in your mind. Getting well—finding a real cure—means accepting that you have the anxiety disease and learning how to care for it in ways that take away most of the suffering and all of the disability that result from the anxiety disorders.

A "cure" is yours when you know what is wrong and what to do about it. This book helps you find your own path to a full life without being limited by an anxiety disorder.

We understand that some readers will be upset by our use of the word *cure* since, to them, a cure means eliminating the problem, rooting it out of their lives for good. Not only is that sort of cure impossible at this time, despite all of the knowledge now available about the anxiety disorders, but, as a practical matter, the search for that elusive goal also makes the anxiety problem worse.

The Universal Antidote

The universal antidote for all anxiety disorders is acceptance.

Acceptance as a cure for anxiety disorders means acceptance of the feelings and the thoughts that are automatically produced in the anxious, sensitized brain. But acceptance does not mean accepting the limitations in your life that anxiety is trying to force on you.

We have found that some people who are unable to think clearly or to benefit from treatment because of their anxiety disorders become able to make use of help once they find the right medicines to quiet their sensitized, overreactive nervous systems. If you are having trouble reading this book and even imagining regaining control of your life, you should consider seeing a doctor who specializes in using medicines to treat anxiety disorders. See Part Four, Chapter 20, Step 6 for more information about the medicines to consider. We have found that medicines do not conflict with or compete with effective therapy. For many anxious people, using effective medicines is the first step to making good use of therapy and other resources, including the Anxiety Cure program.

When you are anxious, it is hard to think clearly. You are afraid and confused because your mind is full of fear, which crowds out all other thoughts. Reading a book or even thinking about the steps needed to get well are impossible when you are intensely anxious. Wait until you feel somewhat calm and then get out *The Anxiety Cure* and begin to use it. If you get overly anxious while you are reading, put the book down for a while and do some simple everyday things to help take your mind off your scary thoughts and feelings. Washing the dishes or the car, vacuuming the rug, or preparing a meal might help. Doing nonstressful activities often reduces anxiety.

Despite emotional pain and the effort and time required, many anxious people are willing to make use of the tools that are available to retake control of their lives. This book is written for readers with anxiety problems who accept the reality of their illnesses and are willing to do the work necessary to get well. Anyone who promises you a way to overcome your anxiety disorder without work is not telling the truth.

Based on our experiences with other people suffering from anxiety disorders, we promise that if you use the techniques you will learn here, you will be able to turn the suffering of your anxiety disorder into a springboard for a better life.

The Program Background

The Anxiety Cure program uses education together with cognitive-behavioral therapy (CBT) to increase your understanding of your anxiety illness. Cognitive-behavioral therapy has been shown to be effective in treating anxiety; *it combines making changes in the way you think (your cognitions) and the way you behave (your actions).*

The Anxiety Cure is supportive of whatever you need and whatever helps you to live the life you choose to lead. Throughout this book, we build a sense of teamwork. You are the coach. You choose how and when to use your players, including if you choose a therapist and/or a psychiatrist and your support person. We recommend that you train your own support person so that you will have at no cost someone who is knowledgeable and dedicated, helping you in your everyday practice.

The Anxiety Cure suggests reading published books to support you in your recovery. We have included a list of suggested reading in the back of this book. The problems with bibliotherapy (the use of books to help you get well) are that many people who buy books do not read them and many people do not do the many things that the authors recommend. We urge you to read the books you select and to conscientiously follow the authors' recommendations. Give your authors a chance to help you. Do not give up without giving your authors a chance to work for you.

If you cannot find a certain book in a bookstore or if it is too expensive, go to your local library to find what they have on self-help for the anxiety disorders. You will find good articles in magazines and newspapers on anxiety disorders and the latest approaches to curing them. We encourage you to be energetic and resourceful in using the printed word to help you get well. Books as well as articles can help, as can chat groups on the Internet and self-help groups in your area.

In addition to books, we also recommend trying more comprehensive self-help programs that deal with anxiety disorders. These are more expensive than books but less expensive than most therapy. You can find information on ordering these programs in the back of this book. At the end of each of the eight steps in the Anxiety Cure, we make specific suggestions about other books you can read to reinforce and extend what you learn from us.

We suggest that you join other people recovering from anxiety disorders in mutual-aid support groups to help you over the long haul. All of these suggestions will be covered fully in Part Four, The Anxiety Cure: Eight Steps to Getting Well. The Anxiety Cure does not compete with any other form of therapy.

This book is different from other books about anxiety disorders in two ways. First, it is written by a family from the perspective that friends and family members are integral parts of the recovery process. Throughout the book we have special sections for friends and family that will help others in your life learn how to help you with your anxiety problem. Second, we have encompassed our two professional areas of training in this book, psychiatry and social work. Psychiatry currently views anxiety as a brain disorder and stresses cognitive-behavioral therapy and medicine. Social work sees a person in an environmental context, so that evaluating that person's family, job, and community involvements is also part of treatment. We work together in our practice, so we know that these two approaches complement each other well, and we have brought this teamwork approach to the Anxiety Cure program.

New versus Long-term Anxiety

The Anxiety Cure provides you with the guidance you need to get moving to overcome the problems created by your anxiety disorder. You can use this boost at any stage of your anxiety disorder—from the time you first have symptoms to suffering a setback after many years.

If you have sought treatment previously for your anxiety problem, you may find that you use the Anxiety Cure program differently from someone who has just had an onset of anxiety. People who have been in and out of treatment typically have many set ideas about how to function with anxiety. You have found some strategies that work for you, but overall, you probably have not found a systematic way to evaluate and treat whatever state your anxiety disorder is in at different points in your life.

If you have some familiarity with anxiety disorders and have had the problem for a long time, you may want to skip reading Part Two of this book, which contains background material about anxiety disorders, and start right in with Part Four, The Anxiety Cure: Eight Steps to Getting Well. You may choose to do the eight steps in a different order, but do not skip a step. You may find that the very step you are reluctant to do is the one that holds the key to help you get control of your anxiety.

If you are newly struggling with anxiety, please take the time to read Part Two, The Basics of Anxiety, to learn more about anxiety prior to embarking on the Eight Steps to Getting Well. Remember that education is crucial to making changes in your thoughts and behaviors, and that will lead to a truly lasting cure.

Working the Program

Little steps will take you where you want to go, if you take repeated steps over a long period of time. The problems created by your anxiety disorder did not start yesterday and they will not be gone tomorrow, no matter how hard you work. The benefit you will get from this program will be directly proportional to the effort you put into the program. Put in a lot of effort, and you will get a lot of benefit. Put in little effort, and you will get little benefit.

The Short Form—a Quick Alternative

For some people, reading this whole book, much less doing all the exercises we suggest, will be overwhelming. Try our shortcut for now if you feel you cannot do the whole program for one reason or another.

Start the shortcut program by reading the table of contents. Mark the chapters of special interest to you, which you hope to read as time permits. But be sure to read the following chapters:

The two most important lessons to take away from *The Anxiety Cure* are: First, change your thoughts about your anxious feelings so that you recognize the physical symptoms as merely false alarms that are being sent to your body by a normal fear response occurring at the wrong time. Second, change your behavior of avoidance to actively seek practice opportunities to systematically disconnect the association you now have between anxious feelings and avoided situations.

If you will do only these two things—change your thoughts and your behaviors—you will begin to get well from your anxiety problem, even if you do no other work suggested in this program. Additional information in this book will speed your cure and help you cope with setbacks on your road to recovery, but even small changes in your thoughts and behaviors are the main part of any cure from an anxiety problem. There is no reason not to do something about your anxiety problem now. Give it a try and when you encounter problems, take time to read the rest of the book and do the other suggested exercises. Above all, *get started!*

What to Do If You Have Doubts

We use this book with our own patients. We know that almost everyone who starts to use this book is filled with self-doubts and convinced that he or she will not benefit. This is your personal "worry machine" turning the good things of your life (such as the opportunities available to you in this program) into trash. This fear-driven outlook is both a reflection of your anxiety disorder and an understandable reaction to the pain and disappointment you have had over the years trying to get well.

Even big problems caused by anxiety disorders can be overcome with repeated practice. *Easy does it. One day at a time. First things first.* Those slogans are just as true when it comes to getting well from an anxiety disorder as they are when it comes to getting well from addiction. In your work of getting well, you cannot go too fast and you cannot go too slow. Both fast and slow get you there if you persist in your efforts.

Use a Journal

We suggest that you create your own workbook or journal to aid you in your work. You will find more uses for your journal throughout the eight steps, but for now get a looseleaf or spiral-bound notebook and write in it your descriptions of your efforts to overcome anxiety. Simply write in it as you would in a diary, every day if possible, but at least once a week. Start with the date and then describe the problems you are facing and your efforts to overcome them. Be sure to record your satisfaction in making progress as you go along.

Over time, you will find it helpful, and surprisingly encouraging, to look back at your journal. You will see that you have made more progress than you thought. You will see that things that were difficult a few months ago have become easy as a result of your practice. Your anxious mind, without the benefit of your journal, will forget your old problems, robbing you of the perspective that comes from recognizing the progress you have made. Your journal is a good way to overcome this tendency to retrospectively minimize your progress. It will also help you gain much-needed, hard-earned self-respect for your efforts to get well for good. You may also find it useful to mark some sections of this book with a highlighter, a paper clip, or a self-stick note so that particularly helpful sections you may want to reread during anxious moments are found more easily.

Start the Journey

Getting well requires that you take your brain off autopilot and take control of your thoughts and behaviors yourself. That means talking to yourself, convincing yourself, little by little, that at root you are neither trapped nor alone. You always have "outs," and you always have someone else who can help you.

An anxiety disorder is cured when you know what is wrong and what to do about it. When you have those two things, then you have regained control of your life.

There is no one right way to get well from an anxiety disorder. There are some good roads that many have traveled with success in the past. *The Anxiety Cure* helps you find and use these roads, but only you can tell which specific roads are the best for you at various times in your life. We will expose you to many roads for you to try for yourself and are glad to have you with us on this journey of recovery from anxiety disorders.

PART TWO

The Basics of Anxiety

CHAPTER 3

The Anxious Brain

There are no laboratory tests for anxiety disorders. Diabetes and high blood pressure can be measured objectively, but, like pain, there are no objective measurements of anxiety. We can only judge someone else's pain and anxiety by the experience of the sufferers as they report it to us.

Brain Chemistry

Scientific research has shown that panic attacks are real, physical events in the brain. The anxiety disorders are chemically based brain diseases that are properly called biopsychosocial, because there are biological, psychological, and social roots to these diseases.

The events in the brains of anxious people when they are experiencing panic and anticipatory anxiety are normal and harmless, although they are triggered abnormally. The fear and panic reactions in the brains of clinically anxious people are the result of chemical changes in the brain involving a variety of neurotransmitters, including norepinephrine and serotonin. The locus coeruleus (LC) is the principal norepinephrine nucleus, which fires when a panic attack occurs. The locus coeruleus is the brain's novelty detector. When it fires, releasing norepinephrine, it signals danger. When it signals an alarm in the absence of danger, as it does in the anxiety disorders, it sends out a false alarm.

Novelty is associated with the feelings of excitement and fear. That brain biology explains why fear and excitement are so often linked. The difference between what causes fear and what causes excitement is in the brain of the person having the feeling. If the situation that gives rise to the feeling and the feeling itself are thought to be safe (or controllable), then a novel situation is likely to be experienced as exciting. If it is experienced as dangerous and out of control, it is experienced as fear. Some people have brain novelty detectors that barely ever swing into action. These people appear to be fearless. Other people have hair-trigger novelty detectors. These people know fear as a common companion in their everyday lives.

As a situation becomes more familiar, the novelty detector does not fire. Familiarity reduces fear. This is called desensitization. The dragon short-circuits this process by leading you in the opposite direction: he leads you to avoidance, which *adds* to your sensitization. Desensitization is central to the Anxiety Cure. We want you to make the things you now fear into familiar experiences. This will help to quiet your overactive, highly sensitized brain.

Anxiety Disorders Are Primary Diseases

The anxiety disorders do not come from or cause any physical illnesses. They are primary diseases. This means they are not secondary to or derived from other illnesses. Most people with anxiety disorders fear physical illnesses—especially brain and heart diseases—but most sufferers are remarkably healthy. Some physical illnesses can mimic anxiety disorders. For that reason it is important to have a physical and laboratory examination, including tests of the thyroid gland, to be sure that your symptoms are the result of an anxiety disorder and not the result of some other medical disorder. Many people with anxiety disorders go to hospital emergency rooms or see physicians because they fear they are having a heart attack or going crazy. The usual physical tests prove that the patient's health is normal. This is good news because although the anxiety disorders are real and serious, the disabilities and suffering caused by the anxiety disorders can be overcome by modern treatments.

Anxiety disorders do not cause auto accidents or insanity, although many people with anxiety disorders fear those outcomes. The anxiety disorders are the result of merely a few normal brain chemicals temporarily out of place. Once these brain chemicals are disordered, they set in motion a chain reaction of disturbed thoughts that sensitize the nervous system, making it more vulnerable to future panic attacks. The anxious brain is like an electrical system that has suffered from a short circuit leading to a breakdown of the insulation between wires so that short circuits then become more common in the future. Medicines and therapy can help to heal the sensitized nervous system over time.

No matter how bad the anxiety disorder becomes, it cannot cause physical or mental illness, other than the anxiety disorder itself.

Sometimes depression and addiction to alcohol and other drugs are associated with anxiety disorders. Most people with anxiety disorders, even when the disorders are severe, do not suffer from either major depression or addiction to alcohol or other drugs. See Part Five, Anxiety and Your Daily Life, for a discussion of these issues.

Anxiety disorders are not caused by some other disorder, and they are not caused by trauma (mental or physical), although trauma and the abuse of certain drugs, such as marijuana, LSD, and cocaine, may trigger the onset of an anxiety in a person who was previously vulnerable to an anxiety disorder. Trauma and drug abuse do not always produce an anxiety disorder, presumably because some people lack a preexisting vulnerability to the anxiety disorders.

Are You a "Born Worrier"?

Most people with anxiety disorders can identify when their anxiety problems began, even though most people with anxiety disorders recognize that they were "born worriers" from the time of their earliest memories. The onset of the full-blown anxiety often occurs between ages fifteen and thirty, but anxiety disorders can start at any age. Sometimes the onset occurs at periods of stress in life, such as after an automobile accident or a bad reaction to a drug. After the anxiety disorder has started for any reason, and most often no specific precipitating cause can be identified, the anxiety disorder has a life of its own. The problems faced by the clinically anxious person are the same whether or not the disorder had an onset that can be explained or identified.

Once the anxiety disorder is understood to be primary and serious, and effective action is taken to deal with the problems caused by the anxiety disorder, there is little likelihood of secondary depression or addiction. *A person who gets well from an anxiety disorder can live a full, normal life with no limitations or disabilities.*

Self-Harm

If you are thinking about hurting yourself or worry that you might act on an impulse to hurt yourself or someone else, please seek mental health care. A therapist or psychiatrist can help you sort out how real this fear is and can keep you safe while you are in treatment to get well.

We have seen thousands of anxious people, many of whom have feared that they would hurt themselves or someone else in an impulsive act (for example with scissors or a knife). Often these feelings are truly horrifying because they are so dramatically contrary to the anxious person's conscientious character. We have never, not even once, seen an anxious person harm himself or herself, let alone someone else (such as a child, who is often the object of such fears). By all means, get your fears assessed, but let your therapist and doctor know you are an anxious person and let them know that we have never seen an anxious person who has hurt himself or anyone else.

CHAPTER 4

The Vocabulary of Anxiety

Worry, along with tension and irritability, are the central features of the six distinctive types of anxiety disorders: *agoraphobia/panic disorder (PD); specific phobia; social phobia; generalized anxiety disorder (GAD); obsessive-compulsive disorder (OCD)*; and *posttraumatic stress disorder (PTSD)*. To understand these common and serious disorders, we need to have a vocabulary that lets us think constructively about what is happening in our minds and bodies.

First, we need to understand the terms *normal fear, normal anxiety*, and *pathological anxiety*. Then we need to understand the three types of pathological anxiety: *spontaneous panic, situational panic*, and *anticipatory anxiety*. Finally, we will discuss *avoidance*. Once we understand these terms, we can think clearly about the anxiety disorders.

The vocabulary of anxiety disorders reflects the brain biology that underlies these disorders. This vocabulary also is essential to understanding these mysterious and powerful illnesses. The Anxiety Cure program relies on this vocabulary and allows you to make the best use of the growing literature about recovery from anxiety.

What Is Normal Fear?

From time to time everyone has fear, the uncomfortable feelings of tension and worry that something bad may happen. These feelings of normal fear are healthy reactions to actual or possible danger. They reflect the fight-or-flight response triggered by two closely related chemicals, norepinephrine (also called noradrenalin), which is a brain neurotransmitter, and epinephrine (also called adrenalin), which is a messenger of danger from the adrenal gland that goes through the bloodstream to every cell in the body. The feelings of fear are the equivalent of having a fire in your home or a burglar alarm going off. Fear signals you to be alert, to look for danger. Physical expressions of fear are sweating, trembling, a tight chest, a lump in the throat, a gastrointestinal system shutdown, and tense muscles. The blood supply in your intestines shuts off, which may even lead to vomiting. Your blood, in stress, is sent to your muscles to prepare for fight or flight, for emergency action. Mental expressions of fear are having thoughts of danger that something terrible is about to happen. A fearful person whose fear reaction has been triggered is hypervigilant, on edge, keyed up, and ready for possible disaster.

The feelings of fear are understandable as the body's fight-or-flight mechanisms swing into action when the danger is real. Even if the fearful feelings are uncomfortable, they are not hard to understand. Moments of impending danger are moments when it makes sense to be keyed up and worried. Anticipation of possible danger is a necessary mental process. In fact, people who are not fearful at such times are in trouble because they are not likely to take action to reduce their risk or to prepare for dangers that may be coming their way.

Fearful reactions are equally understandable in response to something that isn't directly happening to you. For example, you could get a phone call from the police telling you that someone close to you has been injured seriously in an automobile accident. There is no danger to the person being called; the danger is a thought or an idea and is not a threat to the anxious person's own body. The risk is of the loss of, or harm to, a loved one. The threat is the suffering not only of oneself but also of others you care about. In this case, the feelings of dread and terror associated with the adrenal glands pumping out spurts of epinephrine and the brain sending urgent messages by norepinephrine are normal. Danger is real in everyone's life. When accompanying danger, fear is healthy and should be seen as a friend.

What Is Normal Anxiety?

It is helpful to distinguish fear from anxiety, although both emotions use the same fight-or-flight mechanisms. *Fear is the experience of an immediate, real danger. Anxiety is the body's signal of possible future danger, a sort of emotional early warning system.* To think about primitive human experiences that triggered these physical and mental experiences picture a tiger attacking a person holding a flimsy stick for protection. How do you suppose that stick-holding ancestor of ours felt at seeing that tiger poised to spring? Once having experienced and survived such an attack, how do you think our ancestors felt when they thought about the possibilities of such an attack? It is not difficult to imagine panic and anticipatory anxiety in such a setting. A more contemporary example is understandable when you imagine your feeling if your car skidded uncontrollably on an icy street, spinning around and around toward parked cars. When the road iced up again, you would remember that incident and feel anxiety as a result of that experience. The memory of the earlier episode with your spinning car triggers anxiety when you drive on icy streets or even when you hear a weather forecast of possible icy roads. Anxiety is your mind identifying possible dangers and taking the necessary steps to prepare for those dangers.

When you felt your heart in your throat as your car spun out of control on the ice, you felt fear. When you felt your palms sweat and your heartbeat quicken as you looked out of your window the next winter at an icy street on which you were about to drive, you felt anxiety. Anxiety, like fear, is a healthy, normal emotion.

False Alarms: Pathological Anxiety

If you suffer from anxiety disorders you experience the feelings and thoughts that reflect the same basic fight-or-flight mechanisms mobilizing your mind and body for danger. But for you these feelings and thoughts are triggered when there is no generally understandable danger, or your thoughts and feelings are dramatically in excess of the feelings most people have in similar circumstances. This is what makes pathological anxiety. There is no tiger, no car spinning out of control, and no police officer on the phone with tragic news. If your heart sinks whenever you hear a siren or whenever your phone rings because it *might* be the police telling you that one of your loved ones has just been killed, that is pathological anxiety, and you probably have an anxiety disorder. Your body is responding to a false alarm. The idea of a false alarm is such a useful one that it is found in many other resources; for example, it is discussed in *Brain Lock*, by Jeffrey M. Schwartz, M.D.

If you experience panicky feelings when you leave home, drive on a highway, go to a shopping mall, or get on an elevator, then you probably have an anxiety disorder. When thinking about your fears, you are likely to overstate the risks. Ask yourself: "How do most healthy, sensible people react to this situation? Do they experience fear and anxiety or not?" If they do, that is normal fear. If they do not, that is probably pathological anxiety.

If your intense feelings of worry, which most other people do not experience, wake you up at night or come out of the blue at any time of the day, then you have an anxiety disorder. If you spend hours every day thinking about, fearing, and expecting these feelings, if you give up important activities in your life because of these feelings or because of the anticipation of having them, then you have an anxiety disorder. If you worry endlessly and senselessly about feelings in your body, fearing a dreaded illness even when your doctor says you are not ill, then you have an anxiety disorder.

Anxiety is experienced in your muscles as tension. Your muscles are set on edge for hours at a time. They feel stiff and tense. Muscle pain is a common outgrowth of the muscle tension. Irritability is a common symptom of anxiety. As your brain holds worry and fear for hours at a stretch, you feel exhausted and upset. Situations and events that would not otherwise bother you cause you to feel upset and irritable. Relaxation is hard to come by. Sleep is elusive. Especially harmed is the ability to fall asleep, as fear and anxiety come to dominate your life.

Having the feelings of anxiety is always extremely uncomfortable for the same reason that it is uncomfortable when a burglar alarm goes off. These are powerful signals that immediate action—fight or flight—is required. When anxious, your brain is hyperalert, and you search your environment and your thoughts for possible dangers. You find dangers where other people in the same situations do not find them, when other people who do not have anxiety disorders do not hear the burglar alarm that dominates your life night and day.

This is pathological anxiety. It is not the same as normal anxiety because it is not logical. Pathological anxiety is not a useful response that prepares a person for real danger. The unreasonable danger signal of pathological anxiety itself becomes a serious problem that results in major losses in the quality of your life. Imagine trying to live a normal life in your home if the burglar alarm went off without warning or reason *and* if no one else could see the flashing lights or hear the siren.

When you have anxious feelings and thoughts for no generally recognized reason, then you feel not only that you are in peril from a possible external danger but also that you are faced with an even more upsetting internal danger. It is easy to conclude that something is terribly wrong with you, with how your brain and your body are working. Is it any wonder that people with anxiety disorders often think that they are in danger of dying, going crazy, or losing control? Is it surprising that most people with anxiety disorders fear that they are suffering from life-threatening physical illnesses such as brain tumors and heart attacks?

Many people with anxiety disorders think that they have cancer or mysterious diseases that their doctors cannot find. When they go to their doctors to get these problems checked out, they are often told, "Nothing is wrong. It's just stress." Is it any wonder that such information is mystifying and troubling, especially if their lives are no different from those of other people who do not have this problem, and their stress is no different from the stress they had experienced before this anxiety disorder began? How can anything so real be "imaginary"? As we will see, there is indeed something wrong with the brain of the person with an anxiety disorder. This disease is not imaginary or simply the result of stress.

Pathological anxiety is a false alarm that steals the body's healthy danger signals. It has physical manifestations—rapid heart rate, shallow breathing, tight chest, sweaty palms, distorted sight and hearing, and the feeling that you need to empty your bladder and bowels. That is the easy part! The really hard part of pathological anxiety is the thinking that goes along with these distressing feelings. *Discomfort* and *pain* are too mild. *Terror* and *dread* come closer. You think, for example, that you or a loved one are in immediate danger of death from an accident or incurable illness. You must act right now; there is not a moment to lose! Failure to act is intolerable and unimaginable. Everything else is gone from your mind as you devote all your thinking capacity to the urgent demands of the danger you feel and think. That danger, which seems more real than reality, is a false alarm.

Anxiety Is a Disease

A disease is a predictable pattern of problems, with physical components, that has a negative effect on the sufferer's life. Each disease has a range of severities and highly personal expressions. A disability results from a disease when it adversely affects one or more major life function, such as work, social life, recreation, or physical activities. *The anxiety disorders are serious diseases, and they often cause serious disabilities.*

The feelings of pathological anxiety in the body often change, sometimes rapidly, so that just when you finally think that you understand them, there is a new symptom, an unfamiliar manifestation of the anxiety problem, to add new depth to your worry. The feelings of abnormal worry are terribly distressing. The natural, normal reactions to these feelings and thoughts of anxiety are to pull back, to stick close to home, to stay with safe and familiar people, and to stay near someone and someplace that can provide help if you need it on a moment's notice.

Is it any wonder that many people with anxiety disorders stay close to home and limit their activities, especially in unfamiliar places? This tendency on the part of people with anxiety disorders has often been misinterpreted as indicating that they are timid or dependent. Although some clinically anxious people are timid and dependent, most are not.

The anxiety disorders are not the result of a pathological dependency. You are not anxious because you are a dependent person. Rather, the pathological anxiety from which you suffer causes you to be fearful of being alone and of situations that may trigger panicky feelings. Similarly, you are not anxious because you lack self-confidence. Most people with anxiety disorders also develop, sooner or later, low self-esteem because they have so much difficulty doing ordinary things that nonanxious people do with little or no difficulty.

What Are Spontaneous and Situational Panic?

Panic is a sudden burst of anxiety, a sharp surge of norepinephrine and epinephrine. This is the first fear produced by anxiety; it is the chemical signal that came from your own brain to cause the physical sensations of anxiety. Panic frequently comes unbidden to dominate the thoughts and the behaviors of people with anxiety disorders. *Spontaneous panic* occurs when intense feelings and thoughts of panic come out of the blue, for no apparent reason. Whereas *situational panic* occurs when panicky feelings and thoughts are closely tied to particular places or activities that repeatedly cause panic for an individual sufferer.

Agoraphobia/panic disorder usually starts with spontaneous panic and evolves to be mostly or even entirely situational panic, although the situations that trigger panic may be both many and varied. Being tired, stressed, or sick can make panic attacks more likely to occur. In specific phobia, the panic is limited to a particular situational panic, and the panic does not usually shift from one situation to another or involve multiple situations and/or activities, as it does for agoraphobia/panic disorder. Situational panic may arise when driving, flying, shopping, or riding in closed-in places such as elevators. For each person, the specific circumstances that trigger situational panic are usually consistent over the course of many years. People who are psychologically minded can sometimes recognize what particular disturbing thoughts brought on their spontaneous panicky episodes, but often there seems to be no way to understand what triggers them.

The most important fact to know about panic attacks, both spontaneous and situational, is that they will not harm your body. *Panic attacks do not cause heart attacks, strokes, or other serious physical problems.* In addition, panic attacks do not cause you to pass out, go crazy, or lose control of your body. A person having a panic attack can do anything a person not having a panic attack can do, including driving a car or giving a speech. Panic attacks cause terrible feelings—the worst possible feelings—but they do not cause loss of consciousness or loss of control of your body. You might feel as if you will pass out, go crazy, or lose control, but that will not happen. Panic is a normal reaction to danger and, as such, is itself not dangerous. Panic attacks are distressing but not dangerous. They are the body's normal alarm going off inappropriately. And then, because they are inappropriate, panic attacks trigger frightening self-doubt: "What is wrong with me?" This is not part of normal fear reactions.

What Is Anticipatory Anxiety?

The third common type of pathological anxiety, in addition to spontaneous panic and situational panic, is anticipatory anxiety. This is the fear of panic, and it often leads to avoidance or a phobia. Usually panic, often spontaneous panic, comes first in the course of the development of an anxiety disorder. Later in the development of the anxiety disorder, the sufferer comes to anticipate fearfully the reemergence of panic. The panic itself is called the "first fear," and the anticipated panic is called the "second fear." As it was described by Dr. Claire Weekes, the Australian physician who was a pioneer in the treatment of the anxiety disorders, the second fear usually dominates the anxious person's life within a few months of the onset of the illness and leads to the avoidance.

Avoidance Leads to Phobias

It is the avoidance, the "holes in the lives" of anxious people, that creates the disabilities in the anxiety disorders. Avoidance creates a phobia. Anxious people commonly avoid behaviors, situations, or activities that are otherwise a normal part of life. For example, some anxious people avoid elevators, shopping, or flying. Other anxious people avoid public speaking or crowded places. Phobic avoidance is caused by the brain's signals that there is grave danger in otherwise routine situations.

Elevator phobics are not so much avoiding elevators as they are avoiding their panicky feelings that are triggered by going into elevators. Although phobic people often speak of dangers in their phobic situations in their efforts to explain their behaviors to themselves and to others (for example, fearing airplane crashes or losing control of the car on an interstate highway), their fundamental fears are the dreadful feelings these experiences cause them.

To understand anxiety disorders, you must fix that understanding in your thoughts. The central problem is not fear of dying or getting stuck in an elevator. The central problem of all anxiety disorders is fear of the panic, fear of the anticipatory anxiety itself. The central problem is the unpleasant feelings (and thoughts) that are the anxiety disorder.

The serious problem facing the anxious person is found not outside but inside the anxious person. That is why it is not helpful to a flying phobic to explain rationally the low risks of flying or why it does not help the person who is phobic about crowds to say, "There is nothing to fear." There is something to fear, but it is not the airplane or the crowd. The basic problem is the inappropriate brain reactions taking place in the phobic person's brain. That fact explains why nonphobic people cannot understand the behavior of phobic people. Nonanxious people are not having the same experience in the airplane, in the elevator, or in the crowded supermarket because nonanxious people do not have severe alarm signals going off in their brains in these places. Because these inappropriate terror reactions occur over and over again in the same situations, phobic people become conditioned to this fear reaction and begin to suffer from anticipatory anxiety, the second fear. It and avoidance are the central features of this "what if" disease. The anxious person's brain is sensitized to these pathological reactions. That sensitization is the hallmark of the disease, its essential feature.

CHAPTER 5

The Six Anxiety Disorders

Now that we have a basic vocabulary to think about anxiety disorders, we can use these words to identify six anxiety disorders. While anxious people are all unique, most suffer in ways that fit more or less clearly into one of these six specific descriptions:

Agoraphobia/Panic Disorder (PD)

This results in spontaneous panic attacks coupled with situational panic as well as pathological anxiety, with or without significant avoidance. The syndrome often begins with spontaneous panic and evolves over time to include fear of many experiences, most often driving, shopping, traveling to unfamiliar places, and being alone. Typically, agoraphobia shows up as a fear of being away from a safe person or a safe place.

Agoraphobia is the fear of being helpless and alone when perceiving great inner danger. This is why agoraphobia is called "adult separation anxiety." Often this is expressed as fear of dying, going crazy, or losing control of one's behavior and doing something either dangerous or embarrassing. Agoraphobia typically leads sufferers to stick close to safe (and familiar) people and places. At its worst, it can lead to the sufferer's being homebound—unable to leave home.

The Man with the Wild Hair: Agoraphobia

Sam was a twenty-five-year-old man who had his first panic attack after smoking marijuana with friends in high school. He did not connect the panic attack to his drug use, and he continued using marijuana and then cocaine frequently until he was twenty-one. At that point, he had a

---

severe panic attack and was taken to the emergency room in an ambulance. He was told that nothing was wrong with him, which left him
confused and frightened. He began to avoid going out of the house
alone in order to be near the phone if he had another panic attack and
had to call for an ambulance. He stopped using drugs because he was
frightened of being out of control in case a panic attack occurred and he
could not summon help. He lost contact with his friends, and he relied
on his girlfriend to do errands for him to places where he did not feel
safe.

The more Sam avoided situations, the more fearful he became. He
was able to go to his work as a road builder because he was outside, not
closed in a room, and because there was always a team of workers who
could help him if he had a panic attack. He developed a serious fear of
sitting in a barber's chair, and he had a huge, bushy mound of hair and a
long flowing beard when he finally sought help. He feared being
trapped in the barber's chair. If he had a panic attack in the chair with his
hair half cut, he would not be able to leave (fearing embarrassment), and
he would not be able to stay (because he would be afraid he was dying).

Specific Phobia

A specific phobia is a particular form of situational panic such as fear of
flying, fear of heights, fear of insects or snakes, or claustrophobia. Fear of
vomiting or of medical procedures such as injections are common specific
phobias. Specific phobias are usually situational panic of the experience or
circumstance. These are called specific or single phobias to differentiate
them from the more general agoraphobia. Sometimes what at first appear
to be specific phobias are, at root, manifestations of agoraphobia showing
up as multiple phobias, but many people suffer from single, discrete phobias without having either spontaneous panic or agoraphobia.

Fear of Snakes: Specific Phobia

Chantelle was a twenty-eight-year-old woman with a fear of snakes.
Even the word *snake* in a newspaper or a fleeting picture of a snake on a
TV show caused her to have a rush of fear. She feared walking on grass
or going anywhere she might see a snake. Even though she rarely saw a
snake, she lived in near-constant fear that a snake would materialize
anyplace anytime. She avoided hiking and was severely limited by her
phobia.

Chantelle worked as an office manager. When one of her coworkers inadvertently discovered her fear, he began to tease Chantelle about it, leaving the word *snake* or a picture of a snake in unlikely parts of her desk or on her e-mail. Chantelle knew she either had to seek help or find a new job when she realized she was fearful all of the time, which caused her to have trouble concentrating on her work.

Social Phobia

Social phobia is a pathological anxiety expressed specifically as fear of embarrassment, which may be limited to public speaking or it may be part of a global shyness that limits social experiences, including dating, marriage, and friendships. Agoraphobic people are usually afraid to be alone, being more comfortable with a safe person who could help them in an emergency. Social phobics are usually more comfortable alone. People are scary to them.

The Man Who Avoided Meetings: Social Phobia

Kenneth was a thirty-five-year-old middle manager in a fast-growing company. He liked his job, and he worked hard to get ahead. He had avoided public speaking, or even being called on, since he was in grade school. He knew his avoidance hindered his success in his job to a limited extent, and he also knew that to become a key player in his business, he was going to have to give frequent presentations effectively. None of his friends, family, or coworkers was aware of his public speaking phobia.

Although he was afraid of public speaking and avoided it, he was also pragmatic enough not to want a phobia to stand in the way of his success. He set about his Anxiety Cure, using the same methodical, thorough qualities that had placed him in a successful position in the first place.

Generalized Anxiety Disorder (GAD)

Generalized anxiety disorder is a general pathological anxiety, which includes the repeated experience of worry and tension that interferes with one's life and pleasure, but it is without panic attacks, phobic avoidance, or pathological shyness, as well as without obsessions and compulsions. This is both the base of all anxiety disorders (the worry, tension, and anxiety), and the residual category when the defining features of the anxiety disorders are absent. GAD is pure worry.

Worried All the Time: Generalized Anxiety Disorder (GAD)

Blaine was an eleven-year-old who worried about how she would do on tests in school so much that it was hard to learn the material when she studied, hard to give clear answers in class when the teacher called on her, and hard to take tests because she was sure she was doing it all wrong. A few times she faked stomachaches in order to go to the school nurse instead of taking a test, but she found that this avoidance just made her anxiety worse. Her teacher could see that Blaine was nervous in class, but she chose to be unsympathetic in her responses to these worries, as a way to help Blaine toughen up.

Blaine's classmates were tired of her frequent calls in the evenings to check on homework assignments. Blaine's mother and grandmother, with whom she lived, were worried people themselves. These two women wanted to help Blaine so she would not grow up to be like them, worried about everything all the time. They tried to interest Blaine in the swim team, but Blaine complained every day about how many mistakes she made in practice. Every week she counted how many ribbons her best friend won at the swim meets and how few ribbons she won. This was more evidence for Blaine that she was a bad person.

Obsessive-Compulsive Disorder (OCD)

This anxiety syndrome is characterized by obsessions that are unwanted and intrusive thoughts usually of a violent or sexual nature. These disturbing thoughts lead to intense pathological anxiety. People with OCD try to rid themselves of these hateful thoughts. The more they try to get the thoughts out of their minds, the more painful and persistent the thoughts become. One way that short-term relief from the anxiety caused by obsessive thoughts can be achieved is by engaging in compulsions, or ritual senseless behaviors such as repeating a word over and over, or actions such as hand washing, checking on something, or moving in a certain way. Your thoughts cannot harm you or other people, as many people with OCD fear. Thoughts are just that—thoughts. They do not cause things to happen in magical and scary ways. *OCD is a sort of virtual reality experience, as your anxiety convinces you that your thoughts are reality.*

The Safety Checker: Obsessive-Compulsive Disorder (OCD)

Jenny was a sixty-five-year-old woman who had suffered from anxiety problems most of her life. She had used her husband as a safe person and had not had to limit her life much because of his help. However, her husband died the previous year, and Jenny became obsessed with checking to be sure that the doors and windows of her home were locked and that the stove was turned off. She performed other safety checks throughout the house for hours every day. She had to drop out of her bridge club because she spent so much time on this checking, and she was unable to travel with her senior travel group at church on the annual beach trip because she could not imagine being able to get out of her house.

Jenny had diabetes and heart problems. The doctor who monitored her health had recently made several changes in her medication. Jenny had to begin to talk to the doctor about the possible interactions of these medications with her anxiety problem before embarking on the Anxiety Cure. She chose to seek the help of a therapist because she knew that she was still grieving for her husband, and she did not want to burden her grown children or her friends with these concerns or with her obsessions and compulsions.

Posttraumatic Stress Disorder (PTSD)

Posttraumatic stress disorder (PTSD) is a pattern of anxiety that follows a severe stress, such as being in a war, being raped, or being in a terrible accident. PTSD includes flashback memories of the traumatic event that are so real that it feels as though the event is occurring all over again. These flashbacks often involve nightmares about the event. Situations may be avoided out of a desire to minimize triggering thoughts, such as the veteran who avoids going to the airport because the sounds of the airplanes at takeoff trigger flashbacks of being evacuated from a burning village. Not everyone who goes through a severe stress develops PTSD. While reliving a traumatic event is almost universal for everyone who goes through a horrible experience, these thoughts typically fade over the course of a few weeks or months after the trauma. The symptoms are usually minor and do not interfere with the person's life.

In contrast, PTSD is a persistent and severe disorder that significantly disrupts the sufferer's life for many years. The first fear, which is the traumatic event and the flashback reliving it, instead of fading in intensity over time is reinforced by the second fear, the fear of the fear, which can be continuous. This leads to avoidance of triggering situations, which then increases the likelihood of having a fearful reaction when such situations are encountered.

Aftermath of War: Posttraumatic Stress Disorder (PTSD)

Consuela was a thirty-two-year-old immigrant to the United States. She moved here with her son in fear for their lives because their country in Central America had erupted in war. She had watched her brothers' brutal, involuntary conscription into the guerrilla army and had never seen or heard of them again. Then her village was raided by the nationalist army, and she and her son hid in a tree while Consuela's mother and sister were tortured and killed because her family was identified as guerrilla sympathizers. Her house was burned down.

Four years after the violence, living in the States, she sought treatment, as she found that, despite having finally found a steady job with a hotel cleaning service, she could not escape the flashbacks of violence that plagued her. She noticed that her son, now sixteen, had seemed to adjust quickly to his new life, and while he remembered the horrifying scene at their village, he did not think about it often. Her flashbacks, in contrast, disrupted her sleep nightly and left her in tears whenever she saw a police officer or anyone else in uniform. She found herself increasingly isolated in her apartment by her fears.

All of the six anxiety disorders are built on the same underlying foundation of pathological anxiety and abnormal brain chemistry, including false alarms of terrible danger. Although most people with anxiety disorders suffer from one of these six syndromes, the boundaries between the individual anxiety disorders can be blurred. The pattern of anxiety symptoms occasionally changes over time so that a person who starts off with agoraphobia can later be seen to have a social phobia, or a person with panic disorder and agoraphobia may become primarily troubled by OCD symptoms. For most people, it is not difficult to determine which of these six syndromes of the anxiety disorders best fits their problems, and their diagnostic label does not change over time. To rise to the level of a formal diagnosis, the anxiety problem must be persistent (i.e., it cannot simply be a short-term reaction to stress), and it must cause significant distress and/or disability in a major life area (such as family life, work, or recreation).

All of the anxiety disorders afflict the same sort of people (conscientious worri-

ers), and the anxiety disorders generally respond to the same forms of both medication and nonmedication treatments. Although the differences among the particular anxiety disorders can be important for treatment, usually the similarities among the anxiety disorders are far more important. You will learn more about how to evaluate your own anxiety in the next chapter of this book.

CHAPTER 6

Evaluate Your Own Level of Anxiety

The following Anxiety Inventory and Specific Anxiety Disorder Inventory will help you determine if you are suffering from an anxiety disorder and, if so, which one. You may choose to write the answers to these questions on a separate piece of paper—or on a photocopy of the page—rather than writing in this book. In Part Four, The Anxiety Cure: Eight Steps to Getting Well, we suggest that you keep a journal as you do the work outlined in these steps. If you choose to keep your score on the Anxiety Inventory in a place separate from this book, this may be just the time to start a journal to keep track of information as you read *The Anxiety Cure*. You will find that your score on these tests will fluctuate over time, so it is important to date any tests that you take so you can mark your future progress.

After you have taken the Anxiety Inventory, add your score and record it in the top right-hand corner of your evaluation. You can find where your score puts you compared to others with anxiety.

0–16   May be anxious but unlikely to have an anxiety disorder
17–32   Likely to have an anxiety disorder
33 +   Among the most anxious of people with anxiety disorders

Where your score puts you on this chart is likely to confirm your suspicions about yourself rather than be a surprise to you. To learn more about what specific area may be a problem for you, take the Specific Anxiety Disorder Inventory (page 46), answering yes or no to each question.

Anxiety Inventory

Please circle the response that best describes you. Feel free to change the wording of a particular question to fit your situation. Please answer all questions.

0 = does not describe me   2 = describes me mostly
1 = describes me somewhat   3 = describes me completely

1. I am a tense person.	0 1 2 3
2. I worry more than most people do.	0 1 2 3
3. I have a hard time relaxing.	0 1 2 3
4. I have unexpected panic attacks.	0 1 2 3
5. I avoid particular situations, things, or places because of extreme fear.	0 1 2 3
6. When I am anxious, I have physical symptoms.	0 1 2 3
7. I find excuses not to do things because of my anxiety.	0 1 2 3
8. I am embarrassed by the things I can/cannot do because of anxiety.	0 1 2 3
9. I have horrible thoughts that I cannot stop.	0 1 2 3
10. I have to do things over and over because of fear or worry.	0 1 2 3
11. I am usually shy and uncomfortable when other people are not.	0 1 2 3
12. My work suffers/I cannot work because of my anxiety.	0 1 2 3
13. Family/friends notice that I am anxious.	0 1 2 3
14. Family/friends find my anxiety upsetting.	0 1 2 3
15. I depend on family/friends to do things because of my anxiety.	0 1 2 3
16. I have lost contact with family/friends because of my anxiety.	0 1 2 3

Specific Anxiety Disorder Inventory

---

1. **Agoraphobia/Panic Disorder**

   Agoraphobia

   I have extreme anxiety (fear/worry) or panic
   attacks when I am (or even think about being)
   away from a safe person or a safe place. Yes_____ No_____

   Panic Disorder

   I suffer from sudden flashes of panic out of the
   blue, for no reason (spontaneous panic). Yes_____ No_____

2. **Specific Phobia**

   I have extreme anxiety (fear/worry) or panic
   attacks when I am (or even think about being)
   in specific situations such as closed places, high
   places, flying, or about specific things, such as
   animals, birds, or insects. Yes_____ No_____

3. **Social Phobia**

   I have an extreme anxiety (fear/worry) of
   public speaking that leads to avoidance. Yes_____ No_____

   I am shy and uncomfortable in social
   situations that most people are not troubled
   by (e.g., talking in a group or with someone
   in authority). Yes_____ No_____

4. **Generalized Anxiety Disorder (GAD)**

   I am a worrier whose anxiety (fear/worry) has
   risen and fallen over many years, if not my
   entire lifetime, causing me substantial distress.
   I do not have the defining characteristics of the
   other major anxiety disorders. Yes_____ No_____

5. **Obsessive-Compulsive Disorder (OCD)**

   I have intrusive, repugnant, unwanted thoughts
   that I cannot get rid of (obsessions), and I
   engage in ritualized behaviors to reduce my
   fears of these thoughts (compulsions, such as
   hand washing or checking). Yes_____ No_____

6. **Posttraumatic Stress Disorder (PTSD)**

   Following a severe trauma in my life, I
   developed nightmares and flashbacks in which
   I relive the trauma. Yes_____ No_____

Many people suffer from more than one anxiety disorder, as their excessive worry shows up in a variety of ways. If you answered yes to more than one diagnosis, mark those that apply to you, starting with number 1 (the most severe). The usual custom is to assign the diagnostic label for the anxiety disorder that is most severe when more than one diagnostic label applies to a person. Keep in mind that your distress merits a diagnosis of an anxiety disorder only if the problem causes serious and prolonged distress and/or disability.

The Anxiety Cure is useful for people who fall anywhere along this continuum, from mildly anxious to severely impaired. Only a psychiatrist or a therapist trained in anxiety disorders can diagnose you formally as having one or more anxiety disorders. Though it can be useful to know that you have a specific anxiety diagnosis, it is not necessary in order to begin the work of getting well. If fear, tension, irritability, or, especially, worry rule your life, this program is designed for you.

CHAPTER 7

Medicines and Anxiety

One of the two broad classes of medicines that work to reduce anxiety is the antidepressants. They work whether or not the anxious person also suffers from depression. The antidepressants work by reducing the firing of the locus coeruleus and by reducing the reverberations of panic and anxious thinking. Obsessive-compulsive disorder (OCD) in particular responds to the newer class of antidepressants called selective serotonin reuptake inhibitors (SSRIs), such as Prozac (fluoxetine), Zoloft (sertraline), Paxil (paroxetine), and Luvox (fluvoxamine), as well as to Anafranil (clomipramine), which affects both serotonin and norepinephrine neurotransmitters.

The second major class of medicines that help people with anxiety disorders is the antianxiety medicines, which primarily mean the benzodiazepines such as Xanax (alprazolam), Klonopin (clonazepam), Valium (diazepam), Ativan (lorazepam), and Serax (oxazepam). These medicines work though the gamma-aminobutyric acid (GABA) neurotransmitter system, which is the brain's principal quieting system.

In addition, several other medicines that are neither antidepressants nor benzodiazepines have been used successfully to treat one or more of the anxiety disorders. Inderal (propranolol) and other beta-blockers, which are often used to treat high blood pressure, can be wonderfully helpful in the treatment of public speaking and other performance-related anxiety problems. BuSpar (buspirone) is sometimes helpful for generalized anxiety disorder (GAD).

Medicines can help you achieve your goals. Medicines are not crutches. Using medicines is not a sign of failure or weakness. Many people with anxiety disorders need relatively small doses of medicines, although some people need full doses to get the maximum benefit. Do not take the smallest dose of medicine for the shortest possible time. Use medicines to achieve the maximum benefit for you. If the maximum benefit occurs at a small dose taken only occasionally, as is often the case, that is fine. If you find that larger doses taken every day produce a better quality of life for you, by all means use the medicine that way. Work with your doctor in an open and honest way to find the best way to use medicines to live a full, active life without restrictions due to anxiety. Above all, do not view a need for medicines either as a sign of failure or as a reason not to use the Anxiety Cure program to live a full life.

The Antidepressants

The medicines that are known as antidepressants are now used to treat anxiety. They were developed to treat depression, which is why they are called antidepressants and not antianxieties. In fact, antidepressants are used to treat other conditions as well as depression and anxiety. For example, migraine headaches, impulsive aggressive behavior, chronic pain, insomnia, and eating disorders like bulimia and anorexia nervosa are all successfully treated with these medicines even in the absence of either depression or anxiety. There are many antidepressants available, but most can be divided into two groups: tricyclic antidepressants (TCAs) and selective serotonin reuptake inhibitors (SSRIs). The TCAs were developed in the 1950s and 1960s and generally have more side effects than the newer SSRIs, which were developed primarily in the 1990s. More recently, several newer antidepressants have been introduced that are neither TCAs nor SSRIs. These antidepressants include Wellbutrin (bupropion), Serzone (nefazodone), Effexor (venlafaxine), and Remeron (mirtazapine). The good news is that they all work for many anxious patients, so there are a lot of good options.

These medicines do not make people get high, and they are not addictive, so people cannot get hooked. If you do not have an illness that is treated by antidepressants, then they will have no effect on you except for possibly producing unpleasant side effects. They work by affecting the neurotransmitters in your brain and then by slowly changing brain receptor function. Neurotransmitters are nerve messenger chemicals in the brain. One nerve cell (neuron) releases its neurotransmitter into the space between the nerve cells (synapses) in the brain. Other neurons pick up the neurotransmitter. The receiving nerve cells then carry out the activities that the neurotransmitter has "told" them to do. This process is complicated because there are many kinds of neurotransmitters, and each one may have many different effects on the receiving cells.

Because of their mechanism of action, antidepressants do not work quickly. You must take the antidepressants every day for four to six weeks or longer before they are fully effective. Once you have taken them daily for a month or so, they work continuously. This means that if you have anxiety all of the time, you will be getting treatment all of the time, and if you have anxiety some of the time, the medicine will be working when you need it. You only have to take most antidepressants once a day. The two main drawbacks of the antidepressants are: first, that it takes a few weeks for them to start working, and when you are suffering from anxiety and/or depression, that is a long time. Second, you have to take a pill every day, even if you do not have anxiety every day.

Many anxious people want to know whether these medicines will eliminate their anxiety disorder. Unfortunately, the answer is generally no. For most people, anxiety disorders are lifelong. The symptoms of anxiety and panic get better and then worse, and sometimes they go away and then come back. The medicines work when they are taken, but they do not work after you stop taking them. In this way, antidepressants are like antihypertensives, which are medicines that are taken for high blood pressure, and like insulin, which is taken for high blood sugar in diabetes mellitus. These medicines, like the antidepressants, are powerful and generally safe, but they do not eliminate the illness for which they are used, although they do restore normal function if they are taken each day.

Selective Serotonin Reuptake Inhibitors (SSRIs)   The newer antidepressants, called selective serotonin reuptake inhibitors (SSRIs), are often considered first-line medicines for anxiety disorders. They work by affecting serotonin, which is a neurotransmitter. As the name SSRI implies, these medicines act by inhibiting or slowing reuptake, or recycling, of the serotonin. This means that the serotonin hangs around longer in the space between the neurons in your brain so that the receiving neuron has a longer time to pick up the message. There are four SSRIs currently available. They are each a little different, but they work by the same general mechanism:

Brand Name	Generic Name
Prozac	fluoxetine
Zoloft	sertraline
Paxil	paroxetine
Luvox	fluvoxamine

There are several reasons why the SSRIs are often used as the first medicine option in the treatment of anxiety disorders. The first is that they work. About 70 percent of people taking any one of these medicines get better, and if one SSRI does not work, another one probably will. The second reason is that they are well tolerated by most patients. This means that many patients can take these medicines without having unpleasant side effects. The third advantage of these newer antidepressants is that the SSRIs have to be taken only once a day, so they are fairly easy to use. Another important advantage of the SSRIs is that many doctors are comfortable prescribing them, including primary care physicians, gynecologists, gerontologists, and internists. They are easy for the doctor to prescribe for several reasons: each SSRI has a recommended dose that most patients respond to, and they are fairly safe medicines. There is no danger of addiction or abuse, and if a person takes too much by accident or in a suicide attempt, the SSRI is unlikely to do any harm.

Side Effects of the SSRIs   If these medicines are so great, why don't all anxious people take them? All medicines have potential side effects, like getting indigestion from aspirin or diarrhea from antibiotics, but some medicines cause more problems for more people than others. In general, SSRIs have fewer unpleasant side effects than many other medicines, including the TCAs, which they have largely replaced. Because the four SSRIs are each a little different, even if one causes a side effect, another one might not. The most common side effects with the SSRIs are insomnia, jittery feelings, upset stomach, headache, sleepiness, loss of sexual interest, and, paradoxically, anxiety.

When Joe, a twenty-seven-year-old graduate student, heard this list of possible side effects, he yelled, "Anxiety! I thought this was supposed to treat anxiety, not cause it!" It took him several minutes to calm down enough to understand that SSRIs do treat anxiety, but, especially early in treatment, they can also cause it. This and other side effects can usually be reduced or eliminated by starting at a low dose and increasing the dose of the medicine slowly. Joe agreed to start by cutting the pills in half and taking only half of the usual recommended starting dose. After a week he was not having any side effects, and he felt comfortable taking the whole pill.

Another patient, Alice, was also a graduate student. She was not worried about side effects because she'd never had a problem taking medicines in the past. She took the pills as recommended for several days and began to have difficulty sleeping. This was a big problem for her because she was extremely busy and needed her sleep. She stopped taking the medicine and did not go back to see her doctor for six months.

She finally did go back because her anxiety disorder was again affecting her ability to work. The anxiety made her miserable, but she was afraid of trying another medicine because of the difficulties with the first medicine she had tried. Her doctor explained that even though the medicines are similar, each person reacts to each medicine differently. She recommended that Alice try a different SSRI. She asked Alice to call her in a few days to let her know how she was doing. When Alice called, she reported a little trouble sleeping. She was not sure if the trouble sleeping was caused by the medicine or by her newfound anxiety about taking the medicine. She and her doctor agreed to give it a little more time. When Alice came into the office for her next appointment, she reported that she was sleeping well.

Tricyclic Antidepressants (TCAs)   The second main group of anti-depressants are the tricyclic antidepressants (TCAs). They were developed long before the SSRIs and continue to be widely used. They work by af-fecting two neurotransmitters, serotonin and norepinephrine. They work as well as the SSRIs and are also used for many medical conditions includ-ing depression, anxiety disorders, chronic pain, migraine headaches, and insomnia. There are many TCAs currently available. A few of the more commonly used are:

Brand Name	Generic Name
Tofranil	imipramine
Norpramin	desipramine
Pamelor	nortriptyline
Sinequan	doxepin

These medicines are not the first medicine option, because they have more side effects than the newer SSRIs. However, they are effective for some people. Remember, each person responds differently to each medi-cine. The best medicine for one anxious person is not necessarily the best medicine for another.

Side Effects of the TCAs   The most common side effects of the TCAs are dry mouth, constipation, urinary retention (especially in men with prostate enlargement), and weight gain. As with the SSRIs, the side effects can often be minimized by starting at a low dose and increasing gradually. One busy executive put the side effects in perspective: "When I was not taking medicine, I could not go to many important meetings because I was so fearful that I would be called on to talk. Now I go to meetings several times a week. Sure, my mouth is dry, but I would rather have it dry from medicine than dry from fear!" He helped minimize the problem by carrying hard candies to suck on or bottled water. He joked, "So many people carry their own bottled water these days that nobody thinks to question me about it."

Sexual Dysfunction   The SSRIs, as well as the TCAs, can cause difficulty in several areas of sexual functioning, including erectile dysfunction, decreased libido or desire, and delayed or absent orgasm. These are not permanent problems. These side effects go away when the medicine is stopped, but, unfortunately, so will the benefits of the SSRI. Around 50 percent of the people taking these medicines experience some effect on their sex life. For many people the problem is not great enough to warrant their stopping the medicine, but this side effect should be discussed openly with your doctor. Do not be embarrassed to bring up sexual problems or questions. Sometimes the doctor is afraid of bringing it up for fear of embarrassing the patient, and the patient does not want to bring it up for fear of embarrassing the doctor. If this is an important part of your life, discuss it with your doctor.

Sex and Relaxation

Anxiety also can affect a person's sex life even if that person isn't taking any medicine. Many anxious people have trouble relaxing. Glenn had a happy and fulfilling marriage. He loved his wife and found her beautiful and attractive. They had a satisfying sex life until his OCD got control of him. He was embarrassed to admit that in the midst of lovemaking, he would suddenly think, Did I lock the door? or What if I left the stove on? Not only did this affect his sexual enjoyment, but at times it put a stop to intimacy altogether, as he would jump out of bed to check whatever had worried him. His wife was patient for a long time, but gradually it began to affect their marriage adversely. For Glenn, taking an SSRI was a success, and his sex life improved with the decrease in his anxiety.

The Benzodiazepines (BZs)

These useful, generally safe medicines work by promoting quieting of the brain through the GABA neurotransmitter system. In general, they help within about half an hour of taking the pills. Their effects last from four to about twelve hours. The BZs are effective against both anxiety and panic. They are not effective treatments for depression except when the depression is the result of being demoralized by the anxiety disorder. When the depression is secondary to anxiety and the BZ effectively treats the anxiety, then the secondary depression disappears. The BZs are not used to treat anxious people who are also alcoholics or drug addicts because they may be abused at higher than medically desirable doses.

The BZs are safe for virtually everyone else. The BZs have few side effects other than possible sedation (feeling groggy), which usually disappears after a few doses. Because of their rapid effects, the BZs can be used when the anxiety problem is bad and then not used when the anxiety problem is not so bad. Since anxiety tends to wax and wane over time, it is often helpful to use more or less of a medicine, depending on the severity of the anxiety problem at a particular time. Many anxious people find that it helps to know that they can take the medicine if things get really bad. You may want to carry your medicine with you in a pocket or purse, just in case you need it. This medicine can be a powerful tool in your toolbox for dealing with anxiety, as it provides a pharmacological out—relief from the panic trap.

Insomnia   The BZs can also be helpful in the treatment of primary insomnia. We call this experience sleep anxiety, since it is anticipatory fear that you will not fall asleep. Just knowing that you have a BZ and could use it if needed is often beneficial to people with anxiety disorders, including insomnia. See Part Five, Anxiety and Your Daily Life, for more information about insomnia and its treatment.

Beta-blockers and BuSpar

Propranolol is the chemical name for Inderal, the most widely used beta-blocker. Inderal is taken in doses of 20 to 40 mg about one hour before giving a speech. It is often miraculous for public speaking phobia, but it is seldom helpful in treating other forms of anxiety disorders.

Some anxious people benefit from taking BuSpar (buspirone), an antianxiety medicine taken two or three times a day. Like the antidepressants, BuSpar produces its effect gradually after several weeks of use. Also like the antidepressants, BuSpar has no abuse potential for alcoholics or drug addicts.

The Big Picture

Treating anxiety disorders is similar to treating diabetes or high blood pressure. Sometimes dietary and lifestyle changes are all that are needed for those who suffer from diabetes or hypertension to return their blood sugar or blood pressure values to normal. For other people with these disorders, taking medicines is necessary for shorter or longer periods of time, either because the person is unwilling or unable to make behavioral changes or because the behavioral changes are not sufficient to return the blood sugar or blood pressure to normal levels. In either case, whether or not medicines are needed for the effective treatment of anxiety disorders, diabetes, or hypertension, there is no reason to feel either guilt or shame. What is needed is a clear-eyed view of the problem and a commitment to doing whatever is necessary to live the most satisfying and most productive life possible, whether or not that requires medicines.

Most anxious people are reluctant to take medicines, which adds to their interest in trying to work out nonmedical solutions to their anxiety disorders. Sometimes lower doses of medicines can be used once the panic and anxiety have been brought under control and the anxious person's nervous system has begun to heal after a long period of disturbed functioning. Using medicines for weeks or months can sometimes successfully restore the sensitized brain to a more normal state, and the remission of anxious symptoms persists for longer or shorter periods when the medicine is stopped.

Because the anxiety disorders are usually lifelong, it is common for people suffering from them to use medicines either continuously or intermittently throughout their lives. These medicines generally do not cause any problems when taken over long periods of time, so there is no need to fear them. On the other hand, they sometimes do cause unpleasant but not dangerous side effects, which are eliminated when the dose of the medicine is reduced or stopped. Talk to your doctor if you notice any side effects from taking a medicine. Often a simple change of medicine, or a dose adjustment, can have major impacts on side effects.

CHAPTER 8

Understanding the Anxiety Dragon and the Worry Machine

Fear of fear is at the heart of the anxiety disorders, and it is like a dragon that attacks the suffering anxious person. Over the years we have learned a lot about this dragon and how he operates because we have seen so many people who have suffered terribly from his attacks. We have come to view the dragon as male, but you may view the dragon as either male or female. Or neuter! Or as something other than a dragon. Whatever works for you.

The Dragon Wants You!

The dragon wants you to believe that he can kill you, or perhaps even more frightening, that he can make you go crazy, cause you to pass out, or cause you to do something uncontrolled or embarrassing. He does this with an awesome display of feelings and by causing terrifying involuntary thoughts. When the dragon has you on the run, when he has scared you out of your wits, he offers you this deal: "Give up part of your life and I will give you some peace!" What does the dragon want you to give up? It might be public speaking, going to a shopping mall, or flying on an airplane. It might be driving on a highway, going somewhere that is unfamiliar, or talking with someone you fear will reject or judge you, including a boss or other person in authority. The dragon wants to take control of your life, piece by piece.

People with obsessive-compulsive disorder (OCD) see a somewhat different face of the dragon than do people who suffer from the other anxiety disorders. The dragon tells people with OCD that something dreadful will happen to them or to someone they care about if they do not behave in a certain way, such as washing their hands endlessly, checking something a thousand times, or repeating a senseless behavior or thought dozens of times in unusual, ritualized ways. These actions of a person with OCD are called compulsions. They are the equivalent of the phobias, which cause avoidance behaviors in many other anxious people. Once the dragon gets control of their lives, most phobic people eliminate certain normal behaviors from their lives (such as driving or shopping) as a result of anticipatory anxiety.

People with OCD, in contrast, have additional abnormal behaviors as a result of the dragon's influence on their lives. People who suffer from OCD do their best to hide their abnormal (dragon-driven) behaviors, just as phobic people do their best to hide their missing normal behaviors. For those with OCD, the abnormal behaviors are something added to their lives by fear; for other anxious people, phobias lead to the absence of normal behaviors from their lives. Both compulsions and phobias are the result of accepting the dragon's dreadful deals in the hope of lessening uncomfortable feelings. They are both ways of temporarily reducing panic and anxiety and lead to long-term restrictions in the lives of anxious people.

All anxiety disorders come down to the same thing. The dragon tells you, "Reshape your life the way I want you to and then I will give you a bit of peace, a bit of comfort. If, however, you do not comply right now, then I will cause your entire life to be filled with terror." The dragon does not countenance any delay in his gratification. He wants what he wants when he wants it. His approach is, "Give me your life immediately—or else!"

The Dragon Is a Liar

Here are some things the dragon does not want you to know about him. He cannot do any of the things he tells you he can do. He cannot make you pass out or go crazy. He cannot cause you to have a brain tumor, a heart attack, or any other illness. He cannot make you have an automobile crash or do something uncontrolled. He cannot leave you stuck in the terror of a PTSD flashback. People suffering from anxiety disorders, or "dragon attacks," often doubt this because they have believed the dragon. They tell us just how close they have come to awful outcomes as a result of repeated dragon attacks. We have come to call the anxiety disorders the diseases of "this close," as people say, putting their fingers very close together, "I came 'this close' to passing out" or "I came 'this close' to having an accident." When someone tells us that they repeatedly came "this close" to something terrible happening, we know we are dealing with the work of the anxiety disorders dragon.

A woman who was simultaneously dying from metastatic breast cancer and suffering from agoraphobia said: "If I could be cured right now of one of these two diseases, I would choose to be cured of the agoraphobia because that disease ruins my life every single day. The cancer will kill me one day before too long, but until it does I can live a reasonably happy and full life. The agoraphobia wrecks my life all day, every day."

A sixty-five-year-old businessman who was a veteran of the Korean War developed agoraphobia at the age of thirty. He became virtually housebound, traveling only to and from his work. He insisted that his wife be with him whenever he went anywhere except to work or back home. He said: "It is incomprehensible to me that in the war, when I faced death, I felt only ordinary fear, which was not much of a problem for me. I parachuted into battle, and I was decorated for bravery several times. After the war, I traveled alone all over the world without fear. Now that I have this terrible agoraphobia, I cannot go to the supermarket and I cannot drive on the freeways. I cannot visit my brother in New York. I do not understand what has happened to me. My life now is just not my own, even though I have had agoraphobia for more than half of my life."

This man's humiliation from his anxiety disorder was tempered by the memory of his personal history of heroism: "If I had not had that war experience, I might have come to believe over all these years that I really was weak and a coward. But when I look at my medals and I recall my war years, I know for sure that I am not weak and that I am not a coward. I also know that this problem you call my agoraphobia is a whole lot tougher than most people who have not had it imagine that it is."

We tell these two stories to make it clear that we respect the dragon for what he can do. He can produce terrible, terrible feelings. We have learned that these feelings are all that the dragon can do; his other threats are empty.

Here are some other important things we have learned about the dragon:

1. He operates by blackmail. Although the dragon asks you to give up a part of your normal life in return for peace from his attacks, when you do give up the pieces of your life demanded by the dragon, as most anxious people eventually do, he will not give you peace. He will be back again year after year, like all successful blackmailers, asking for more and more of your life. The dragon has no pity and no honor. His goal is to make you his hostage. He does not want you to roam free in your life. He wants you to stay behind the bars he has constructed for you. "Stay here and you will be safe. Go outside these bars and you will feel my full wrath," the dragon shouts through his bared teeth and multicolored, fiery breath.

2. The dragon can eat only one food—your fear. Nothing else except your fear of him can sustain the ever-hungry dragon. The more you fear the dragon, the more you feed him and the bigger and more terrible he grows. Stop fearing the dragon and you stop feeding him. Without your fear, he withers away and eventually dies of neglect.

3. The dragon's greatest strength is his talent for disguise. Just when his attacks become familiar to you, just when you resolve not to fear him, the dragon changes costumes and comes at you with entirely new symptoms, often pretending to be yet another deadly physical disorder. People with OCD sometimes experience the dragon as threatening not only themselves but also others, especially the people whom they love the most. The dragon may have threatened you with a brain tumor at the start, but then he shifted to threaten an ulcer or heart disease. The anxious pain may at first have been mostly in your arms or your back, but then your stomach or your bowels become affected. The dragon will scare you about the medicine you take and the food you eat, convincing you that they are poison and that any unfamiliar symptoms are life threatening. There is no limit to the dragon's skill at disguise. One telltale feature that is usually part of the picture when the dragon is involved is the extreme worry produced by the dragon's pretending to be a physical disease.

4. When you start to get well, the dragon grows more and more desperate. As he senses your possible escape from his prison, he pulls out his last trick. It is one of his best. He lets you go for days, weeks, or even for years without any trouble. He encourages you to think that you have defeated him. You grow more and more confident about your achievements and secure in your new, fuller life, free of the dragon and your fear of him. You come to think that your panic is part of a distant and unpleasant past.

Then one day when you least expect it, sometimes when you are under stress and sometimes when you are under no stress at all, the dragon comes back with full force. Panic grips you once more. You suddenly remember, as if for the first time, how awful the experience of panic has been. You are confused and afraid. You feel weak and defeated. Then, facing a severe relapse, you confront the true test of your work to recover from your anxiety disorder. See Part Seven, Chapter 26, for more about dealing with relapses.

Taming the Dragon

Jerry, a patient who owned a delicatessen, said that for twenty years he had gone only between home and work and nowhere else. He came for help in desperation when his daughter was getting married. He feared being "trapped" at the wedding ceremony when he would have to walk down the aisle. He had been in psychotherapy for years but had not gotten any better from his panic disorder and agoraphobia. He learned about the dragon and how he could find freedom by facing the dragon respectfully but without fear.

Accept the Dragon

My previous therapy, which I had over all these years, told me that I needed to understand why the dragon chose to attack me, of all people. I needed to know why he attacked me just exactly when and how he did. Every therapist I saw taught me techniques for protecting my life from the dragon, closing my house and sealing the doors and windows so that the dragon could not get to me. I learned complicated, detailed breathing and relaxation techniques to help me stay calm. I never could keep the dragon out of my life, but I dared not give up my ever more complex and frantic efforts to banish him.

You were the first to advise me to open the doors and windows of my life and to accept the dragon without fear and with no—absolutely no—defenses. When the dragon showed up before the wedding, I invited him in. I set a nice table for him and gave him good food and drink. Then I told him to enjoy himself and that although I would be back shortly, right now I needed to do some things outside of the house. I asked him to make himself at home and to know that I would be back to help him a little later on. Amazingly enough, the dragon seemed to be satisfied with that treatment. He got what he wanted, and I got my life back.

That is the way with this anxiety disease: it comes for no reason, and the sufferer is not responsible for having the disease. Nevertheless, a cure—knowing what is wrong and what to do about the problem—can only be earned one person at a time by that person's own hard work over a long period of time. A cure is regaining control of your life, not being free of panic or anxiety.

The first time you have a panic attack is always the worst, because that time you did not know what was happening to you. You were not only unprepared but you also had no way of knowing that even though these were bad feelings and bad thoughts, you would not die, go crazy, or lose control. The single most important part of getting well is knowing what you are up against, knowing what the dragon can and, even more important, cannot do. That knowledge comes only over time from experience and hard work.

Understand the Worry Machine

People with anxiety disorders suffer from anticipatory anxiety—the second fear. Because of the great importance of the anticipatory anxiety, we have labeled the anxiety disorders the malignant diseases of the "what-ifs." Anxiety disorder sufferers project themselves into the future and foresee disasters just around the corner. When they think about what might happen, they only think of bad outcomes, never good. It is as if they have worry machines in their brains that crank out nothing but worries—the "what-if" scenarios of troubles and disasters. The worry machines spin the precious gold of clinically anxious people's lives into straw.

Awfulizing Dominates Your Life

One anxious patient described the cruel and relentless working of his worry machine: "I have had a terrible life—only most of the bad things never happened." Another patient called his worry about terrible things that might happen to him "the if-ies," noting that most of his suffering was not from panic or even from avoidance, but from "the if-ies."

Worry takes on a life of its own for many clinically anxious people. One patient of ours told us that his wife called his routine anxious thinking "awfulizing." He scanned not only own his own life, but also his family, and the whole world through the media—focusing on awful things, upsetting and frightening things. He found a lot of them over the years! These awful things got stuck in his mind. He could not get free of them. While some anxious people find that their worries are limited to one or two things (such as elevators or airplanes), most anxious people do a lot of involuntary awfulizing about an amazing range of worries. Life, especially through the modern media, provides an endless supply of material on which to awfulize.

Another anxious woman explained how the worry machine affected her: "I get so upset about potentially bad things that may happen to me or to my family that I cannot think of the good things that happen all the time to all of us. In fact, when something good happens I immediately think of how it could turn into something bad. I must do this because a pessimist is never disappointed. If I never let myself think of good things in my life, then I cannot be disappointed. If something bad happens, I can tell myself, 'I told you so.' If something good happens, I am pleasantly surprised, but I quickly change the good to what bad might come from it so that I don't risk getting disappointed if I lose the good experience in the future."

A Positive Side to Worry

We have noticed one good result of these otherwise distressing workings of the worry machine. *When anxious people find themselves in genuinely dangerous situations, like a serious automobile accident or the major illness of a family member, they usually behave admirably.* They do not panic when confronted by real danger, even though many so-called normal people do. We have come to think of this as the result of the anxious person's always being in mental training for disaster. Disasters do not happen very often in anyone's life, but when they do happen to anxious people, they are the only people who are always prepared!

Rehearsing for Disaster

Sally was forty-five, a teacher, mother, and an agoraphobic whose big problem was driving. She struggled over many years practicing her driving and had become able to drive to her children's school and to shopping and to work. An even bigger problem for Sally was her husband, Mike, who was a tremendously successful corporate attorney with little patience for her driving phobia.

One evening while Mike was driving, they were involved in a multicar accident on a major commuter road. Neither of them was injured seriously but other drivers and passengers were. The accident scene was frightening, with people bleeding and crying in the lights of flashing rescue and police vehicles. Mike was confused and no help at all as he ran around the accident scene. Sally got Mike calmed down and managed to help several injured people. She drove herself and Mike home because Mike was too upset to drive.

The next week Sally came to therapy with a new self-esteem and new respect from her husband. She explained that she had not been upset at the accident because she had anticipated an auto accident for decades and had rehearsed her role thousands of times in her anxious mind. When an accident happened, she was calm and efficient. Mike, in contrast, had never thought about an accident and had no idea what to do. He told Sally the next day that he appreciated her helping him. He was embarrassed by his behavior. She was glad to have been able to reassure him and to play the role of the strong and understanding spouse.

Practicing Problem Solving

Margaret was an artist whose husband was a physician. Margaret had GAD and used medication every day to help her manage her anxiety. She had been through a lot of psychoanalytic therapy many years ago, which she now thought had not helped her, but her more recent cognitive psychotherapy had helped her to accept her illness and regain better control of her life. Margaret was certain that her heightened sensitivity, stemming from her anxiety, was a big help in her art, as she was tuned into intense feelings in visual ways that she compared to the power of a laser beam.

When their daughter, Becky, developed epilepsy at the age of seventeen, Margaret's husband had a hard time coping. He was worried about Becky and skeptical about her medical treatment. Margaret took over the management of Becky's care, doing what everyone agreed was a great job. Margaret put this all in perspective:

"My anxieties are hard to pin down. They come at me from every direction. When one leaves, another appears. With Becky's epilepsy, scary as it was for all of us, I knew what the problem was, and my usual systematic approach to life worked. I just took it step by step, and it all worked out. My irrational anxiety made this realistic problem seem easy. What amazed me was not that I handled Becky's problem reasonably well but that everyone else, especially my husband, was surprised and therefore quick to congratulate me. That shows me that they just do not know how hard the anxiety problem is to deal with compared to the problems that overwhelm most people in life."

PART THREE

Helping the Anxious Person

CHAPTER 9

Elizabeth's Story

A Sister

In the Introduction and Chapter 1 of this book, you learned about Bob's and Caroline's firsthand experience with anxiety disorders. This story will be a familiar one for friends and family members of sufferers from anxiety disorders. As Caroline's older sister, I was not her parent and not her support person, and yet I spent many years with Caroline as she struggled with her anxiety.

I felt helpless as I watched her suffer. Caroline's childhood fears were terrifying and unsettling for her and for me. I remember the time we were trapped in a closet while playing hide-and-seek as small children. Although I was five years old, I was not frightened by the experience. Sure, it was dark, and the dust on the closet floor made me sneeze, but I knew that an adult would be along soon to find out where we were. I called out for help. I put my arm around her and felt her shiver with fear in the dark. Could such a short experience explain the terror that she thereafter experienced? It seemed to be the only way to understand why in future years she was so frightened of closed spaces.

I learned to be protective of Caroline, since it was so easy to avoid the things she feared and the consequences were so terrible for her if she had to face her fears. She was eight and I was ten and the dragon of anxiety had convinced both of us to give in to his demands. We would meet at recess in elementary school so I could hold open the door to the bathroom for her. I knew if I didn't do that, she would wait all day to use the bathroom until she got home. On the other side of protectiveness, however, was resentment. I never got to the best swings first on the playground because I had to wait behind with my younger sister. I resented the intrusion of her anxiety into my life. Since I did not know then that it was an illness, I simply saw the problem as Caroline limiting my life.

Caroline's anxiety also limited my life because she was afraid not only for herself but also for the rest of her family, fearing something terrible would happen to the people she loved. This meant that none of us could ride an elevator or walk up the stairs without holding the door open without risking her screams of fear. Sometimes I felt the urge to do something she did not want me to do just to hear her scream. More often I stumbled unaware into a fear-generating situation, like the time I came out of a bathroom in a fast-food restaurant to find her in tears outside the door, certain that I had been locked inside and would never be seen again.

When Dad learned about treating phobias and anxiety and began to help Caroline with her fears, our family life changed dramatically. Suddenly there was a way other than avoidance to help Caroline deal with her fears. We had a language to communicate how scared she was, with the ability to rank the intensity of her fear from 0 to 10. With consistent practice, the fears shrank amazingly quickly. It was a miracle. After all those years of having to submit as a family to the dragon's self-centered will, life was again unmarred by avoidance and tantrums.

It seemed that once Caroline had the tools to deal with anxiety, her fears fell like a row of dominos. Suddenly she could close doors to bathrooms at school, at first with me standing just outside and then on her own.

Having considered myself immune to anxiety problems, I was surprised one day when I stood in front of an elevator and felt my heart hammer and my mouth go dry with fear. I was a student at Columbia University in New York, and I lived on the eighth floor of a freshman dormitory. This occurred several weeks into the fall semester, and I had ridden that elevator daily during that time. Yet suddenly I could not get onto the elevator. My experience made clear to me that anxiety is truly a family disorder.

I got over my brief fear by realizing that I had set myself up for having an anxiety problem. The first weeks of college are tremendously stressful. Additionally, I had been staying up later than I was used to and, consequently, drinking more coffee during the day to stay awake. By that time, after my years of learning about anxiety, I knew to cut back on the coffee, get more sleep, and use relaxation techniques to calm myself prior to attempting to ride the elevator again. I rode the elevator alone the next morning—a quiet time, and after having had a good night's sleep. I had only mild anxiety and have continued riding elevators ever since. Even now I have some anxiety every time I step into an elevator. I look on the anxiety as a reminder that I need to keep up my own work or risk being entangled with the dragon once again.

People with a family history of anxiety disorders are genetically vulnerable to having anxiety problems. Not everyone is going to have the same degree of difficulty, but I know that I am definitely at risk. I use my knowledge of anxiety treatment to reduce the risk that anxiety will become a problem in my life, and I generally avoid medications and caffeine that might cause me to have a panic attack. When I have a tooth filled, for example, I request novocaine formulated without epinephrine, since I have found that regular novocaine causes me to have unpleasant physical symptoms of anxiety.

Now I have two sons. Will they have anxiety problems? Probably not, but the risk is in our family. I do not wish such a painful problem on my sons, but if either (or both) should develop an anxiety problem, I am ready to help them not only overcome it but also to learn from it as others in my family have—including me.

CHAPTER 10

Friends, Family, and Anxiety

The person who has the symptoms of anxiety is not the only one who suffers in a family struggling with an anxiety disorder. Many of the high costs of phobic avoidance are paid by family members. A vacation is a lot less fun if your friend, child, spouse, or parent has a phobia that prevents him or her from going along or which turns the joyous experience of a vacation into a torture for the anxious person and, because of this suffering, everyone else.

Sometimes frustrated friends and family think the clinically anxious person is malingering or trying to manipulate them to get his or her own way in difficult situations. This may have some truth as the anxiety takes over much of the person's life, but in the end it is never the whole, or even the most important part, of the story. This is because anxiety is so terribly painful. No one would choose to have an anxiety disorder, no matter how desperately he or she sought to manipulate someone else to do something. The pain of the anxiety is simply too great to permit that sort of manipulation.

It is hard for children to understand why their phobic mothers or fathers do not drive them to school or to after-school activities the way other children's parents do. Even when a friend or family member tries to understand and to help solve anxiety problems by talking with the anxious person, the words of the anxious person can be confusing and disturbing because this is not a rational disorder. If the kitchen is a mess, why does a mother with OCD not allow her teenage son to clean it? How can a teacher understand that a child would restrict the intake of liquids all day at school because he or she is so scared of going into a bathroom without windows? It is often hard not to be angered by the explanations given for phobic behaviors.

Our family's confrontation with an anxiety disorder was relatively brief

70

and had a happy outcome, as Caroline no longer has symptoms of the claustrophobia that plagued her as a child. Brief though this interlude was, however, it clearly had a profound impact on our lives, and as a result the anxiety disorders have become the focus of our professional work. Each of us has incorporated the techniques that are used in the Anxiety Cure into our own lives not only to deal with our own anxieties but also to deal with many of life's problems. Each of us has devoted much of our professional lives to helping people with anxiety disorders. Not only have our experiences helped us in our professional work, but we also have learned from our experiences to respect the suffering that is part of anxiety disorders while maintaining a tough-love stance—filled with hope, no matter how many prior efforts have failed—to overcoming these disturbing problems.

Frustrating Attempts to Help

One of the first signs of trouble for friends and families confronting anxiety disorders is often the control over the behaviors of others that anxious people exert in order to decrease their intense anxieties. These attempts at control may include incomprehensible tasks that make others feel unimportant or enslaved by the anxiety dragon, an unreasonable taskmaster. Friends and family members are being victimized as they are pulled into the anxious person's world. The passion surrounding this type of irrational behavioral control can be intense, often leading to the capitulation of nonanxious people, who would rather yield than suffer through the worry of having done something "wrong." Powerful feelings of fear and anger can erode relationships, alienate friends and family members, and, ultimately, cause all concerned to feel alone, rejected, and hopeless. This is a common but terrible consequence of allowing the anxiety, fear, and panic to become more real and more important than the caring bonds among friends and family.

Most anxious people try to hide their manipulations of their friends and family members because they know their needs are unreasonable. All too often, friends and family members are either oblivious to the deep-seated irrationality behind certain requests or preferences or they are willing to give in to get along. Only in extreme situations is the anxious person willing to come out and label the request for what it is: a do-or-die requirement for any sort of peaceful family life. The power of the anxiety disease is so great that no matter how loving and easygoing the anxious person is in other aspects of family relationships, when it comes to phobic avoidance or obsessive-compulsive rituals, no compromise or reason can be tolerated. This is a surefire recipe for family crisis.

Imaginary Victims

Mary was a twenty-four-year-old woman with OCD. She had a terrible fear that while she was driving, or even riding as a passenger in a car, she would hit or witness the hitting of a pedestrian. This had been a problem for her since she was sixteen years old when she took a driver's education course that showed a movie about drinking and driving. The movie ended with a scene of a pedestrian having been struck and killed by a hit-and-run driver. At the time she came to us for help, Mary did not drink at all for fear that she suddenly might have to drive. She lived in the city, so she could usually take the subway. Her mother drove her to her part-time job on the weekends. Whenever Mary had the obsession that her mother had hit a pedestrian during their drive to work, her mother gave in to Mary's request to turn around and retrace their route to search for the imagined victim. This took them so much extra time that they routinely took twice the ordinary driving time to get to their destination. Mary's mother had to choose between going on a fruitless search or enduring the pain and anger of the anxious passenger. Years before she had chosen the easy route of going along with Mary's fear, although the mother knew the search was pointless. This had become so much a part of their lives that they rarely discussed the fact that Mary's request was outrageous and wasteful.

In situations where this type of behavioral control has gone on for many years, it may seem normal to the nonanxious friends and family members to do things in odd ways. They may have adapted to cover up the anxiety problem by ignoring the strange ways that they are all forced to act. Often families in which this has happened are quite isolated socially, because often they are defending the anxious person from the scrutiny of the rest of the world.

Families and friends who have protected a person with an anxiety disorder have a difficult task during treatment, as they have to unlearn all of the unreasonable, protective, and limiting behaviors that they performed previously. Instead they have to see that their protection is keeping the anxiety disorder alive and that it is a disservice to an anxious person to give in to the tyrannically anxious feelings because it reinforces the anxious person's perception that this behavior is acceptable. *Once friends and family members stop giving in to the unreasonable demands of the anxious person and begin to do things in a more healthy manner, anxiety and stress will lessen for both the anxious person and for those who care about that person.*

This reduction in anxiety is especially true for nonanxious family members and friends who have been supporting the anxiety, since these people often do things the "wrong" way. They do not have the powerful, irrational internal feelings that would dictate the oddly specific way in which things must be done, and they are repeatedly being taken to task for this by the distressed anxious person.

Stop Supporting the Anxiety Disorder

No longer supporting the anxiety disorder can be easy for some friends and families, but for most it is a difficult process filled with moments of uncertainty. If the person suffering from an anxiety disorder is motivated to overcome the disability of the anxiety-driven behavior, then this process is much easier.

Mary sought help in a crisis because her job transferred her to the suburbs, which necessitated her driving to work daily at the same time that her mother developed an illness that forced her to restrict her driving. What had been a stable pattern for Mary and her mother for years suddenly collapsed, and both of them had to confront the fact that Mary was unable to continue as before, when she had been relying on her mother. Mary's mother felt bad when she realized that her loving support of her daughter had allowed Mary to stay relatively free of anxiety but only at a high price. Mary suffered because of her limited life, especially socially. Once she sought help, Mary worked hard on learning new techniques and practicing new behaviors because she was motivated to keep her job. Mary's mother was extremely supportive of her and praised her hard work. This story ended successfully, with the daughter able to drive herself directly to her destination without having to retrace her route and without severe anxiety.

In situations where a friend or family member has decided not to tolerate the dragon's dictates any longer, but where the anxious person is not a willing participant, there will be many difficult decisions to make. It is easy to imagine how this story would have gone if Mary had not wanted to change her behavior. Her mother would have been caught between her desire to help her daughter live a normal life and her desire not to upset her anxious daughter. This sad dilemma happens frequently and leads not only to breaks in friendships and family bonds but also to increased limitations and increased suffering for the anxious person. It is truly important to keep the message of tough love for the anxious person and anger at the anxiety disorder dragon's tyranny clear at all times.

Once Mary's mother learned about OCD and how to treat it, she could say that it was out of love for her daughter that she no longer drove her to work. She learned that trying to minimize the symptoms of anxiety at the time they first occurred by giving in to Mary's illness in reality had prolonged and intensified her daughter's suffering. If, despite the best efforts of friends and family, the anxious person insists on continuing to give in to anxious thoughts, it may be time to move on without that person.

What if Mary's mother had learned about the treatment for OCD and shared her knowledge with Mary, but Mary had not wanted to confront her fears. If her mother then decided to move to another city to convalesce from her illness, that would be an example of moving on and forcing the anxious person to change the present anxiety-driven behavior.

The most common example of this type of situation is in families where one member has agoraphobia or a flying or driving phobia, and a family vacation, an out-of-town wedding, or another obligation is scheduled months in advance. It may be necessary for the family to choose to go on the trip and to lovingly encourage the phobic family member to join them but not to alter their plans if the anxious person chooses not to attempt to confront his or her fears. It is important to stress that this is done out of a desire to help the anxious person get well and to show that there is no reason to give in to the fear. If the dragon is allowed to control the family's activities, then the dragon puts not only the anxious person in prison, but also the entire family is held hostage.

There may be complicating reasons why a person fails to get well from an anxiety disorder. For example, posttraumatic stress disorder (PTSD) can be complicated by depression, addiction, or legal and financial consequences of the event, such as liability lawsuits and disability payments. Work on PTSD with the Anxiety Cure may be severely hampered if there are financial reasons for a person to benefit from having the anxiety problem. People who have secondary gains from PTSD and other anxiety disorders associated with liability have a conflicted motivation for recovery: if they get better, they lose the "perk" of having the problem. This is important to evaluate early on in your recovery because we have found that people with secondary gains do not fare well in terms of long-term recovery from their anxiety disorder. One way to handle this is to settle the lawsuits before trying to begin to get well. That solves the problem of secondary gain. People who are receiving disability payments for an anxiety disorder have a more difficult problem and may need to get off the disability before they can get well.

Friends and family members can be a major source of hope during the recovery process because they are not bound by irrational anxious thoughts and feelings. Instead healthy friends and family members can offer their own realistic assessments of a situation in an effort to reeducate the anxious person about the risks involved in a particular situation. For example, Mary's mother told her daughter that when Mary was not in the car, she herself *never* feared hitting a pedestrian while driving and *never* turned around to retrace her route. This was a great surprise to Mary and a big step forward in her process of recovery.

Support Efforts to Get Well

Friend and family confrontations about anxious irrationality can succeed only when nonanxious family members accept the intensity and reality of the suffering of the anxious person. Mary's mother did not feel anxious about hitting a pedestrian when she drove. She did not have obsessions, and she did not have panic and dread when she drove. Mary did have terrible thoughts and painful feelings. Only when Mary's mother respected those serious, painful thoughts and feelings, and just how hard it was for Mary to confront them, could Mary begin, in small steps, to confront her fears.

Friends and family members cannot help anxious people by minimizing their suffering or by humiliating them. The thoughts and feelings of the anxious person are real, not imaginary. They are false alarms of the anxious brain, false signs that are experienced as more real and more important than any other part of the anxious person's life. It is only with time and great effort that anxious people can reclaim their lives from being hijacked by the anxiety disorder dragon. Friends and family members need to be patient and respectful, as well as firm and supportive, as they gradually confront the anxious person's pathological thoughts and feelings.

What Do You Tell People?

Many people with family members who suffer from anxiety disorders are confused about what to tell others about the problem, especially what to tell children about their parents' anxiety problems or what to tell other children about their anxious child's problems. While there is no point in wearing a figurative signboard advertising any illness, including anxiety disorders, it is generally wise to let people know the facts if they will be interacting with someone who has an anxiety disorder. That means telling teachers about children's anxiety problems and family members about anxiety disorders. It sometimes means telling employers if the anxiety disorders show up in workplace behaviors. See Part Four, Chapter 15, Step 4, and Part Five, Chapter 20, for more thoughts on whom to tell about anxiety disorders and what to tell them.

It is important not to let outrage at the anxious person drive you apart. Instead both of you be angry at the anxiety disorder. Think of the dragon as your common adversary. Use your outrage to fuel the family's recognition of having a shared problem and finding a good family-based solution. Together you can act out new, healthy responses to the dragon's distorted message. Do not let him take back the new freedom you are finding. As a united family, you can be strong for one another, and you can be your own best teachers.

There are rewards for a family that has gone through this process together. Just as everyone suffers with the person who is limited by anxiety, so also does everyone benefit once the anxiety is conquered. As one wife whose husband recovered from severe agoraphobia put it, "I never knew we could be so happy or that we could have such a wonderful life together."

Provide Hope

We ask you to be patient and to build hope for a better life for your anxious person. Getting well starts with acknowledgment of the disease, with acceptance of the pain and the losses that are caused by the disease. Without that pain, and the honest acceptance of it, it is not possible to make the effort needed to get well. In that important sense, the pain of an anxiety disorder is constructive. It is motivating, or it can be. The next step is hope. Your anxious person has to have hope that life can get better, that he or she can get well. Without hope, even with pain, your anxious person will not do the work needed to get well. The third necessary ingredient is to see a path to getting well. That is what the Anxiety Cure offers.

CHAPTER 11

How to Be a Support Person

When a person is ill with a physical disease, be it a broken bone or a long-term chronic illness, there is usually a support person to offer care. Because anxiety disorders, and mental health problems in general, are often not acknowledged to be as serious as physical ailments, there is seldom a recognition of the need for a support person. Far from being given encouragement for the hard work that you do to support your anxious person, you may instead have been unsure of your role in his or her recovery, and you even may have been accused by others of prolonging the illness.

The support person is vital to the Anxiety Cure program. Without you, the program works much less well. A support person can be a parent, a child, a spouse, a friend, or a neighbor. We want you to learn how to be helpful in the process of recovery. You do not have to be an expert in anxiety disorders or a genius in the treatment of mental disorders to have a success with the Anxiety Cure. As a support person, you need patience and persistence. You need to respect your anxious person and his or her efforts to succeed in the program.

Choose to Accept or Decline Being a Support Person

You may find that you have unintentionally become a support person, for example, if your child has developed an anxiety problem, or you may have been specifically recruited for this job by your anxious person. Either way, we ask you to think carefully about taking on the tasks that we outline here. It is not in the interest of either your anxious person or you to take this responsibility if you feel upset or overburdened by the obligation. Sometimes being too close to the problem could keep you from being empathetic and prevent you from understanding the necessity of some important recommendations, such as breaking up the work needed into manageably small steps. Carefully read through this chapter to see what is expected of you and then have an honest conversation with your anxious person about your willingness to fulfill this important role. If you would rather not be a support person, remember that there are other ways for you to help your anxious person, and there are other people who can be his or her support person. Even if no other candidates seem possible to you right now, be sure to review Chapter 15 about selecting a support person to get new ideas.

Responsibilities of the Support Person

To be useful as a support person, you must be genuinely interested in the welfare of the anxious person and be willing to take the time to learn how to help. There are two main commitments that support people must make to be effective:

1. Take the time to understand the anxious person's problems.
2. Make time for a regular practice to overcome these problems.

To learn more about anxiety, you should start by reading this book. You will learn that anxiety diseases are complex, painful, humiliating, and ever changing. Nevertheless, anxiety disorders are ultimately understandable and manageable. Words like *panic* and *obsession* will take on new meanings for you as you see just how powerful these experiences are. They are not similar to the ordinary anxiety experienced by people who do not suffer from anxiety disorders. The painful feelings of clinically significant anxiety are so devastating that they bring even the strongest people to their knees.

Respect, but do not fear, these distressing thoughts and feelings. Above all, respect your anxious person for what he or she is up against and for whatever efforts he or she makes to get well. Acknowledge that you do not understand his or her feelings and (unless you have an anxiety disorder yourself) that you never will fully understand them. Even though you do not understand the experiences of your anxious person, with help from the Anxiety Cure program you can understand the disorder and what it takes to get well. You will not understand your anxious person or be able to help him or her unless you honestly respect the great suffering and disability these disorders cause.

Practice, Practice, Practice

As you will see in Part Four, The Anxiety Cure: Eight Steps to Getting Well, your anxious person must practice in his or her discomfort zone at least once a week in order to get well. We ask that you participate in at least one practice session a week. Initially, this may mean simply meeting to talk about the problem, which in itself may cause your anxious person to be in his or her discomfort zone. Ultimately, practice will require you to accompany your anxious person to the anxiety-provoking situation to practice. During these practice sessions, ask your anxious person to describe his or her feelings every step of the way. Ask him or her what you can do to be helpful. The best way to be helpful changes rapidly, so you will need to understand how to be the most helpful at each specific time during practice sessions. You will be surprised by just how beneficial it is for you to be there, being both supportive and encouraging. These practice sessions should last at least thirty minutes to give you time to use the Silver Five antianxiety strategies you will learn in Part Four, Chapter 13, Step 2.

You do not need to have answers. If you join your anxious person in becoming a student of anxiety, you will have been tremendously helpful. Ask what his or her feelings and thoughts are as the practice goes on. Ask what you can do to help. Remind your anxious person how you see the situation at the time. Tell your anxious person how he or she looks to you during practice. You will be surprised that your anxious person thinks he or she looks bizarre or distraught, although you and any other outside observer are unlikely to see any manifestation of the inner panic. It is likely to be surprising (and reassuring) to your anxious person that he or she looks pretty normal, even though feeling a high level of panic. If your anxious person asks you a question you cannot answer, say that. No one expects you to be an expert. You job is to be patient and supportive while you learn from your anxious person more about the problems that anxiety causes.

During this practice time or at a different time, we ask that you review the journal entries or practice sheets that your anxious person will use to record his or her practice and future goals. You job is to be supportive, encouraging, and patient. Progress may be slow at times, but that is fine. As long as there is regular and repeated practice, there will be progress. Always give praise and always give outs. That means that when your anxious person asks you to let him or her get out of a situation, you always say yes. You will learn more about this approach in Chapter 15.

You will learn that an out is different from an excuse or fleeing a situation. While it is wrong to avoid an unpleasant activity due to anxiety, it may be necessary to ask for a six-month delay in jury duty, for example, to permit an agoraphobic person to practice for the experience. That practice usually involves visiting the court and jury setting and watching the process. The principle is always to break the task down into small steps and to repeat them over and over until they become manageable, if not easy.

During practice and as you review the practice journal, be sure to show sincere interest and optimism. Keep the warming fire of hope alight at all times. Do not be harsh or judgmental. Do not say, "Go do it. Don't be a wimp!" Say instead, "I know it is hard for you, and I am sorry about that. Can I help break it down into smaller steps for you to practice?" Your job is a hard one in the sense that you need to be both firm and gentle at the same time. You need to be persistent and patient, too. We have tremendous respect for the challenges you face in dealing with your anxious person. We hope that you and your anxious person can find the serenity of recovery and the gift of self-esteem that comes from doing a hard job well.

Seek Professional Help for Troubling Situations

Sometimes a person with an anxiety problem is unwilling to do the work needed to get well. Although he or she suffers and lives a crippled life, there can be too much fear or worry to enable effective action to solve the problem. Such a person has our sympathy because we are aware of just how terribly painful these illnesses are. Anxious people who suffer without working on a cure are among the most difficult people to help.

Most anxious people will use this program effectively and practice on a fairly regular schedule. If, however, your anxious person does not practice regularly, which this program encourages, then as a support person, you have no good moves. If you criticize or pressure your anxious person to practice, this will lower his or her already low self-esteem. If you accept the passivity and avoidance and find ways to make life easier for the anxious person despite the disability caused by the disease, then you are enabling the disease to continue to control the anxious person's life. Either way, with criticism or avoidance, both you and your anxious person lose.

It is important to remember that you are a *support person*—ultimately, this is your anxious person's problem, not yours. Point out the bind that you are in, and to help with your work, suggest finding a psychiatrist or therapist who specializes in treating anxiety disorders. Perhaps some medicine or help from an experienced professional therapist can get both of you back on track. Recall that support people can be helpful in most situations, but you are not likely to be able to handle the most difficult problems by yourself. Do not hesitate to get help if you feel overwhelmed.

Four Trouble Signs for Support People

When to seek professional help:

1. Your anxious person is not practicing in his or her discomfort zone regularly.
2. No progress is being made toward achieving your anxious person's goals.
3. Your anxious person's anxiety level has not dropped in practice settings, even with repeated exposure.
4. You feel overwhelmed and unprepared to deal with your anxious person's level of distress.

PART FOUR

The Anxiety Cure: Eight Steps to Getting Well

In this part, you will find a practical guide for using the principles contained in Parts One, Two, and Three to achieve the goal of living a full, normal life without restrictions as a result of anxiety. Do each step once and then go back to specific steps as you need them later on. Every step will take each individual anxious person a different amount of time. Some people can do all eight steps in eight weeks, but for others, each step will take several weeks. Throughout these steps, we refer to each step taking a week in order to establish a practical time frame. If you find too much is expected at a given step and/or if you decide to take more time, simply translate the weekly goals into a time frame that works for you.

The key to getting well is to be accountable to your support person about the work you are doing and the progress you are making every single week. It is important to do each step, but it is also important to make progress, moving from step to step. Here is a list of the topics covered in the eight steps:

Step 1: Become a Student of Your Anxiety
Step 2: Use the Silver Five—Build Your Own Armor against Attacks
Step 3: Practice—Put Yourself in Your Discomfort Zone
Step 4: Use Support People: Relate to Others about Your Anxiety
Step 5: Eliminate External Causes of Anxiety
Step 6: Evaluate Your Need for Medicines and Therapy in Your
        Anxiety Cure
Step 7: Structure Your Life without Anxiety
Step 8: Plan for Lifelong Recovery

In each step you will find new ways to think about your anxiety and new ways to overcome the limitations it puts on you. At the end of each step is a homework assignment. These assignments build on the topic in the step. Through your structured writing in a journal, they will help you write your own self-help book specifically tailored to your unique anxiety disorder. The reading, writing, talking, and practicing we outline will take some time every day. You may initially feel overwhelmed by what we recommend.

Remember: You are already spending far more time with your anxiety disorder than any program could demand. The time you spend worrying about your symptoms is wasted. The time you spend on the Anxiety Cure is invested in a better future for you, your friends, and your family. You may be dealing with anxiety in some way every hour of your waking life if your anxiety is severe—avoidance, worry, excuses, and guilt all take their toll. If you follow every step we suggest in the Anxiety Cure, you will ultimately spend far less time on your anxiety than you spend now. That is our goal together—to help you get yourself out of the prison of your anxiety.

Many people feel tremendous relief to have a constructive way to direct their anxious thoughts. Far from being burdensome, it could be exactly what you have been looking for—answers to questions that trouble you and at long last solutions to problems.

You will find in the following chart a list of all the homework assignments, step by step. Notice that each assignment asks you to do something a little different. Importantly, each step (after the third week) asks you to do one important activity: *Practice! Practice is the most important element of the cure for anxiety disorders.* If you do nothing else, set goals each week and practice once a day or at least once each week. Even without all the other assignments, you will find that you slowly improve. You will learn that practice is not the same as testing. To avoid this common error, be sure to read Part Four, Chapter 14, Step 3, carefully before setting goals and starting to practice.

Some readers will eagerly use all the forms and make daily records. Others will do none of the paperwork we suggest. We want you to make this your own program. Take what helps you and leave the rest behind. But by all means regularly practice by putting yourself voluntarily in situations that produce fear and panic. You get well only by working, over and over, in your anxiety discomfort zone. If you do this, you are sure to get better.

Each step of the Anxiety Cure refers you to further readings from recommended books we have used to supplement our program. Use these books, which are available at most bookstores and libraries, as you go through the eight steps. The books we suggest do not all agree with one another or with every element of the Anxiety Cure, although these books are highly regarded by us and have been useful to many anxious people. We are open to alternative paths to recovery, and we encourage you to be open to many alternatives—just so you find the ones that work best for you.

Look for Tips to Help with Anxious Moments

Throughout the eight steps, you will find highlighted tips to help you through anxious moments. Some of them are concrete things to do; others are ideas to hold in your mind when you feel your level of anxiety rise. We have included techniques that come from our clinical practices. Not all of these tips will work for any one person. For example, some people find cold drinks helpful in reducing anxiety, others find warm drinks calming, and some people do not benefit from drinking any kind of liquid when they are anxious.

Try the tips that make sense for you, and be sure to record in your journal what you try and how it works. You or your support person may come up with other tips that you find helpful, and you should record these in your personal journal also. Think of these tips for dealing with anxiety as tools, and keep them in your journal as if they were in a toolbox, so that you can pull them out to use whenever you need a tune-up to cope with your anxiety.

Schedule for the Anxiety Cure Homework

Assignment	STEP							
	1	2	3	4	5	6	7	8
Read Part Four	x							
Read This Step	x	x	x	x	x	x	x	x
Read Additional Specified Assignments	x	x	x	x	x	x	x	x
Anxiety History	x							
Daily Anxiety Cure Journal	x	x						
Goal Setting	x							
Personal Progress Log		x		x	x	x	x	x
Weekly Practice Worksheet			x	x	x	x	x	x
Practice			x	x	x	x	x	x
Recruit Support Person				x				
Meet with Support Person				x	x	x	x	x
Share "Dear Friend" Letter				x				
Evaluate Stress, Exercise, and Caffeine					x			
Practice Breathing and Relaxing					x			
Review Medication Use						x		
"Structure of Your Life" Evaluation							x	
"How My Time Is Spent" Evaluation							x	
Review Need for a Group								x

CHAPTER 12

Step 1

Become a Student of Your Anxiety

Notice that this step will not ask you to make changes in your behaviors and thoughts but ask you to begin to notice these behaviors and thoughts and how they are caused and affected by anxiety. Remember that anxiety is caused by the first fear, the powerful physical symptoms, as well as the second fear, the fear of the symptoms. You will explore the relationship between the first and the second fears further in this step. Only by studying your current behaviors, physical symptoms, anxious thoughts, and fear levels will you know where to start making changes to take back your life from the anxiety dragon. Changes can wait. Now just observe and learn.

Study the dragon of anxiety, which has you on the run. You are likely to be not only scared out of your wits, but also unable to look at the monster that is driving you crazy and ruining your life. To get well you need to stop running. Turn and face your tormentor. Check out his face and his claws. Look at his teeth and feel his fiery breath. This what it means to become a student of your anxiety. This first step in the Anxiety Cure is about getting organized to do the work that you need to do to get better.

Use Your Journal

The best way to get organized about your anxiety disorder and to stay organized over time is to keep a journal. Without this permanent record, it is hard to make progress and even harder to acknowledge the progress that has been made. For your journal, use a loose-leaf notebook, a binder, or any other blank booklet that you can carry easily. This is not a journal in which the profound or the monumental need be recorded. Rather, it is your personal workbook, which you create as you cure your anxiety disorder. You may have started your journal already by recording your answers to the Anxiety Inventory and Specific Anxiety Disorder Inventory from Part Two, Chapter 6. If you have not already done so, please take these tests now and record your answers in your new journal. You will continue the journal by writing an anxiety history and a list of goals, and then use it daily to record your practice. This will help you keep a concrete record of your successes and your setbacks. Date all of your entries so you can keep track of changes over time.

Dan's Journal

Dan was a forty-five-year-old man who lived alone. A year ago his prosperous business restoring art went bankrupt with no warning. Dan went from being comfortably middle-class to being on the verge of homelessness. He began working at nighttime as a clerk in a copy center to pay his bills. He believed that he had lost his business because his lifelong problems with anxiety and depression had finally become so severe that his worry and the resulting preoccupation led him to treat his customers badly when he failed to deliver their art on schedule. Dan abandoned his friends when he went bankrupt because he was feeling too depressed, anxious, and humiliated to face them.

Dan had no idea how to reclaim his life when he began the Anxiety Cure. Writing his anxiety history, he realized that he had been anxious and, because of his anxiety, depressed his entire life. Nevertheless, he had managed to function despite these problems until the previous year. He also realized as a result of writing his history in his journal that the recent worsening of his problems had started soon after the death of a close friend. When he took the Anxiety Inventory, his score was high, which confirmed his own sense that he was suffering terribly. He began to record his daily anxiety levels and found that he was never below a 4. With these objective measures of the severity of his current problems in mind, Dan wisely decided to find a psychiatrist and evaluate the possible role of medicine before continuing with the rest of the eight steps.

Your journal is the place to keep on hand the tips you would like to try or those that have been beneficial to you. If you are in therapy, have your therapist help you set up reasonable, concrete, and small goals for yourself based on your work together. This will give you another way to make therapy more effective. Throughout the eight steps of the Anxiety Cure, we will give you suggestions about how to use your journal. Try these ideas as you adapt your journal to the format that is most helpful to you.

Begin Your Journal by Documenting Your Personal Anxiety History   This will help you now and in the future, should the anxiety problem ever return. You will be able to use this as a reference point to tell if you become better or worse than you are now. Answer the following questions in your journal:

1. How old were you when your anxiety disorder started?
2. What were your first symptoms of anxiety?
3. How and when did your anxiety disorder first seriously interfere with your life?
4. When was your anxiety disorder at its worst? What were your major problems then?
5. What treatments have you tried? Include therapists' and/or physicians' names and dates seen, medications, dosages taken, and results of treatments.
6. What have you found most helpful in the past in dealing with your anxiety disorder?
7. Add any other comments, remembering that you will reread this history months, and even years, from now.

Every day this week write down in your journal the characteristics of anxiety as you experience them, separating the event, the physical symptoms, the thoughts, and the level of fear that characterize your own personal torture.

Use the Anxiety Cure Daily Journal form found at the end of each step as your guide in making your own journal, or make many copies of this form, always leaving one copy blank so you can make new copies for future use. In the journal, describe where in your body you feel anxiety and precisely what those feelings are. Use words to describe these experiences. Notice carefully exactly when the anxiety is worse and when it is not so bad. *Notice precisely what makes it go up and what makes your anxiety level go down.* Are you surprised that your fear level can change so quickly? Are you surprised that it goes down if you just wait and let it run its course over a few minutes? This week is meant to get you in the habit of noticing the details of your anxiety: where, when, and how anxiety appears. Your first week is your baseline. It is ground zero for your recovery.

Label your level of fear from 0 (meaning no fear at all) to 10 (meaning the worst, the most intense panic/fear you have ever experienced). You will probably notice that your fear of the fear (the second fear) makes the first fear grow larger, and that your activities and immediate involvement with other people make the fear grow smaller.

Fear Level Scale

0 = no fear at all; completely relaxed
10 = the worst fear you have ever had; pure panic

This is a standard way to evaluate fear. Begin labeling your fear levels as they change from hour to hour and from day to day. Keeping track of your fear level will give you a reference for change over time and will help you explain your state of fear to anyone you talk to, from friends and family to therapists and doctors.

Touching someone else's hand often makes the fear level fall, as does carefully describing your fear in words to another person. When you are afraid, it is often helpful to tell another person what you are feeling and what you want that person to do to help you. The simple but difficult act of thinking of answers to those questions will bring your level of fear down as your mind jumps free of the dragon's grip and functions more normally.

List your major goals in your journal and put them in order, starting with the easiest to the hardest. Make the hardest goal the one that, if you could do it, you would know that you were functioning as a fully normal person without restrictions on your life because of anxiety or panic. Use the following to guide you in making your list in your journal:

1. List four goals that you think will be fairly easy to achieve.
2. List four goals that you think will be fairly hard to achieve.
3. List four goals that you think will be very hard (or impossible) to achieve.
4. List the one goal that you think will be the hardest of all for you to achieve.

Record your goals in three sections, from the easiest to the hardest, with that final, hardest-of-all goal highlighted at the bottom of the page.

Tips for Friends and Family

This is the week for you to get organized. You may want to start your own journal, documenting difficulties caused by the anxiety problems as they arise. Your journal is a place for you to record the frustrations you feel over the anxiety problem, since most friends and family are often unhappy and feel anger about the impact of this problem on their lives. Think about what you have tried in the past to help your anxious person. Have you forced him or her to do something? Have you acted as if nothing was wrong? Have you covered for your anxious person to a boss or a child? Write down all of your failed attempts to help.

Also document the books about anxiety problems you have read or the professionals or groups from whom you have sought help. Have any helped you? What has been helpful? What has not been helpful? Continue or begin this type of outreach by doing the reading assignment suggested at the end of each step and recording your thoughts about what you have read. Also write down when you have tried these suggestions and what the good and bad results have been.

Homework for Step 1

1. Read Parts One and Two of *The Anxiety Cure* if you have not already done so.
2. Read Step 1.
3. Record your anxiety history.
4. Record your anxiety levels daily as described in the Anxiety Cure Daily Journal.
5. List your goals in your journal.

Readings for Step 1

1. Schwartz, J. M., with B. Beyette. *Brain Lock—Free Yourself from Obsessive-Compulsive Behavior.*
   Step 1: "Relabel, 'It's Not Me—It's My OCD'"
2. Markway, B. G., C. N. Carmin, C. A. Pollard, T. Flynn. *Dying of Embarrassment—Help for Social Anxiety & Phobia.*
   Section II: "Preparing for Recovery"

Six Tips for Using Your Mouth to Help You

1. Sip ice water.
2. Drink a soda.
3. Fix a cup of herbal tea or warm milk.
4. Suck hard candy.
5. Chew gum.
6. Whistle or sing.

Anxiety Cure Daily Journal

Date	Situation/Event	Physical Symptoms	Thoughts	Fear Level*	Comments

*Rate 0–10

CHAPTER 13

Step 2

Use the Silver Five—Build Your Own Armor against Attacks

Anxiety disorders are disorders of ideas and actions. If you blindfold someone who is phobic about bridges and then drive him or her over a bridge, there is no panic. It is the link between the idea (the cognitive function) and the action (the behavior) that creates the heightened anxiety and panic. In this step, you will learn the techniques that will break this link by reducing the way your automatic thoughts and behaviors feed your fear. Notice that we are not asking you to change what you are doing in this step. We are not asking you to begin to practice yet, nor are you going to begin working toward your goals. Rather, you are going to build on what you learned in the last step, your baseline week of anxiety observation. This week you will use the new ideas you are learning to change your thinking and actions about your daily activities as they exist now.

The Three Cycles of Anxiety

Three cycles illustrate how anxiety is sustained and how the Silver Five work to break the escalation in fear. The first two cycles are probably quite familiar to you, especially when you consider what you already learned about your own anxiety in Step 1. As you read about Cycles I and II, think about how they apply to you.

Cycle I is the anxiety cycle associated with avoiding possible anxiety-generating behaviors, such as shopping, traveling, or leaving the house without checking to be sure the stove is turned off. Anticipatory anxiety

Cycle I
DON'T DO IT

Think of Anxiety-Generating Situation
"What-If" Thinking
Anticipatory Anxiety Rises

Decreased Self-Esteem   Avoid Anxiety-Generating Situation
                                         Anxiety Falls

leads to avoidance, which in turn feeds self-doubt and self-criticism. This is the vicious cycle of the anxiety disorders experienced by most anxious people before treatment, when their lives and self-images are dominated by fear and avoidance. Fear causes avoidance, avoidance causes fear. This cycle is called the "Don't Do It" cycle of anxiety.

Cycle II (page 96) is labeled the "Do It and Flee" cycle of anxiety. This is similar to the first cycle, but instead of avoiding the anxiety-generating trigger behavior, the anxious person enters the situation, feels increased anxiety, and fears it with a mind full of "what-if" thoughts. Cycle II also perpetuates the self-defeating cycle of avoidance and eroded self-esteem.

Instead of these cycles, which lead to increased anxiety, we are going to help you create for yourself a suit of armor against dragon attacks by using the Silver Five antianxiety techniques. The Silver Five make an especially effective armor because you build the armor yourself, customizing it to fit you just right. Remember that the dragon is produced by your own thoughts and actions, and no amount of reassurance from others is going to change the way the dragon attacks you. Remember also that the only food the dragon can eat is your fear. You let the dragon grow by feeding him with your fear.

Cycle II
DO IT AND FLEE

Enter Anxiety-Generating Situation
"What-If" Thinking
Anxiety Rises

Decreased Self-Esteem   Escape Discomfort Zone
                                        Anxiety Falls

Think of all the people—friends and family, doctors, emergency room workers, and others—who have told you that everything in your body is all right. Your only thought was that if they understood how bad you felt, they would not be so sure. Dragon armor is built specifically to defeat this type of negative internal dialogue. Only when you make your own cognitive and behavioral changes will the dragon stop being a threat to your quality of life.

The Silver Five

1. *Allow* anxious thoughts and feelings to reappear.
2. *Recognize* that these thoughts and feelings are not dangerous but are normal bodily reactions.
3. *Function* in your discomfort zone and notice your achievements.
4. *Wait* for the anxiety to pass. Notice when it fades.
5. *Move on* to new goals.

Cycle III, "So What-If?" asks you to use the Silver Five. Use the first two parts of your armor—*allow* and *recognize*—to get into the anxiety-

Cycle III
SO WHAT IF?

Enter Anxiety-Generating Situation
So "What-If" Thinking
Anxiety Rises

Increased Self-Esteem   Stay in Discomfort Zone
                                         Anxiety Falls

producing situation. This helps to overcome the anticipatory anxiety, which is defeating in Cycle I. Then *function* in your discomfort zone as the anxiety increases, and *wait* for the anxiety to pass. This leads to increased self-confidence, which in turn diminishes both anticipatory anxiety and the likelihood of panic. Use *function* and *wait* to break the second cycle of fear and flight.

Cycle III is named "So What If?" Many anxious people call this approach "I Don't Care" or "Letting Go." It is effective when facing anxiety-triggering experiences. Instead of answering the "what if" anxiety-generated question by avoiding or running away from the panicky feeling, the stance in Cycle III is a calmly assertive "so what" to the dragon's threats. So what if you have anxious feelings? Anxious feelings eventually fade. So what if you have a panic attack? The panic will not hurt you.

Peace Lies on the Other Side of Panic   Go through your panic and find the peace you seek—a peace based on pride resulting from your hard work.

Say to yourself, "I don't care." Instead of trying (and always failing) to control your panic and anxiety, let go, let the feelings come and go. Since the dragon feeds on your fears, this approach starves the dragon and keeps your anxiety from growing in a vicious cycle of fear and avoidance. Self-esteem rises in Cycle III. It falls in Cycles I and II.

The Silver Five

It is important to clearly understand the way the Silver Five work in order to begin using them in your anxiety cure. In Cycle III, you saw how the Silver Five can help you move forward toward your anxiety cure. Now we will break apart the five parts and examine each one in detail.

1. Allow anxious thoughts and feelings to reappear. You know from the study of your anxiety problem, which you did in Step 1, that before you began the Anxiety Cure you were experiencing anxiety frequently even though you were likely to have been avoiding and fleeing from anxious situations, as in Cycles I and II above. No matter how many changes you made in trying to avoid anxiety, you were still cowering from the dragon. To take back your life from the dragon, you must end your flight from the fear. Whether you avoid or do not avoid, you will feel crippling anxiety until you can permit these disturbing feelings to do what they want to, without your fighting or fleeing from the anxiety-generating experience.

When you use the first of the Silver Five, the change in your thinking about anxious thoughts—simply knowing that at times you will have anxious feelings and thoughts—helps begin to break the connection between the biological fact that you have a tendency to have anxious feelings because of your sensitized nervous system and your pattern of trying to avoid situations in a self-defeating effort to minimize the anxiety. Expect to have anxious thoughts and feelings in your life. Some will be minor, and some will be major, but both exist. Do not feed the dragon with your secondary fear of the fear. Anxiety is normal for an anxious person.

2. Recognize that these thoughts and feelings are not dangerous but are normal bodily reactions. You may want to review Part Two, The Basics of Anxiety, to remind yourself that these thoughts and feelings are not dangerous. If you have had multiple medical evaluations for these problems, then you know from your doctors that there is nothing physically wrong other than the anxiety disorder itself. The feelings of anxiety are real and they are physical. They are distressing, but they are not dangerous. This is another change in your thinking about the feelings and thoughts that anxiety provokes. Your body is simply misinterpreting anxious feelings as an alarm that danger is occurring when, in fact, there is nothing dangerous going on. Your anxious feelings and thoughts are painful, but they are harmless *false alarms* from your sensitized, overreactive alarm mechanisms.

Remember that if you were in a dangerous situation, you would know that it was appropriate to have these thoughts and feelings. As with the first of the Silver Five, you know from your work on Step 1 that avoidance does not prevent anxious thoughts and feelings. In fact, over time, avoidance makes your anxiety disorder worse. You have suffered from this anxiety disorder for a long time without having bad physical consequences, such as a stroke or a heart attack, and the worst anxiety is behind you.

3. Function in your discomfort zone and notice your achievement. Recall that anxiety is measured on a 0–10 scale, with 0 representing no anxiety and 10 representing the worst anxiety you have ever had. Your discomfort zone is the block of numbers representing heightened anxiety levels within which you can more or less get on with your life. For most people that means numbers between about 4 and 8. Below 4 and you have only slightly anxious thoughts and physical symptoms. Above 8 it is hard for most anxious people to focus on anything but their fear. We will talk more about levels 8 and above in Step 3. For now, think about this middle range of panic as *your discomfort zone.* You are clearly aware of your anxious thoughts and feelings, and it is easy to add frightening thoughts and push the fear up to a 9 or 10 level. Try, though, simply to do what you can in your discomfort zone in a low-key, steady, and unspectacular way. Do not flee the anxious situation. Give yourself lots of credit for this hard work in your discomfort zone. No one likes the discomfort zone, and by voluntarily entering it, you are beginning to break your "Don't Do It" and "Do It and Flee" cycles.

4. Wait for the anxiety to pass. Notice when it fades. Simply letting time pass is a powerful antianxiety technique because the dragon lacks stamina even though he has plenty of short-term force. As you stay in your discomfort zone, you will notice that even though you do not change the fear-inducing situation, your anxiety level will gradually begin to fall. You are no longer feeding the dragon with your fear of anxious thoughts and feelings. The dragon, without your fear-food, loses his hold on you. Let go of your tension and impatience so that the dragon can do his thing and you can do yours. Anxiety cannot be rushed or wished away. Staying put and letting time pass will let your level of pathological anxiety fall. Most people with anxiety have learned to focus exclusively on the upsurge in anxiety and not to notice the more important times, when the anxiety begins to fade. As you wait for your anxiety to pass without fleeing from your anxiety-generating situation, notice that your anxiety level numbers go down. Appreciate every drop in anxiety while staying with a difficult situation. It is a big, big accomplishment.

5. Move on to new goals. Once you have gone through the first four parts of the Silver Five, you will have begun to experience increased self-esteem and decreased anticipatory anxiety as a result of breaking the anxiety cycle. This self-confidence will lead you on to tackle other goals, goals that you once believed to be out of your reach. In the next step, "Practice—Put Yourself in Your Discomfort Zone," we will describe further how to choose appropriate goals. For now it is important to remember that the ultimate sign of progress is taking back your life from anxiety. You have the right to choose for yourself what you do with your life. No longer let the dragon control all of your choices. This is the final marker of progress—you set your goals without interference from the anxiety disorder. Build on your successes. Look for the next challenge.

Incorporate New Attitudes

To make the Silver Five your own, copy them into your journal. If you are artistic, consider using a piece of silver paper or writing them with silver ink! Keep them nearby, so when anxiety strikes, you can look them up easily. Make notes in your journal about how long it takes before your anxiety level begins to go down, even if you do nothing but wait. It is important to begin now these cognitive, thought-based changes about how you look at your anxiety symptoms.

Change your relationship to the dragon and the worry machine. Regain control of your life. Get out of the dragon's dungeon by accepting the distressing feelings and by not adding frightening thoughts to the painful, but not dangerous, feelings of anxiety. Remember that these experiences are the normal workings of your healthy fight-or-flight responses, which are triggered inappropriately. Your body and your mind will let you do what you choose to do, even with panic and anxiety.

Track Your Progress

Keeping track of your progress is another way for you to take charge of your anxiety. Look at the Personal Progress Log at the end of this step. We suggest that from now on you evaluate your overall anxiety every week as compared to how you felt the week you started the Anxiety Cure. Last week you wrote about the anxieties you felt at that time. Now you have a permanent record of how you were doing when you began this program. Even years from now you can compare yourself to how you were last week. This documented starting point is important in many ways. Seeing improvement, or the lack of improvement, or backsliding in numbers, is a helpful way to quantify your emotional state. Use the Personal Progress Log as it is or copy it into your journal. We have suggested some questions to evaluate your progress, but you will come up with others that are specific to you.

There will be ups and downs in your progress from week to week, month to month, and even year to year. Even if you have steady improvement over a long period of time, you most certainly will have a bad week occasionally. Do not get discouraged by day-to-day fluctuations or even a week or two of setbacks. What you want is overall improvement over the long haul. If you stick with the Anxiety Cure, that is likely to happen faster and better than you can believe right now. If, however, improvement does not occur and if, even more dramatically, you see yourself becoming worse over the course of months of steady work, this is a clear sign to reevaluate this situation with your support person and consult a therapist or physician.

Peace lies on the other side of anxiety. Only by voluntarily going through anxiety can sufferers find peace from anxiety, release from the dragon's grip. This is what practice means, and what you will be working toward in Step 3.

Tips for Friends and Family

The easiest thing to give to an anxious person is reassurance: "You will not have a heart attack," "You do not have cancer," "You cannot get AIDS from using a public telephone," "Your plane will not crash," etc. Reassurance is like avoidance; it buys peace from the dragon for the moment, but it strengthens the anxiety in the long run as the anxious person comes to depend more and more on the reassurance. All friends and family, as well as all physicians and other health care professionals, get caught in the reassurance trap. If anxiety disorders were rational, then a single episode of reassurance would be sufficient.

Reassurance for an anxious person is similar in one important way to giving heroin to a heroin addict. It brings a sense of peace right after it is given. The problem with this approach comes later, when the reassurance (or the dose of heroin) deepens the dependence so that the sufferers who have chosen those seductive solutions find that their lives are ever more dominated by their diseases. Reassurance, like avoidance, is a trap.

So how do you know when you should give reassurance to your anxious person? Ask yourself this: if I, as a nonanxious person, were in this situation, would I need reassurance? If the answer to this question is an honest yes, then go ahead and be reassuring. If the answer is no, as it usually is with an anxious person, help that person use the Silver Five to find his or her own reassurance through doing the activity. This success will be much stronger than any reassurance you could give. This approach leads to freedom and release from prison, for you and your anxious person.

In this step, we ask you to stop continuing to give the reassurance to your anxious person. Instead, gently return to the techniques in the Silver Five and remind your anxious person that external reassurance has never worked before. Stopping reassurance can only work when it is combined with real compassion and respect for how hard it is for the anxious person to face his or her fears and do the things that are necessary—working in the discomfort zone—to get well.

Remember that in this step, we are not systematically practicing anxious situations, but rather we are applying the Silver Five techniques to life as it is now. The next step will be to practice systematically, and that will be covered in Step 3.

Homework for Step 2

1. Read Step 2.
2. Continue to record answers to the Anxiety Cure Daily Journal.
3. Fill out your Personal Progress Log.

Readings for Step 2

1. Burns, D. D. *The Feeling Good Handbook.*
   Part One: "Understanding Your Moods"

2. Wilson, R. R. *Don't Panic—Taking Control of Anxiety Attacks*, rev. ed. Chapter 13: "How to Inoculate Yourself against Panic: The Eight Attitudes of Recovery"

Touching Anxiety—Four Tips for Comforting Yourself

1. Hold your pet.
2. Hold a smooth stone in your hand.
3. Hug a stuffed animal.
4. Squeeze a friend's hand.

Six Tips to Distract Yourself

1. Look at a favorite cartoon book.
2. Go for a short walk, preferably with someone else.
3. Watch a videotape of a favorite movie or sports event.
4. Call a friend who likes to talk.
5. Bring a tape player and listen to a relaxation tape or music.
6. Look at a photo of a favorite place or a favorite person.

Personal Progress Log

Use this progress log to rate your progress weekly. Compare your anxiety each week to how you were the week you started the Anxiety Cure. Always date your log so you can watch for changes over time. The blank spaces can be used to list your own standards for judging your improvement. Rate each item, using the Rating Scale listed below.

Today's Date: _____

Date I Started to Use the Anxiety Cure: _____

Signs of Progress	My Rating
1. I enjoy life more	
2. I am less anxious	
3. My anxiety interferes less with my life	
4. I feel more in control of my life	
5.	
6.	

Rating Scale:
- −3   Much worse
- −2   Worse
- −1   A little worse
- 0   No change/the same as the week I started the Anxiety Cure
- +1   A little better
- +2   Better
- +3   Much better

CHAPTER 14

Step 3

Practice—Put Yourself in
Your Discomfort Zone

In Step 1 you started your journal and listed your goals. In Step 2 you learned to use the Silver Five to protect yourself against the dragon. Now with this step we get down to the heart of the Anxiety Cure program. You need to commit yourself to active practice, putting yourself in your discomfort zone for preferably thirty to sixty minutes each day. That means voluntarily and routinely putting yourself in anxiety-provoking situations.

Practice in Your Discomfort Zone

Recall from your work in Step 2 that anxiety is measured on a scale of 0 to 10, and your discomfort zone is from about 4 to 8. These numbers typically represent the heightened anxiety levels within which you can function even though you feel more or less discomfort. Remember that it is important to work voluntarily in your discomfort zone in order to reclaim your life from the dragon of anxiety. Remember also that you are changing the faulty wiring in your brain by not responding to the false alarm that is being sounded. If you work at lower levels of anxiety, say at 3 and below, you will usually have only modestly anxious thoughts and physical symptoms. Most people with severe anxiety function at this level of anxiety on a daily basis, even when they are avoiding their anxiety-provoking situations, so it will usually be necessary to move your work higher up into the discomfort zone in order to see meaningful improvement.

Improvement comes when you voluntarily enter your personal discomfort zone. All anxious people have times when the dragon pins them down, producing anxiety levels of 4 and higher involuntarily, even when they do not voluntarily choose to enter anxiety-provoking situations. This discomfort, then, is the same as the discomfort of being in the situation voluntarily. The big difference is that involuntary exposure to high levels (when you avoid and when you flee) actually increases your sensitization. *Only repeated, voluntary exposure will cause your levels to fall over time.* Only active practice will *de*sensitize your nervous system.

While you are working in your discomfort zone, adding frightening thoughts is likely to cause your anxiety level to jump to a 9 or 10 level. Instead of adding frightening thoughts, simply do what you can in your discomfort zone. Apply the Nike slogan "Just Do It." Little steps will get you to your goals—all of them, even the hardest. Give yourself lots of credit for this hard work, especially for taking repeated small steps. By staying voluntarily in your anxiety-provoking situation, you are beginning to break the "Don't Do It" and the "Do It and Flee" cycles you saw in Step 2.

The dragon will try to surprise you. He will give you a hard time at a level 3 or 4 sometimes—jumping the level to an 8 or 10 without warning or reason. At other times you will do something you are sure will produce a level 10 and you will have no anxiety at all. That is the unpredictability that is standard operating procedure for the anxiety dragon. Just accept his unpredictability and do your practice tasks whether the anxiety level is low or high. Give yourself credit for your efforts regardless of the dragon's behavior, regardless of the level you experience.

Functioning with High Levels of Anxiety

Most people find that an anxiety level above 8 makes it hard to focus on anything but their anxiety. This makes it difficult to use calming techniques such as you learned with the Silver Five, the tips throughout these steps, and the deep breathing practice you will learn in Step 5. It is likely that you will have times during your practice sessions when your anxiety level becomes higher than you had anticipated. It is wise to prepare ahead of time and write a plan for yourself about what to do when experiencing high levels of anxiety. This plan will help you avoid adding frightening thoughts to your anxiety during practice, making it less likely that you will need your plan. Mark your plan in your journal with a paper clip, since you will need to find it quickly if your anxiety gets too distressing.

The most important thought to keep in mind at an anxiety level of 8 and above is: this is unpleasant, but not dangerous. The feelings at this high level of anxiety are so overwhelming that it is easy to respond to the false alarm your body is sounding by concluding that real danger is at hand. Remind yourself that nothing dangerous is happening. Would a nonanxious person experience fear in this situation? Look around you. Are other people scared now? It is your body's false alarm to a common situation that is causing your anxiety to get so high. Nothing is actually wrong. Panic is a false alarm, a few chemicals out of place in your sensitized brain.

At high levels of anxiety it is important to keep in mind that it is wise to have an out. This is true because panic is fed by these two mistaken ideas: you are trapped and you are alone. An out is any way to change your feelings about the anxiety-provoking situation so your high anxiety can return into the more manageable discomfort zone, going from a level 10 to a level 6 or so. An out is different from running away from a situation. Fleeing anxiety never works because the dragon feeds on his victory. You are, in a sense, reinforcing your faulty beliefs when you flee high anxiety. When you flee and your anxiety level falls, you conclude that you must flee to regain your composure, to drop that terribly high level of anxiety. That is exactly what the dragon wants you to think and what he wants you to do (avoid or flee). With active, voluntary, repeated practice, you will learn that your anxiety level will fall if you stay in your anxiety-provoking situations. That is exactly what we want you to learn and what the possessive dragon hopes you never learn.

By taking an out, in contrast, you contract with yourself to take a break and return to the situation in a more manageable way in the near future. Best of all, most of the time when you have an out, a good out, you are so reassured by not feeling either alone or trapped that you do not need to leave the panic-causing situation at all. If you do take an out, return to the situation as soon as possible. It is like the old proverb: get right back on the horse that threw you. The longer you wait to return, the harder it will be to get on that horse again.

Write down some fairly modest goals to work on for this week, and think of some ways to practice them. Look at the goal sheet you wrote in your journal in Step 1 to think of where to begin, but do not pick something too hard this week. Begin with the easiest goals. Remember, persistence is the key to long-term success, not fast starts!

Planning Your Outs

John is a twenty-two-year-old graduate student with social phobia. Prior to working on finding a cure for his social phobia, John went out for pizza after class with a small group with whom he was assigned to do a project. He was frightened by the prospect of eating in this social setting, but the group was planning the required project during lunch, so he felt there was no way out of the frightening situation.

As he entered the restaurant, his anxiety was a 7. He was so anxious he could not understand any of the plans that were being discussed, and he could not eat. Suddenly, his anxiety soared to a 9. John jumped up, grabbed his books, and fled the restaurant without a word to his startled classmates. This was not an out; this was terror-driven flight.

John almost dropped out of graduate school over this humiliating crisis. Fortunately, however, he sought help and began to work voluntarily in his discomfort zone. He planned carefully for his next social encounter, a date with a woman in his program. She had asked him to go to dinner, but after thinking it over, John suggested an alternate plan of seeing a popular movie and having coffee afterward. This, he thought, would be less intense for him (i.e., he would feel less threatened) than would a long period of face-to-face conversation in a formal restaurant. During the movie he began to feel his level of anxiety rising. He quietly leaned over to his date and told her he was going to get a soda and asked if she would like anything. When he was in the lobby of the darkened theater, he pulled from his pocket a piece of paper with antianxiety tips and reminded himself to steer clear of avoidance and "what-if" thoughts. He used several techniques that he found helpful. He returned to his seat with his cold drink and was actually able to enjoy the rest of the movie because he felt so successful about his use of the out.

Once John began to use planned outs, he found that he had much better control of his social interactions, and in turn, these successes led him to feel confident enough to face even more challenging social situations.

Imagery Practice

To achieve the goal of working in your discomfort zone, it may only be necessary at first to spend time thinking about the place or situation that makes you anxious. That is fine. If going to a place or being in an anxiety-provoking situation would push your anxiety level above the discomfort zone, simply set your goal as something that is manageable. Many people find that imagery practice is useful because it allows you to control the intensity of the anxiety level. Most anxious people have overactive imaginations, which is part of what causes "what if" fears to grow so large. Imagery practice capitalizes on this imagination. For example, a woman who was afraid of flying sat in a chair, closed her eyes, and imagined that she was on a flight. She felt the chilled cabin air, smelled the coffee brewing, and heard the captain announce how high the plane was flying. Her anxiety quickly soared to a level 7, despite the fact that she was still sitting in her living room!

Be sure to use your senses during your practice to heighten the sense of reality. Imagine the taste, feeling, sight, sound, and smell of your anxiety-provoking situation. During this imagery practice, if your anxiety gets to be higher than your discomfort zone, it is easy to give yourself an out—just open your eyes! During your out, remember that nothing dangerous is happening to you. You are in a safe place, and the events are all in your mind. Once your anxiety level is again at a manageable level, close your eyes and pick up your practice where you left off.

Imagery practice is especially useful for people with fears that are difficult to practice regularly, such as flying, fears of specific bridges that are far away, and public speaking. Imagery practice is also useful with OCD. To work on obsessive thoughts, allow yourself to imagine in detail the images that you are afraid of. Let your imagination go, and as your anxiety level rises, remind yourself that this is a false alarm—not real—and not even really happening.

You can assist yourself with imagery practice by first writing a script of your anxious situation and then reading the script into a tape recorder. To practice, simply listen to the recording. You can also use this technique for OCD, by counting or using phrases that are "stuck" in your mind or your recording. You will find that it does not take too many times listening to that same tape to become bored with the repetition of the same fears and that your mind begins to wander. When this happens, you have desensitized yourself to that fear, and it is time to record another fear on tape or to be in the actual setting.

The ultimate goal of the Anxiety Cure is not to desensitize you to any particular situations or experiences, but to help you to desensitize yourself to the painful feelings that are the heart of the anxiety disorders.

You will find many activities in your daily life that constitute practice. For example, if you fear sharp objects you may deliberately use a knife to prepare dinner, or if you fear talking to people you may call information for a phone number instead of looking in the phone book. Opportunities for practice are all around you if you look for them.

All anxiety disorders, whether triggered by public speaking, flying, contamination, or whatever, are, at root, fear of the same feelings of fear. The difference between your anxiety disorder and someone else's anxiety disorder is primarily what triggers the fear reactions, not the reactions themselves, in your brains and in your bodies. As you change your behaviors, we want you to begin to correct the unrealistic thoughts that both result from and provoke these horrible feelings and negative behaviors. When you no longer fear the anxiety dragon, you stop feeding him. Then, and only then, does he begin to die of neglect.

Here is another image for those who are sensitive to the concept of hurting (let alone killing) the dragon: if you stop feeding the dragon, he can return to the wild where he belongs.

What has happened to you when you have entered your personal fear-generating situation in the past? When have you had success and when have you had failures? What made one practice experience a failure and another a success? What has happened to your self-esteem and to your resolve to work hard to get well when you have had a setback or a slip? In other words, what if one day you can ride an elevator three floors with low or no anxiety levels, and then suddenly you have an anxiety level of 10 when going only one floor on the same elevator? Record your practice and your fear levels on copies of the Weekly Practice Worksheet, which is given at the end of this chapter. Record the feelings and thoughts you had when you actually did your practice.

Testing versus Practicing

Some people have pointed out that if all it took to get well was to have panic on a regular basis, they would have been well long ago. Correct! The trick to getting well from this disease is to have panic voluntarily, to let the dragon come without resisting him. That changes "testing" into "practicing" and lets you develop a solid and realistic sense of confidence and mastery.

Testing sets you up for failure. Sooner or later you will fail one of your "tests" and your self-esteem will shrivel.

Voluntary, Repeated, and *Regular* are the Key Words   Feel good when you complete a practice step with high levels of fear, not when you complete the task with no levels of fear. Practice with high levels of fear takes courage and hard work, for which you deserve praise from yourself and others. Practice with no fear levels at all is easy and is much less deserving of praise.

Feeling good about those practice experiences that provide low levels of fear and feeling bad about those practice experiences that produce high levels is rooted in the old way of thinking about getting well. It equates getting well with not having any painful, anxious feelings. This new way of thinking about getting well sets you on a path to working toward having a full normal life, *with* or *without* your painful, anxious feelings. The new way puts you in control. The old way leaves the dragon in control of your life and your self-esteem.

Testing may work for a while, but it always fails. Set up a test, and sooner or later you will fail. But when you practice, you always succeed. This is how it works, because testing is based on the idea that you will do something as a test to see if you can do it without fear and with low levels of anxiety. When the dragon strikes, as he surely will, you chalk it up as a failed test. With practice, you work regularly and moderately in your discomfort zone. You do your practice whether or not the dragon shows up. You always win when you practice. You win if the dragon shows up (because you do what you have set out to do) and you win if he does not show up. When you test, the dragon controls the game. When you practice, *you* are in control, and the dragon loses all of his power over you.

Tips for Friends and Family

It is finally time for you to begin changing the way you interact with your anxious person so that you no longer reinforce the anxiety problem. With this step your anxious person begins to practice regularly in anxiety-provoking situations. Now it is time for you to gently and respectfully begin allowing your anxious person to experience the situations that you have been helping him or her avoid. Do not metaphorically dump your anxious person into deep water, letting him or her learn to swim under the threat of drowning. You need to make the transition into deep water gradually. Start in the shallow end. Start with short episodes of having your anxious person put his or her head under the water voluntarily, briefly at first.

If you have been doing the driving for your anxious person because of a driving phobia, plan to start allowing your anxious person to drive him- or herself for short distances at times when it does not interfere with work. If you have been touching only those dishes in the kitchen that your anxious person with OCD says are safe, use a few of the "unsafe" dishes at each meal. Remind your anxious person during this transition that you are no longer supporting the anxiety disorder because you care about him or her. Supporting the anxiety disorder reinforces the belief that the dragon is right. It is time for you to show your anxious person that the dragon is not right. There is a healthier way to do things. Give outs, and always praise your anxious person for hard work done. You cannot go too slowly—easy does it. Being persistent is what works, not taking big steps. Going too fast risks discouragement and quitting the effort. Just like starting an exercise program, if you do too much too fast, you may get injured and quit altogether. Better to take it easy and build up slowly so that control and confidence can grow slowly.

Homework for Step 3

1. Read Step 3.
2. Practice in your discomfort zone daily, preferably for thirty to sixty minutes.
3. Select and record a goal for this week's practice.
4. Record your practice on the Weekly Practice Worksheet.

Reading for Step 3

1. Ross, J. *Triumph over Fear—A Book of Help and Hope for People with Anxiety, Panic Attacks, and Phobias.*
   Part Three: "Recovery from Panic Disorder and Phobia: A Self-Help Program"

Six Action Thoughts for When Your Anxiety Is High

1. Remember that anxiety is unpleasant but not dangerous.
2. Think of panic as a false alarm.
3. Take a few deep breaths.
4. Think of outs.
5. Remember that you are not trapped and you are not alone.
6. Plan to return to the anxiety-provoking situation when the anxiety is more manageable.

The Anxiety Cure Weekly Practice Worksheet

Your Goal for This Week: _____

Each day record the minutes of practice and the expected and actual levels of fear or panic. Record your general level of satisfaction with your life for that day, from 0 (completely unsatisfied) to 10 (completely satisfied).

Date	Practice Activity	Maximum Expected Level*	Actual Duration (Min.)	Maximum Actual Level*	Satisfaction Level*	Comments

*Rate 0–10

CHAPTER 15

Step 4

Use Support People—Relate to Others about Your Anxiety

When it comes to recovery from anxiety disorders,

You alone can do it,
But you cannot do it alone.

You can get an anxiety disorder on your own, but you are not likely to get well alone. Getting well from an anxiety disorder usually takes the help of others. The first step is facing that *you* have the problem. You need to face that vital fact without embarrassment or shame and without denial. That is not easy because of the societal stigma that anxiety is the result of weakness, poor coping skills, or laziness. Getting well can be done, just the way you would face any other illness or problem.

Be Honest about Your Anxiety

If you have been following the Anxiety Cure step by step, or if you have read any other part of this book, you know that we do not believe that weakness, poor coping skills, or laziness are the causes of anxiety. Rather, this is a biological and conditioned response of your nerves to inappropriate signals of anxiety when no danger exists.

Do you believe you have a clear understanding of your own anxiety problem? It is important that you do before you try to explain the problem to others. If you are feeling unsure at this point, back up and review your score on the Anxiety Inventory in Part Two, Chapter 6, and your own anxiety history in your journal from Part Four, Chapter 12. For most people, this will not be necessary, but if you are a highly anxious person, you may find that your thoughts about your own suffering are chaotic because of your anxiety. This may make it hard to focus on the information you have read about anxiety. If this is true for you, either continue with this step, being careful to find a trusted person to be your support person with whom you can learn this information together, or seek professional help from a therapist or psychiatrist.

Honesty is a good place to start—honesty with yourself and with those who care about you when it comes to your thoughts and feelings. Even if people do not understand your symptoms, if they care about you, you are better off to be open with them in most cases. Please realize that this does not necessarily apply to people in your place of work or others who are in authority over you. We are only talking here about people who truly care about you, such as friends and family. For more ideas about honesty at work, see Part Five, Chapter 20.

Honesty is an important starting point precisely because it is so easy to be dishonest with yourself and with friends and family when you have an anxiety disorder. Most people with anxiety see these types of dishonest communications as "little white lies," but they are untruths nonetheless, and they always worsen your anxiety problem, lower your self-esteem, and reduce your ability to get well.

Everything Is Contaminated!

Joy was a thirty-five-year-old woman with severe OCD. She had particular trouble with the laundry and felt that she had to wash the clothes "just right" to make them safe for her family to wear. She spent three or four hours a day doing the laundry, and yet each family member only had a few pieces of clothing that Joy would let them wear. All of the clothes looked worn and faded because of the many times they had been laundered. To keep her husband and five-year-old son from wearing other clothes, which she considered to be "contaminated," Joy would explain that the other clothes were torn and needed mending, or that the water in the apartment had been shut off during the day for repair work, which prevented her from doing the wash, or that she had run out of laundry detergent. No one else was allowed to touch the dirty laundry. Joy became fiercely angry with her husband when he attempted to do a load of wash himself, telling him that he was too dirty from his construction job to go into the laundry area.

Joy's husband sought help because he could not understand what was wrong with his wife. Her lies had him completely confused. He had been embarrassed once during a conversation with a neighbor when he commented about the chronic problems with the water being turned off in the building, only to have the neighbor reply that the water had never been turned off.

Joy could not explain her OCD to herself and was frightened to tell her husband the thoughts she knew were unreasonable about the laundry. Her anxiety dragon told her that if she did not do the laundry "just right," her family would become sick and die. In her mind, she was trapped between giving in to the OCD and keeping the people she loved safe, even though they were angry with her, or ignoring the OCD and risking losing them to illness from the germs she believed were on the clothes.

Our secrets keep us sick. By not admitting the problem to herself or her husband, Joy prevented herself from finding help. Only honesty about the OCD that was driving the lies could explain to Joy's husband what was happening. Once Joy was not secretive about her anxiety problem, they could find help together.

It is important to be direct about telling friends and family what is wrong with you and what they can do to help you regain control of your life over the anxiety disorder. We have included a sample Letter to a Friend at the end of this step. Make copies of it to give to people you want to understand more about your anxiety disorder. It is not a short or a simple letter because it is not easy to explain the anxiety experience. You can also use the letter as a starting point to write your own Letter to a Friend, which can be a more personal description about your experiences and which more fully explains what you want from the person to whom you are giving it.

The only way to overcome any disability, including an anxiety disorder, is to work harder than people who do not have this disability. There never was any other way and there never will be any other way that works over the long haul. The bonus of facing your anxiety disease and working hard to conquer it is that when you have admitted the problem with your anxiety disorder, you can start building your self-esteem on a solid foundation. Confronting any problem and working hard to get well builds self-esteem. Other people can understand your effort and can help you along the way, if you will take the time and be unself-conscious enough to let them know what the problem is and what they need to do to help you.

Choosing Your Support Person

Once you have been open and honest about your situation to people who care about you, you can enlist other people in helping you get well. Although many people will help you as you continue with your recovery, it is useful to have one particular person to work with on a regular basis. This support person will assist you in evaluating your anxiety, choosing goals, practicing, and being accountable for your actions. This final role is especially important as you recover because it is easy to let yourself fall back into the pattern of dishonesty with yourself over small things. Do you really want to skip the museum tour on a family vacation or are you afraid you will not be able to see an exit sign at all times? Did you not volunteer for an extra assignment at work because you are too busy already or because you did not want to have to present the information to a group of people?

When considering how you function at work or in other situations where you do not choose to be completely honest about your anxiety, it will be important to have your support person help you evaluate your actions. Think of your support person as an extension of the healthy part of your brain—someone to help you gain perspective on the thoughts and feelings that bombard you when anxiety is high.

Perhaps your choice of a support person is obvious. Perhaps it is not so clear. Begin by making a list in your journal of all the possibilities for support people. Next to each name write down the advantages and disadvantages of working with that person. If you have social phobia or are withdrawn from people because of your anxiety, you may have no one to choose from, or your list may be of people who all seem not quite right for one reason or another. Clearly, one of your goals will be increasing your social contacts, and reaching out for help to someone whom you do not know well can be a good way to begin to get to know a person better. You may find it helpful to go to an anxiety support group to meet others with similar problems, and pick someone who you think would be a good support person from the people at the meeting. If you are truly feeling stuck with this step, it is probably wise to find a therapist to be your support person for now. Eventually you will get to your goal of having a nontherapist friend as a support person, but for now it is simply important to have someone to help you get started on your work. See Part Four, Chapter 17, for some ideas about how to find a therapist.

Once you know who you want to have as your support person, your path is relatively clear: ask the person to read the section for support people in Part Three, Chapter 11, and then let you know if he or she is willing to volunteer for this role. Once you have found a support person, set up a regular weekly meeting time so that the two of you can practice together and review the practice you have recorded in your journal. Allow your support person to give you praise and to help you through anxious moments.

Let your support person praise you, and accept the praise without hiding behind an apology such as "I should have done more" or "That was nothing. When I tried to do something really hard, I failed" or "Normal people do that stuff with no effort. Why should I get praise for doing such a simple, ordinary thing?" Those are self-defeating and hurtful thoughts produced by your worry machine. Such thoughts undermine your self-esteem and mock your hard work. Instead, just say to your support person, "You are right. It was hard for me, and I am proud I did my practice and grateful to you for sharing this experience with me."

With a good support person, you can accomplish more goals faster than you believed to be possible. Keep up the work between practice sessions by repeating the work on your own. For example, if you have a fear of elevators, practice at a mall with your support person one week. At the end of your practice, set up a meeting for the following week at a tall building for longer elevator rides. During the week return to the mall and practice on the same elevator on your own.

Some anxious people never get around to practicing. While unfortunate, this is also uncommon. Many more anxious people practice, but they fault themselves for not doing more. We recommend practice once a week with your support person and for thirty to sixty minutes each day on your own. That is a high standard. But give yourself some slack. Take some days off, take some weeks off, but always come back. The more you practice (the longer and more frequent your practice), the faster you will get well. But slow will get you to the same place as fast. Set your pace but do not quit. Keep at it, and your results will be far beyond your best hopes.

Tips for Friends and Family

Whether you are a designated support person or not, there are plenty of opportunities for you to help your anxious person relate better to others. Review the people with whom it is better to be open and honest about the anxiety and the people with whom it is simply better to learn how to relate without explanation about anxiety. If you have friends and family in common, talk about these specific people and review the pluses and minuses of honesty.

It is also useful to talk over how your anxious person handles specific interactions, such as talking to a boss at work or returning items to a store. You will find that anxiety often leads anxious people to have difficulty with these types of situations. Practice role-playing particular situations with your anxious person by first acting as the anxious person and having your anxious person pretend to be the boss or sales clerk or whatever the specific situation suggests. In these roles have a dialogue that your anxious person has feared. Then switch roles and do the same role-playing again. After you have done both roles, talk over how each of you felt during the roles. You may need to repeat the same situation several times before your anxious person feels confident about being able to handle it in real life.

Homework for Step 4

1. Read Step 4.
2. Select and record a goal for this week's practice.
3. Practice in your discomfort zone daily and record this practice on your Weekly Practice Worksheet.
4. Recruit your support person.
5. Meet with your support person to practice together.
6. Fill out your Personal Progress Log.
7. Discuss with your support person the potential people to be honest with about your anxiety disorder.
8. Talk to people about your anxiety disorder, if this is what you decide to do.

Readings for Step 4

1. Ross, J. *Triumph over Fear—A Book of Help and Hope for People with Anxiety, Panic Attacks, and Phobias.*
    Chapter 13: "Sylvia: The Impact on the Family"
2. Schwartz, J. M. with B. Beyette. *Brain Lock—Free Yourself from Obsessive-Compulsive Behavior.*
    Chapter 6: "OCD as a Family Disorder"

3. Wilson, R. R. *Don't Panic—Taking Control of Anxiety Attacks*, rev. ed. Chapter 20: "The Fear of Being Seen: How to Face Social Anxieties"

Five Venting Strategies

1. Cry into your pillow.
2. Pound your pillow.
3. Curse and pound the steering wheel in your car—with the windows closed.
4. Talk to your support person.
5. Go for a walk, a run, or a bike ride.

Letter to a Friend

Dear Friend:

Although at first it may be hard for you to understand, I want you to know that I have an anxiety disorder. It is characterized by feelings of panic and fear in situations where other people do not have those feelings. It is embarrassing to admit that in situations where other people are calm, I experience dizziness, sweating, breathlessness, the "shakes," and other alarming body sensations. All anxiety disorders are forms of claustrophobia. The experience of feeling trapped and alone with unbearable feelings is at the heart of panic.

An anxiety disorder can cause these physical responses—the same responses as those suffered by people who are facing imminent peril—when an anxious person is in a seemingly safe situation, such as driving a car, going to a shopping mall, getting on an elevator, or flying in an airplane. Panic is a false alarm. Because the anxious person is not in imminent external danger when the alarm sounds, these reactions are irrational, and anxious people recognize that they are irrational. Everyone sometimes experiences feelings of anxiety, but those universal, normal feelings are not related to the intense and overwhelming feelings those of us with an anxiety disorder experience when we are in panic-generating situations.

Recently, there have been important scientific discoveries in the understanding of anxiety disorders. These disorders are not related to laziness or insanity, they do not lead to bizarre or dangerous behavior, and they do not lead to physical illness such as heart attacks or strokes. Anxiety disorders often run in families, affecting about 20 percent of women and 8 percent of men in their lifetimes. An anxiety disorder usually waxes and wanes over a lifetime. The good news is that anxiety disorders can be successfully treated.

It will be easier for me to get well if you understand what I am facing and how I am coping with it. I am learning specific techniques to enter and remain in the situations that produce feelings of panic and dread. It takes courage to do that because the feelings and thoughts are all-consuming and extremely painful. As you can imagine, it is unnerving to feel that you cannot trust your own body in many everyday situations.

That is why anxiety disorders often lead to avoidance of the situations and experiences that trigger these reactions and why they lead to a loss of self-esteem and a desire to hide the problem. I know other people cannot see the danger and do not understand my reactions. They cannot see my inner terror. That fact makes me feel even more strange and hopeless. Think about what it would be like trying to explain the color red to a person who was born blind. In the end, that is the problem I have in explaining to you the inner experience of my anxiety disorder.

It will help me if you ask me what I am feeling and what you can do to help in any of these situations. It is always the right thing to give me "outs" from any circumstance in which I feel trapped. Paradoxically, knowing that I have an out helps me to stay in the difficult situation. It also helps if you acknowledge my accomplishments and give me praise and support for my efforts to practice my antipanic techniques. I know it may seem ridiculous to you—as it does to me sometimes—to praise me for doing something that for most people is perfectly easy, but believe me, it is not easy for anyone with an anxiety disorder to do this practice.

If you would like to know more about my anxiety disorder, please ask me. I appreciate your efforts to understand my problem. Thank you for your concern. It means a lot to me that you have taken the time to read this letter and to think about how you can help me.

Regards,

[Your Name]

CHAPTER 16

Step 5
Eliminate External Causes of Anxiety

In this step you will evaluate possible external causes of anxiety. By external causes, we mean events that happen in your life and outside of your brain. This contrasts with the main sustaining force of your anxiety, which is the fear of having the anxious and panicky feelings again—having the dragon arise within your brain. It is important to evaluate external causes in your anxiety cure, as there may be simple changes you can make, such as cutting down on caffeine, that will make the work of finding a cure much easier. Some of the external causes of anxiety we cover here may not apply to you at all. If this is the case, simply skip over this section and move on to the next one. We suggest that you document this skip in your journal, however, and review your decision in the future with your support person, since it is possible to be so close to the problem yourself that you do not realize that the piece you skipped over is a place to begin future work.

Medicines and Drugs

Some medicines and drugs cause significant increases in anxiety for susceptible people. Remember that anxiety disorders are triggered in genetically susceptible people by events that may or may not be clear at the time. People who do not have this hard-wired susceptibility can use medicines that potentially cause anxiety and never have a problem. People with anxiety, however, should be wary of medicine that lists anxiety, agitation, insomnia, or tremors as possible side effects. Be sure to discuss your anxiety disorder with any doctor who prescribes medicines for you for other reasons. Read package inserts from over-the-counter medicines carefully. While we believe that no one should use street drugs, anxious people have an especially powerful reason not to use them, as many people report their first panic attack occurred following use of marijuana, cocaine, and other nonmedical drugs.

The following is a list of medicines that may cause increased anxiety. This list is a good place to start, but it barely scratches the surface of substances that cause anxiety. If you have any questions about a specific medicine you are taking, check with your doctor or a pharmacist.

Potential Anxiety-Causing Medicines

Caffeine—in some headache remedies, coffee, tea, colas, chocolate

Pseudoephedrine—in cold medicines, decongestants, appetite suppressants

Epinephrine—in novocaine, EpiPens

Nicotine—in tobacco products, smoking "patches"

Theophylline/prednisone—and other asthma and allergy medicines

---

Note in your journal what medicines or vitamins you are taking now and if you believe that any changes are warranted. Call doctors or pharmacists for more information if necessary. Be sure to review this list with your support person.

You do not know for sure whether any of these substances or medicines contributes to your anxiety, and neither does your doctor or pharmacist. They can give you useful advice, but in the end, the best way to figure out whether any particular substance is contributing to your anxiety is to try a period of time—usually a week or so—off of the medicine to see if that significantly reduces your anxiety. Then, if you are still in doubt, start taking the substance or medicine again. Did you see a change or not? Recording your levels of anxiety and panic in your journal before, during, and after these trials will help you work through what can be a difficult decision-making process. Just as you would work with a person who has an allergy to a food or other substance, you can use the scientific method to reach your conclusions. You can conduct a personal experiment to decide whether your life is improved by avoiding a substance or medicine that is sometimes known to cause anxiety.

When it comes to prescription medicines, the *Physicians' Desk Reference* (*PDR*) lists virtually all possible side effects for virtually all medicines.

These exhaustive lists are almost certain to contain "insomnia," "anxiety," and "agitation" for any medicine you look up in the *PDR*. But we do not want you to avoid medicines that can help you simply because they may have one of these possible side effects. That is one more way to let the dragon run your life. We want you to consider the question of medicines causing anxiety and to work with your prescribing physicians to sort this out, one medicine at a time. Many medicines, such as antidepressants used to reduce anxiety, can add to anxiety in the first few days or weeks, but in the long run they reduce anxiety and insomnia. We want you to think of the long term in such situations and not to be turned away from medicines that can help because of anticipatory anxiety about possible side effects.

Do not stop taking any prescribed medicine out of concern over anxiety without talking with your prescribing physician. We cannot know all the facts of your particular case. Only your own doctor can. Sometimes it is hazardous to your health to simply stop a medicine to see if it is part of your problem with anxiety. When it comes to either starting a new medicine or stopping an old medicine, we want you to work closely with your doctors so that your decisions about the use of particular medicines are right for you.

Stress and Anxiety

Stress and anxiety are not synonymous, but they are linked through your brain. Stress is externally located, while anxiety is an internal state. Change causes stress. Anxiety is a feeling usually associated with tension, worry, and irritability. It is not easy to distinguish between stress and anxiety because many people erroneously use the two words interchangeably. Early on in the process of your anxiety cure, you also may have difficulty separating stress from anxiety. This is especially true if you have a high level of anxiety.

Most people with anxiety find that reducing social commitments and work obligations does not diminish anxiety and, in fact, may increase anxiety. You may find, for example, that weekends and vacations are especially anxious times for you. For many anxious people, social and work commitments actually liberate them from anxiety. These obligations are *not* sources of stress. This is exactly the opposite of the conventional thought that working causes anxiety.

To feel anxious—to feed the anxiety dragon—you have to focus on your own fear. When you are busy meeting obligations in your life, you have less time to focus on your fear. This reduces your anxiety. When you relax, when external demands are lowered, you have more opportunities to focus on your inner experiences, and for many anxious people, that means you focus on your fear and panic, which makes the anxious feelings worse. This becomes a vicious cycle as more fear leads to more focus on the fear, which in turn leads to more fear.

We do not believe that reducing life's external stress will, on its own, either cure or even reduce your anxiety. Rather, in this step you will evaluate the interaction between stress and anxiety. Make a list in your journal of sources of external stress that occur in your life now. Some of these will be things you cannot change, such as the stress of having a parent who is ill and in need of extra assistance. Other situations will be within your control, especially as you begin to recover from your anxiety disorder.

Family Stress

Jenny, a thirty-two-year-old woman, suffered from severe agoraphobia when she first began working on a list of stresses in her life. She lived at home with her father and her sister, who was twelve years younger than Jenny. Her mother had abandoned the family when the sister was, as an infant, found to be disabled. Jenny became a caregiver at an early age. The year her mother left was the first time Jenny had a panic attack.

Her father now drove Jenny to and from work. Because of her agoraphobic fears, the drive was so hard for Jenny that she would wear a Walkman and listen to gospel music because she was sure they would have an accident and be killed during the short journey. Other than that drive to and from work, which she felt forced to make because her father and sister counted on her income, Jenny did not leave her house.

When she first evaluated stress in her life, Jenny regarded her relationship with her father to be a problem because her father told her that she was too dependent. Her relationship with her sister was stressful because Jenny resented her sister's need for Jenny's income. Jenny thought that she had no personal life and that she was missing any opportunity to date, marry, and have a family of her own. Her job, which was the same one she had held since she graduated from high school, had become boring.

All of these negative thoughts were a big problem because Jenny had too much free time to worry about her anxiety symptoms. She felt trapped in the job, but she did not believe she had the skills to do anything better. Because of her phobia about driving, she could not imagine how she could work at a different location. Most days she rated her average level of anxiety at about 7 or 8. Her stress list read as follows:

Jenny's Initial Stress List

1. My father wants me to drive, and I can't!! I am afraid he will make me lose my job one day because he will refuse to drive me anymore.
2. My sister. I know it is selfish, but I am tired of taking care of her and having my pay go to support her.
3. No social life.
4. Being trapped in a dead-end job.
5. Being lonely and isolated in my home.

One year later, Jenny's list of stresses looked considerably different. She had worked hard at the Anxiety Cure assignments and had finished a semester at a community college. Her grades were so good that she won a scholarship to study at a local university. She had bought a car and was practicing for her driver's license. Jenny regularly attended church. She had a new job, which she had found through one of her college professors. Her new life was hardly stress free! Yet her anxiety level was quite low, usually no higher than a level 3.

Jenny described an especially busy week in which she had ongoing problems with her sister, taken a college final exam, interviewed for a new job, and had a date with a man she met at church. Yet Jenny noted that the final three stresses on her list were positive changes because they brought enrichment to her once terribly limited life.

Jenny's Stress List—One Year Later

1. My sister. I still wish I did not have to care for her both financially and physically.
2. My final exam. I am so proud that I finished this course. I hope I can show on the exam how much I learned.
3. My job interview. This sounds like a wonderful job; I hope I get it.
4. Going on a date. I am so excited! He is a really nice guy, and he seems to like me.

As you see from Jenny's first stress list, her anxiety caused all of her stresses except her problem with her sister. Jenny's progress in treating her anxiety disorder resulted in external stress changing from having negative to positive effects on her life, which resulted in lowering her anxiety symptoms.

Remember that people are like the bones and muscles that support us. Our bones and muscles need to be used to keep strong. In space, which is without gravity, the bones of astronauts rapidly become brittle because they do not have the stress of working against gravity to keep them strong. People need positive stress to grow and to learn new things. External life stress is not negative; it is what we do with it that makes it negative or positive.

Notice in Jenny's example that there is no way to solve her stress about her sister. Social services possibilities had been explored to the fullest and private respite care alternatives had been used. Still Jenny felt overworked. Even so, she did not want to institutionalize her disabled sister, which was the only other alternative left to her. Jenny joined a support group for caregivers and felt at least a bit better understood in her long-term dedication to her sister.

How Is Your Thyroid Functioning?

Jenny's example brings us to another important cause of anxiety that is not related to the fear of the feeling of fear brought on by the dragon. It is, however, internal to the brain, but not in any conscious way. Jenny found out early in her anxiety cure that she had a thyroid deficiency. She had not had a medical examination for years when she first began her treatment for anxiety. She noted that her menstrual cycle was unusual. She scheduled a gynecological appointment and made sure her doctor knew that anxiety was a problem for her.

Routine blood work confirmed the doctor's guess that her thyroid was not functioning properly. She was referred to an endocrinologist who stabilized her on Synthroid, and Jenny found that she had a dramatic reduction in her spontaneous panic attacks. Review the box at the end of this step for symptoms of thyroid problems. If you have any questions about whether or not this is a part of your anxiety problem, ask for a thyroid screening by your primary care doctor, a gynecologist, or an endocrinologist. Very few clinically anxious people find that they have a thyroid problem, but it is worth checking because it is so easily solved with supplementation and can make such a dramatic improvement in anxiety levels.

Some other medical disorders can cause symptoms of anxiety. It is a good idea to see your doctor to check out your medical status. Most people with anxiety disorders, even after many years of suffering from panic and other symptoms of anxiety, are remarkably healthy. Most people have seen many physicians about their symptoms before they conclude that their problems are the result of an anxiety disorder.

Breathe the Anxiety Away

Tension is both a mental and a muscular expression of anxiety. Once present in your body, tension signals your brain that you are anxious. This pattern of anxiety—where increased muscular tension leads to an increased perception of anxiety—can be maintained perpetually. This cause-and-effect relationship explains the chronic headaches, jaw pain, muscle stiffness, and general aches and pains so commonly experienced by people with anxiety disorders. One of the first places to try to break free of anxiety is to learn consciously to relax your body, which in turn will signal your brain that you are relaxed, that there is nothing to fear.

Some people scoff at the idea that changing the way you breathe can significantly lower your anxiety level. It is true that breathing practice certainly will not solve all your anxiety problems, and it may not even make much of a difference in your anxiety. Breathing practice does help many people, however, and it is so simple that it is worth trying.

Begin to calm your anxious breathing by taking a few nice, easy breaths, moving your abdomen up and down as you breathe. You may find it helpful to lie on your back on the floor or your bed to practice this simple breathing technique: place one hand on your stomach and a second hand on your chest. Feel your hand on your stomach move up and down when you breathe deeply. Feel how far into your abdomen you can swell with air when you relax your shoulders and allow yourself to breathe fully.

This focus on the simple, natural body movements associated with deep breathing helps to quiet anxiety. It helps you to think about your body as your friend, not as an enemy. It is important to understand that your brain will get all the air it needs no matter how scared and upset you become. Many anxious people fear that they will suffocate or not be able to get the air they need. This never happens, period. *You will get all the air you need.* If your brain's mechanisms that control breathing required you to be calm or to work hard at breathing correctly, all the anxious people in the world would have died of asphyxiation long ago!

Anxious, irregular breathing will move plenty of air so that your lungs keep your blood full of oxygen. That is not the problem with anxious breathing, although fear of not getting enough air is often a symptom of anxiety. The problem with anxious breathing is that it adds to tension and fear. It signals danger to your sensitized brain. This triggers the false alarm of panic and the more chronic danger signal of anxiety. Anxious breathing both results from and causes anxiety, but it does not cause low oxygen levels.

A Wonderful Antifear Strategy

Now try a paradoxical intention exercise: breathe as abnormally as you can. Hyperventilate as much as you can to see if you can make yourself panic or pass out. Alternately, hold your breath for as long as you can. Most people with anxiety are surprised at how hard it is to do these exercises for more than a few seconds. In fact, what makes breathing normally so hard for anxious people is trying so hard to do what is best done with no effort—by letting go. Breathing is natural and unconscious, like walking. If you try to walk carefully, you are likely to trip over your own feet.

Even during the worst anxiety, your body is not poised on the brink of disaster with respect to breathing. Learn to trust your tense and anxious body; it will get you through what you need to go through. In the words of Dr. Claire Weekes, "Jelly legs will carry you." We could add, "*Abnormal breathing will still get you all the air you need.*"

Record your deep breathing and paradoxical breathing practices in your journal. Include the length of time you hyperventilated and held your breath, and record any changes in your anxiety level during these exercises. Try taking three deep breaths when you are anxious.

As you do, remind yourself: "*My breathing is good enough.*" This positive thought will encourage you to continue and will begin to take the place of the negative thoughts that you have been bombarding yourself with and that only make your breathing more difficult.

Relaxation and Guided Imagery Practice

Deep breathing practice can be effectively combined with relaxation and guided imagery practice. Relaxation and imagery are relatively easy for most anxious people because part of their anxiety stems from an overactive (fear-generating) imagination. In doing these exercises, you will be harnessing this imagination and using it to help yourself, rather than allowing it to be destructive, as it has been in the past.

Relaxation reduces distress for many people, including people who are suffering from chronic pain and people undergoing cancer treatment. Anxious people also benefit from learning relaxation techniques, although many find sustained concentration difficult early in their cure because they feel too anxious to concentrate on anything but their fear. We have purposely kept these exercises short so you will not have to concentrate for too long. The goal of practicing relaxation is to be able to summon a physical and a mental feeling of peace and calm whenever you need it during the day. Try each of the several relaxation exercises we suggest.

Make your own personalized relaxation tape by recording yourself saying these instructions in a slow, calm voice or have your support person or someone else close to you record the instructions for you. After you have made your personalized relaxation recording, practice these techniques for fifteen minutes or so every day.

During your relaxation practice, you will need to use thought-blocking to consciously let go of anxious thoughts from your mind. As anxious thoughts interrupt you, simply let them slide from your thoughts, reminding yourself that you will be able to worry about them again at the end of your practice time if you choose to. In thought-blocking, it is essential to have a specified period of time within which you are firmly preventing yourself from thinking anxious thoughts. Start with a short goal. Perhaps initially you can do only a five-minute, modified relaxation tape without being interrupted by unwanted anxious thoughts. As you gain greater experience from your practice, you will be able to extend the time that you set aside from worry. You may need to set a kitchen timer so that you know when you have achieved your goal. This technique is especially helpful for people who have OCD that involves having upsetting images or GAD, which seldom lets you stop worrying. As these images and worries appear while you are doing your relaxation exercise, consciously say to yourself, "I will think about that upsetting thought again after this practice session is done," or simply, "*Not now.*"

Many people with anxiety do not realize prior to this practice that it is possible to put aside, at least for a while, their anxious thoughts. Rather, they feel so carried away by their anxious thoughts and feelings that they believe these thoughts and feelings are unstoppable. This is the first time you are saying to your dragon: "This is as far as you go. You may not have my attention right now. This is my time to relax. Later you can do your worst. Not now." When you get to the end of the prescribed time, you will be faced with a choice: to let the dragon back in or to continue blocking him for another set time—say another fifteen minutes.

Eventually, one of two things will happen: either you will have gotten on with the things you are doing and realized with surprise sometime later that the dragon has not been back to bother you, or you will be exhausted from keeping the anxious thoughts back for even the minimal time and find they rush in on you as soon as your guard is down. Most people will find the former to be true most of the time.

Script for Relaxation Exercise

Read this—or your own version—slowly and calmly into a tape recorder. Pause for five to thirty seconds at each *

Begin to relax by finding a comfortable position. Settle yourself, finding relaxing places for your arms, your hands, and your feet. * Close your eyes gently. * Now that you are settled, take three calming, deep breaths. Feel your stomach expand with each breath. Feel the tension leave your body each time you exhale. Think the word *calm* each time you exhale. * Continue to breathe deeply and slowly as you relax by focusing on letting tension drift out of your body. Do not fight tension. Instead, let it slide away.

Scan your body, and when you find places where you are tense, focus your attention on that area. Hold your focused attention on an area of tension while you breathe deeply. Imagine that tense place becoming warm, loose, and relaxed. * It is as though you are shining a spotlight over your whole body. You are illuminating each place that is tense. When you find a tense area, hold the light on that place. As the light rests on that tense area, you feel the warmth from the light entering your skin, warming your muscles, relaxing that part of you. *

Now direct your attention to your head, and feel the muscles in your scalp and face become soft and relaxed. * Feel the skin around your eyes and mouth become smooth as you relax. Focus especially on the muscles in your jaw. Feel the muscles release the tension they have been holding. Feel the warmth of your illumination lengthen and relax the muscles. Perhaps your mouth will open slightly with this relaxation. * Continue to breathe slowly and deeply.

Direct your attention to your neck and shoulders, feeling the tense, tight muscles gradually relaxing and become smooth and warm. * Allow the warmth and calm to travel down your arms, around your elbows, and down your forearms. Feel your arms settle down as they become heavy, warm, and relaxed. Let your wrists and hands become limp and relaxed, feeling the tension drain out of your hands. *

Take another deep breath and bring your attention to your stomach and back. Think of your back. Let it relax, slowly. Follow the relaxation down your abdomen, feeling the muscles and inner organs relax and calm. * Feel your hips settle with relaxation. Let your thighs and knees relax. Feel your lower legs and calves relax and become warm and heavy. Feel the tension from your body flow out your feet, and feel your feet become warm and relaxed. *

Savor the feeling of being completely relaxed and loose. * Let your body learn how it feels to be warm and calm. * Now that you know this feeling, it can be yours anytime you want. Simply recall the words *relaxed* and *calm*, and breathe easily, slowly, and deeply. Peace will return to you. * *

Now it is time to begin to focus on the world outside your body again. You may feel like shifting in your seat. Blink and open your eyes. Think about how good it feels to be alert and yet relaxed and calm. Give yourself praise for taking the time to do this relaxation exercise. You deserve to feel this calm and relaxed. Take this peace with you as you rejoin your day.

Script for Travel Imagery Tape

*Personalize it to fit you. Make choices about
mode of transportation and destination prior
to beginning. Customize a script, and read
slowly into a tape recorder. Pause for five to
thirty seconds at each ***

It is time to go to your special place. This is the trip you have been longing and waiting for, to go to the most wonderful place you know. Find a comfortable position, and close your eyes. Imagine yourself climbing on board your personal shuttle. Transportation just the way you want it, just when you want it. Feel the ergonomic seat on your first-class shuttle. It fits you perfectly because it was made just for you. Guide your imaginary shuttle on its journey. Fast or slow, the pace and the destination are yours. * Feel the breeze as you move along. Feel the warm air surround and carry you. Breathe deeply as you feel totally safe. *

You are getting close to your destination now. See it ahead? This is the place you have been hoping to find. Your own perfect place. Safe, warm, relaxing—it has everything you need. * Settle into your perfect place. What do you see? * What do you hear? * Are there fragrances surrounding you? * Feel your arms rest lightly and comfortably on your magic seat. Settle yourself even more comfortably. Relaxation at last. Let the feeling of relaxation flow over you like warm sunshine. * If you like you can get up and explore. * Examine this wonderful place. You feel welcome and safe here. Take a few minutes to relax and enjoy all the sights, sounds, smells, and feelings that surround you. * * * *

Now it is time to leave your special place. Your shuttle has arrived for you. Take a minute to feel the relaxation and peace you have experienced here before you go. * Know that this special place is all yours and that you can return here anytime, as often as you like. The ride back seems to be over more quickly than the ride to your special place.

Begin to reacquaint yourself with the here and now. This too is your special place. This is the unique life you have created for yourself. You may find yourself shifting and moving as you return from your journey. As you fully return to the present, blink and open your eyes. Remember, your special place is yours to travel to whenever you wish. Remember that wherever you are, right then, is your personal, special place. Know it, appreciate it, explore it.

What do you think of these suggested relaxation exercises? There are many commercial tapes available, so if you find that these do not suit you, try looking for others in a bookstore or a library. In your journal write down your impression of these relaxation and breathing exercises. We suggest that you try them or other relaxation exercises for a week and then again evaluate how you feel about them. Be sure to date these observations in your journal, and give yourself credit for doing the work, whatever the results.

Exercise Helps Every Body

Most anxious people need to learn, or relearn, to trust their bodies. One good way to do that is to start a regular program of aerobic exercising. Aerobic means any activity, even if it is not intense, that is rhythmic and continuous and raises your heart rate to your target heart rate (THR) zone. See the box at the end of this step to calculate your target heart rate. Most anxiety, and especially panic attacks, is associated with a feeling of rapid heart rate, but this usually is less than 100 beats per minute even during a level 10 panic. Learn how to check your pulse when you are anxious and when exercising. Learn what your resting pulse is. For many people, their resting pulse is between about 70 and 80 beats per minute. Aerobic exercise, depending on your age, brings it up to between about 110 and 140 beats per minute. It surprises many anxious people who worry about their heart rates that when they exercise, even moderately, their pulse is higher than it is during a panic attack. Panic does not hurt your heart, it just gives it a minor workout. Exercise regularly and moderately to help both your mind and your body.

You can feel your pulse on the inside of your wrist at the base of your thumb. You can also feel it in your neck on either side of your windpipe (trachea). Push your fingers into your neck and count the beats for 10 seconds. Multiply that number times six to get your heart rate (beats per minute). In general, exercise so that your THR is between 70 percent and 85 percent of your maximum heart rate as calculated in the box at the end of this step. For most people, this means a pulse rate above about 100 and under about 140.

For most people, the best aerobic exercise is walking, which can often be done with someone else, making it more fun. Aerobic exercise need not be difficult or strenuous. But the activity does need to be regular and sustained. The simple goal for healthy aerobic exercise is to exercise for thirty minutes four times a week, but start out with five minutes two to three times a week. This simple exercise routine will not only help your mind, it will also help your body, too. If you have heart disease, if you are over forty and in poor health, or if you have any doubts about exercising, you should check with your doctor before starting a program of exercise.

In your journal write your current level of exercise and your ideal weekly exercise routine. Record your total minutes of aerobic exercise each day and add up the daily numbers each week. Your goal is 120 minutes, or more, each week. Begin to think how you could move toward that goal. If you need to see a physician prior to exercising, schedule that appointment. Otherwise, begin with some simple, easy-does-it exercise. If you have concerns about your ability to engage in moderate aerobic activity, check with your physician before you start to exercise.

Yoga, Tai Chi, and Other Good Options

Some anxious people find great benefit in a program of yoga or tai chi. If you are attracted to either approach, you will find many useful books and videotapes at libraries and bookstores. Some public television stations broadcast yoga or tai chi classes in the early morning. These programs can be taped to play at your convenience and are an excellent way to try a new approach for free.

You will also find many professional programs ready to help you. In contrast, many anxious people do not significantly benefit from either biofeedback or formal meditation—both of which require much effort and time—but some do. Try several approaches for yourself if you are interested.

Food and Anxiety

Examining the role of food and eating in an anxiety disorder is another area that may or may not be helpful to you. Some people find that eating sugar or chocolate, or skipping meals, triggers panic attacks. Unless you have a food allergy or a problem with blood sugar, it is probably sufficient to do some detective work on this connection by yourself. Try keeping a list of all flare-ups of your anxiety symptoms, whether panic attacks or OCD symptoms, and then trace back what you have or have not eaten over the previous few hours. If you believe you have found a link, make a change in the direction that you predict will reduce your anxiety problem. See over the course of several days if this link continues to hold true. If you feel better, try a planned return to the problem-provoking food or eating pattern to see if the anxiety problem worsens. Many changes along this line are possible, and while most people with anxiety find no difference in anxiety levels from eating particular foods, others feel that they do. Caffeine is a special case, as discussed earlier. Many, but not all, anxious people find that caffeine is a trigger for anxiety, including caffeine in foods and beverages.

Tips for Friends and Family

Many of the tips for handling external causes of anxiety mentioned in this step are useful for people other than just the person with an anxiety disorder. Consider making some changes in your own life to support the changes your anxious person is making. For example, why not set up a schedule of walking together? Perhaps you also would like to try tai chi, and the two of you could sign up to take a class together one evening a week. Another possibility is for you to evaluate your eating and set a goal for change, whether it is to lose weight or to cut out caffeine. Whatever you do, be sure to encourage each other's success at sticking to your goals and following through on your commitments.

Homework for Step 5

1. Read Step 5.
2. Select and record a goal for this week's practice.
3. Practice in your discomfort zone daily and record this practice on your Weekly Practice Worksheet.
4. Meet once to practice with your support person and to review your journal.
5. Fill in your Personal Progress Log.
6. Evaluate stress, exercise, and caffeine in your life.

Readings for Step 5

1. Norden, M. J. *Beyond Prozac—Brain-Toxic Lifestyles, Natural Antidotes & New Generation Antidepressants.*
   Part II: "Natural Prozac"
2. Wilson, R. R. *Don't Panic—Taking Control of Anxiety Attacks,* rev. ed.
   Chapter 10: "The Calming Response"
   Chapter 11: "The Breath of Life"

Common Indications of Thyroid Disorders	
Hypothyroidism	*Hyperthyroidism*
Tiredness/fatigue	Nervousness
Forgetfulness	Difficulty sleeping
Dry, coarse, hair	Bulging eyes, unblinking stare
Loss of eyebrow hair	Goiter
Puffy face and eyes	Rapid heartbeat
Goiter	Increased sweating
Slow heartbeat	Unexplained weight loss
Cold intolerance	Light menstrual periods
Weight gain	Frequent bowel movements
Heavy menstrual periods	Warm, moist palms
Constipation	Fine tremor of fingers
Brittle nails	Irritability

Calculating Your Target Heart Rate (THR) Zone

The first step in calculating THR is to estimate your maximal heart rate. Complete the following:

220 – age (years) = age-adjusted maximal heart rate
Example: For a fifty-year-old person:
220 – 50 = 170 beats per minute

The second step is to calculate the THR zone:

70 percent maximal heart rate = low end of THR zone
Example: 70 percent of 170 beats per minute = 119 beats per minute
For you: .70 × _____ beats per minute = _____ beats per minute

85 percent maximal heart rate = high end of THR zone
Example: 85 percent of 170 beats per minute = 145 beats per minute
For you: .85 × _____ beats per minute = _____ beats per minute
Your THR is between 70 percent and 85 percent of your maximum heart rate.

Within five seconds after stopping exercise, count the pulse rate at your neck or wrist for ten seconds. Heart rate decreases rapidly after you stop exercising, so you must monitor it quickly if it is to be a good estimate of your exercise heart rate. Multiply the ten-second heart rate value by six to calculate the heart rate in beats per minute

Source: The President's Council on Physical Fitness and Sports

Three Tips for Staying in the Here and Now

1. Splash cold water on your face.
2. Put a rubber band around your wrist and snap yourself lightly.
3. Buy or rent a portable phone, and use it to call a friend when anxiety is high.

CHAPTER 17

Step 6

Evaluate Your Need for Medicines and Therapy in Your Anxiety Cure

It is important as you continue to do the work of practicing daily in your discomfort zone that you evaluate your need for medicine and therapy with your support person. You may have found at this point, for example, that you need more help from your support person than he or she feels can be offered. Or you may be proceeding well with your practice but finding that there are other problem areas of your life that the anxiety has masked. These are signs that you would benefit from having a therapist. Similarly, you may have found that even after using many different techniques to deal with your panicky feelings, you are still routinely having high levels of chronic anxiety or spontaneous panic attacks. These are indications that medicines may be particularly useful to you to give your brain a break from the biologically caused panic feelings. Once you have a supportive therapist or helpful medicine, you may find that you are able to make great strides in overcoming your anxiety.

Many anxious people feel guilty about taking medicines or seeing a therapist. They may reject medicines or therapy without even trying them. That is usually a mistake. If you can live a full normal life with your anxiety disorder without undue discomfort and without using medicines or seeing a therapist, then you do not need to use these resources. But if your discomfort is substantial, and if you find your life is limited by your panic and anxiety, then consider using medicines or seeing a therapist to help you reach your goals. We encourage clinically anxious people to try medicines and therapy to see if they produce significant benefit. If you do use them and they do not benefit you, at least you have tried, and you will know what medicines and therapy can and cannot do for you.

As described in Part Two, Chapter 7, of *The Anxiety Cure*, there are three types of medicines useful in the treatment of anxiety disorders: the antidepressants, the benzodiazepines (BZs), and other medicines such as the beta-blockers and BuSpar (buspirone). Prozac (fluoxetine) is the most widely used antidepressant, and Xanax (alprazolam) is the most widely used benzodiazepine today. The beta-blockers, including Inderal (propranolol), are used in the treatment of public speaking phobia.

In general, it is wise not to drink alcohol within at least twenty-four hours of taking any medicine for anxiety. The effects of alcohol can be magnified by simultaneous use of these medicines, which is especially dangerous when driving or doing anything else that requires you to be fully alert. Alcohol also negates the positive effects of antianxiety medicine. See the tables at the end of this step for a listing of the most widely used medicines to treat anxiety and the typical maximum daily doses of each.

One of our patients, who had been through countless years of intensive therapy for agoraphobia when she started the Anxiety Cure, found that using very small doses of Valium (diazepam) for acute anxiety when she needed it, combined with the shift in thinking and behavior that she learned from this program, were just what she needed to help her be able to go with her husband to Europe for a family vacation. This was all the more remarkable to her because she had never been so far from home, and a few months before this trip she had been nearly housebound from her disorder, despite her best previous efforts to overcome it. Here is a letter she wrote describing her joy while taking a trip that had terrified her before she took to the air and crossed the Atlantic Ocean:

I wanted to drop you a note to let you know how well I'm doing! You definitely were a *much* better predictor of how things would go than I was. As usual, my anticipatory anxiety was way out of range with the reality of things.

I did take much more Valium than before (2.5 mg about every four hours, with a total of about 15 mg over the course of the day) on the day of the flight. I felt almost completely free of anxiety, and the flight was fine.

Since I've been in London, I've been able to do everything—including very crowded buses, subways, sightseeing, restaurants, etc., feeling quite comfortable. Again, as you predicted, I've been doing well on about 2.5 mg two or three times a day.

I can hardly believe I'm here in Europe—leaving for Paris Monday morning. This is not only a wonderful family trip that we'll always remember, but also a great lesson in what I can do. I am so relieved that I am actually *enjoying* myself (also, as you predicted), not just getting through each day painfully. That is a great gift for me.

Thank you! It helped me so much to see you right before I left. And guess what? I'm not even walking around "ga-ga" from the medication. I believe I appear to be a normal person.

The usual maximum dose of Valium for anxiety is 40 mg a day. This woman did not take more than 15 mg a day, and most days she was using 5 to 7.5 mg. She used small doses of Valium and had a good response. This is typical of anxious people. She was concerned about her use of Valium and had been afraid she would be a zombie if she took more than a tiny dose. Those concerns and fears are also characteristic of how anxious people often feel about the use of all medicines. Valium helped her use cognitive and behavior techniques. The medicine helped her escape from her phobia prison and enjoy her life.

Feeling Guilty for Taking Medicines?

Many anxious people do. They feel that using medicines is a sign of weakness or failure, but they do not have such feelings about using medicines for most nonmental diseases. Both medicines and therapy are ways of coping with many serious but solvable mental problems, including the anxiety disorders. They are complementary, not competitive. Using neither medicines or therapy is not a sign of weakness. Both are signs of strength, of doing what it takes to live a full, normal, and reasonably comfortable life. Using medicines does not interfere with effective use of nonmedicine therapies for anxiety disorders. The opposite is more often the case. Only when medicines have quieted the overreactive, clinically anxious brain can the anxious person make the best use of psychotherapy and of practice as outlined in this book.

The Problem of Addiction to Medicines

Is an anxious person addicted to a medicine? Addiction is characterized by two features: loss of control and denial. If the anxious person lies about the use of alcohol and other drugs, obtains drugs from more than one physician without telling all the physicians the truth about the use of medicines, and/or uses the medicines despite obvious harm that is caused by the use of that drug, then that is addiction.

In contrast, if the anxious person uses medicines that produce benefit instead of harm and if that use is entirely honest and openly described to all physicians (and family members), then that is not addiction. The same thing is true for therapy. If the anxious person tells the truth about seeing a therapist, and if that relationship is helpful, then it is not an "addiction." These simple distinctions are often not made, which leaves many anxious people who use medicines feeling guilty, as though they were "addicted" to their medicines. Equally bad is the fear of addiction, which inappropriately leads many anxious people not to use medicines that could genuinely benefit them. For more about anxiety and addiction, see Part Five, Chapter 23.

When to Take and When to Stop Taking Medicines for Anxiety

Anxiety problems usually come and go repeatedly over the lifetime of an anxious person. That means that they are worse at some times and better, or even absent entirely, at other times. Medicines can quiet down the panic dragon and let the sensitized nervous system heal. On the other hand, antianxiety medicines work only while they are taken. When they are stopped, they no longer help. Since the anxiety disorders are usually chronic and often lifelong, it is not surprising that many anxious people find that medicines are necessary for them to lead more normal lives for long periods of time and even for their lifetimes.

While there can be no simple rules for every anxious person, below are some guidelines for your own personal needs for medicine for your anxiety disorder.

Should I Take Medicines Now?   *Use medicines when you find your quality of life is diminished by anxiety.* If you are doing well without medicines and if you are getting help from nonpharmacological forms of treatment, then you do not need medicines. But if you use nonmedicine treatments and find that you are still suffering from your anxiety, it is usually wise to give medicines a try. If the first medicine you try does not help, or if it has side effects that are bothersome to you, try another medicine. There are many good choices, and no one can say which is best for any particular person until several have been tried. However, if after trying several you find that medicines do not help you or if the side effects continue to be more bothersome than the anxiety, then you may be better off not taking medicines. This is not common in the treatment of anxiety disorders, but it sometimes happens.

When Do I Stop Taking Medicine?   After six to twelve months or so of successful medical treatment, you can try a period with no medicine. Do not stop medicines abruptly, since that may produce heightened anxiety as your brain is jolted by the sudden loss of the medicine. Work with your doctor and/or therapist to establish whether you still need the medicine. Gradually reduce your dose of medicine over the course of one to two months. It will probably take two months or so for you to be off medicines entirely to know whether you need them or not, because the symptoms of your anxiety disorder may not come back immediately when you stop the medicine. On the other hand, when you stop a benzodiazepine, you may have a temporary upsurge of anxiety when you get close to or actually reach the zero dose. Often this rebound anxiety will pass after a few weeks. For these reasons, it takes several months of being medicine free to know for certain whether you continue to need medicines or not. If when you try this gradual dose-reduction experiment you find that your anxiety gets so much worse that the possible gains of being medicine free are more than overbalanced by the increased distress you feel, then it is usually desirable to go back to your regular dose of the medicine for an additional six to twelve months and then consider trying another discontinuation experiment.

How Do I Stop Taking Medicine?   If you have trouble about how to stop taking medicines, talk with your doctor to work out a plan of discontinuation. The most likely explanation of the difficulty is the recurrence of your underlying anxiety disorder.

It is desirable to discontinue medicines gradually so that your nervous system has a chance to get used to a lower level of medicines over a longer period of time. Two months of gradual dose reduction to reach zero dose is about average, but even six months is reasonable if you have been using medicines every day for a year or longer.

How Much Medicine Should I Take?   Many anxious people take too little medicine to get the full benefits from the medicine. Talk your dose over with your doctor. It is often desirable to use higher doses early in treatment to quiet your oversensitized nervous system and to explore the maximum potential of the medicine. After a few months of a good result, it is sometimes possible to lower the dose by half or more without losing the therapeutic benefits. Lowering the dose can also reduce whatever side effects you may be experiencing. In general, do not use doses above the listed maximum doses unless you discuss this with your physician. In some cases higher doses are desirable and safe.

With respect to the benzodiazepines (BZs), such as Xanax (alprazolam) and Valium (diazepam), concerns over taking too much are common. In general, the treatment of panic may require doses higher than the listed maximums to control the panic initially. Usually this is not the case because most often panic is controlled at lower doses. Even when higher doses are needed at first, the dose can usually be reduced to levels below the listed maximum doses after a few months of successful treatment.

We use a green light, yellow light, and red light system for benzodiazepine doses for anxiety. The green light zone is half the maximum dose or less. The green light zone for Xanax is 2 mg or less a day, for Valium it is 20 mg or less a day. The yellow light zone is between one-half and the full maximum dose. For Xanax the yellow light zone is doses above 2 mg and at or below 4 mg a day. The red light zone is above the maximum listed dose. Most anxious patients, even with panic attacks, do well at doses in the green light zone. Doses above the maximum (in the red light zone) are rarely needed except for short periods of time for the treatment of panic disorder/agoraphobia. If you find yourself in the yellow or red light zones, discuss this with your physician. Sometimes alcoholics and people addicted to drugs who are prescribed benzodiazepines for anxiety move into the red light zone because of their unique tendency to addiction.

The typical anxious person using a benzodiazepine will find no need to raise his or her dose above the green light zone, no matter how long the person uses the medicine. The benzodiazepines do not lose their effectiveness over time (i.e., there is no tolerance to the antianxiety or antipanic effects of these medicines).

We have seen many anxious patients who are inappropriately worried about their benzodiazepine use. They then take terribly small doses and find that their response is inadequate. They complain to their doctors that they are addicted (because they feel a need to use more of the benzodiazepine). These people are never suffering from addiction. They are suffering from inadequate doses of the antianxiety medicine. If this description fits you, try raising your benzodiazepine dose slowly higher in the green light zone, and see if you can find a dose where you are more comfortable with significantly less panic and less anxiety. Most anxious patients who do not have preexisting problems with addiction to alcohol or other drugs find this modest dose escalation in the green light zone works well for them.

Will I Need Medicine Again?   Even after you have been medicine free for a period of weeks, months, or even years, you may have an upsurge of anxiety problems in the future that is so severe that it would make sense to use medicines again for a period of time. Often when a relapse occurs, patients wait too long to restart medicines. This can make the relapse both more severe and more prolonged than it would have been if medicines had been started earlier. In general, if an upsurge of anxiety symptoms is severe and if it lasts more than a week or so, it is desirable to restart medicines and to continue them for at least a month after the upsurge of symptoms has abated.

Do I Have to Take Medicine?   It is desirable not to use medicines at all if you can do well without them. On the other hand, *if you find that the quality of your life is degraded by the anxiety problem and if medicines help you by improving the quality of your life, then you are generally wise to use the medicines.* This advice is no different from that given for the treatment of depression or other mental disorders. It is also no different from advice given for any other diseases, from arthritis and diabetes to high blood pressure and ulcers. The important thing is to remember that the anxiety disorders are just as real and just as serious as these diseases and that you are no more guilty or weak if you need medicines for anxiety than you are if you need medicines for these other diseases. The medicines used to treat anxiety are generally safe, even when taken every day for many years. It is important that your prescribing physician have all the facts about your use of all medicines and your use of any other substances that can affect your brain, including alcohol and illegal drugs. If you are not telling your doctor the complete truth about your use of medicines or drugs, then you are at risk for serious problems.

How Do I Find a Therapist or Psychiatrist?

There are many ways to find a therapist or a psychiatrist. If you know someone else who can give you a referral, that is an excellent way to find a good mental health provider. Often, however, people are reluctant to talk about these problems, so you might have no idea which of your friends has found a good therapist or psychiatrist. You can ask your family doctor for a referral. You may also call the Anxiety Disorders Association of America (ADAA), a nonprofit organization. There is more information about ADAA listed in Resources, in the back of this book; the ADAA's phone number is 301-231-9350. ADAA keeps a national list of therapists and psychiatrists who are experienced in treating people with anxiety disorders. Another good source of referrals is anxiety self-help groups in your area. Even if you are unable or unwilling to go to the group, you can often call the group leader and ask him or her for recommendations. People in self-help groups are a wonderful source of information about locally available resources, since members of these groups have been through many of the same things that you are facing. You can also call the National Self-Help Clearinghouse, listed in the Resources, for a list of groups in your area.

Dealing with Managed Care

The ongoing evolution in managed care leaves you with another factor to consider when you work out your own care for your anxiety disorder. You need to think about how your health insurance coverage can meet your needs within the financial constraints your managed care or indemnity plan and your budget create.

We suggest that most people first try to work within their managed care network to find the best care they can. More and more first-class health care providers are joining managed care networks. That may mean your educating your network providers so that they can better understand anxiety disorders and the new ways to treat them with medicines and with cognitive behavioral treatments. You can use *The Anxiety Cure* as a test in your educational efforts. Recall from the Introduction that Bob first learned about this new form of treatment for agoraphobics from a patient of his who brought him an article about new treatments from *Glamour* magazine. Even highly educated professionals are often educated by their patients. Do not be shy in your efforts and do be persistent—as Bob's patient was in 1977.

If you cannot get the help you need inside your managed care network, then we suggest that you become an educated consumer outside your network, seeing just how many of these costs can be covered by your health insurance. We do not work in any managed care network. Many other doctors and therapists work outside networks. Many of our patients find that our costs are relatively modest when budgeted over a year and when compared to the value of the changes they are able to make in their lives. You will need to work this out for yourself with the providers in your area.

Unlike the costs of open heart surgery or the inpatient costs of managing many chronic illnesses, the costs of outpatient care for anxiety disorders can often be budgeted successfully by people who are by no means rich, since these treatments are relatively affordable, even without the help of health insurance. For many anxious patients, the fact that managed care plans are increasingly providing options for partial payment outside the network is a big plus, since many patients know about some good providers outside their managed care networks.

Managed care companies hire talented people who wish to provide high-quality care and are motivated by many factors, including both economic factors and sincere concern for your welfare. As managed care matures and recognizes that anxiety disorders are very common, often severely crippling, and highly treatable in affordable ways, it is doing an increasingly good job handling these problems. Give your managed care company a chance to help you. Help it help you before you go outside the system. If, in the end, you find your needs are not met, consider writing to the managed care company, or your employer, or both, and encourage them to do a better job in the future of helping people with anxiety disorders. Taking this step may not help you, but it may help other anxious people in the future when they try to use this particular managed care network.

Do not let the financial issues get between you and your recovery. Be realistic about what you need and what you can afford. Be determined to get well. You can often use self-help organizations in your area to help you meet your needs and to find knowledgeable providers of health care services that you can afford.

What Kind of Therapy Do I Need?   There are many forms of the talking cure, or psychotherapy. The traditional form of treatment is psychoanalytical therapy, which focuses on childhood traumas and enduring emotional conflicts. In this view, anxiety is a symptom of deeper conflicts, which can be resolved in the psychotherapeutic relationship, often with frequent visits over a long period of time. The new form of psychotherapy for anxiety disorders is called cognitive-behavioral therapy (CBT). The visits are less frequent and the course of treatment is less prolonged. It focuses on thoughts (cognitions) and behaviors (avoidance), often using journals and structured readings and active practice in the anxiety-generating situation.

There are many other forms of psychotherapy as well, some provide more support and some provide more education. Most real-life therapists today are not doctrinaire practitioners of any particular school of therapy but can best be described as eclectic, meaning that they select components from many sources to fashion the best treatment they can do for each individual patient. No form of psychotherapy works for every anxious patient, and no form of therapy fails to work for any anxious patient. We recommend having an open mind and doing an active search for the best treatment for you at this time in your life, recognizing that your own needs may change over time.

M.D. or not M.D.?   Just as there are many approaches to psychotherapy, so are there several categories of caregivers. Psychiatrists are medical doctors who specialize in mental disorders (often including anxiety disorders, the most common of all mental disorders). Psychologists are Ph.D. doctors of psychology who are trained in clinical treatments, including the anxiety disorders. Licensed clinical social workers have master's degrees in social work and are licensed to provide clinical care. All three categories of treatment providers—M.D.s, Ph.D.s, and L.C.S.W.s/M.S.W.s—are licensed by the states to provide psychotherapy. They are well trained and usually highly experienced. Within managed care networks, it is common to see a social worker or psychologist for talking treatment and an M.D., not necessarily a psychiatrist, for prescribing medicines.

Some people find it helpful to see one doctor for both therapy and medicine (which tilts you toward using a psychiatrist, since only psychiatrists are specialists in mental disorders who are also medical doctors), while other anxious people find it desirable to see a non-M.D. therapist for the talking part of their treatment and to see a psychiatrist or other M.D. for medicines. Often particular M.D.s and non-M.D. therapists are experienced in working together as teams.

We are open to all of these approaches to getting well, and we have seen both good and bad outcomes for all of these many patterns of care. While the professional status of the treating person may be important, we have found that experience and personal characteristics are often more important, and that the therapist who does well with one patient may not necessarily be right for another patient. We recommend that you proceed in therapy as you do with medicines, getting as much information as you can—with an open mind, with a determination to get the best from each provider of care that you see, and with a willingness to try something new if you do not get your needs met in a particular relationship. See the back of this book for a discussion of handling insurance and managed care.

How Should I Prepare for an Appointment with My Psychiatrist? If you have decided to see a psychiatrist to evaluate whether you would benefit from taking medicine, take a few minutes to get organized prior to your appointment. In your journal, review the anxiety history you prepared in Chapter 12 and any prior history you have of taking psychiatric medicines.

List in your journal all the medicines you have ever used in your efforts to reduce anxiety and insomnia. List the names of the medicines, the maximum dose you used, and the approximate dates you used each of the medicines. Also record the benefits you got from each medicine, the side effects you experienced while on the medicine, and why you stopped using each medicine. This information will be helpful to you and to your prescribing doctors in working out the best care for you in the future.

We have found that many anxious people have tried medicines and then stopped using them without giving the medicines a full chance to work (which for most medicines is two to three months at adequate doses). This happens because anxious people are often frightened of taking medicines and of any possible side effects, so they commonly quit prematurely. We have also found that some anxious patients use medicines alone, without full use of therapy and antianxiety techniques at the same time, concluding that medicines do not work for them or that the medicines do not work well enough. We recommend using medicines long enough at high enough doses to get the full potential benefits from them and using medicines along with therapy and diligent practice in anxiety-provoking situations to achieve the maximum benefits from antianxiety medicines.

Answer the following questions in your journal in preparation for your medicine evaluation:

1. What are my feelings about taking medicines?
2. What do I worry about the most with regard to taking medicine?
3. What do I hope to gain by taking medicine?
4. What do I think my friends and family, and my support person in particular, would think about my taking medicine?

5. What questions do I have about medicine options that I want to ask my doctor about?

Tips for Friends and Family

Many people have strong feelings about medicines. Having seen your anxious person working on finding a cure for his or her anxiety, you may feel the need to quickly find a pill that will relieve his or her suffering. On the other hand, you may not like the idea of your anxious person taking medicine of any sort. If you know others who are part of your anxious person's life, you will find that they, too, are likely to have strong feelings about medicine, and they will not always agree with you.

It is important for all of you to step back from this decision so you do not jump to a conclusion that is not the best one for your anxious person. Answer the questions posed earlier in this step about choosing whether to take a medicine or not, and then share your answers with your anxious person or other friends and family.

Do the reading that is suggested for this step, and look in libraries and bookstores for books with current information about psychiatric medicines. You may also want to talk to people in an anxiety support group about their personal experiences with medicine. No two people ever have the same experiences with taking medicine, even if they have taken the same medicine.

It may be helpful for you to find a knowledgeable psychiatrist to help you sort out the risks and benefits of medicine. Even if your anxious person is not ready to take this step, you can certainly have a consultation appointment to review the information that you present. If your anxious person does want to see a psychiatrist, find out if you could go along, or at least submit a list of questions for the psychiatrist to answer. Some psychiatrists will allow a session to be audiotaped, and then you and your anxious person together can listen to the doctor's advice in a quiet, nonstressful environment and talk about the information and your feelings together.

Homework for Step 6

1. Read Step 6.
2. Select and record a goal for this week's practice.

3. Practice in your discomfort zone daily, and record this practice on your Weekly Practice Worksheet.
4. Meet once to practice with your support person and to review your journal.
5. Review your current or potential use of medicine and therapy with your support person.
6. If you have a doctor or therapist, review medicine use with him or her.
7. Fill out your Personal Progress Log.

Readings for Step 6

1. Appleton, W. S. *Prozac and the New Antidepressants.*
   Chapter 2: "What Are Antidepressants?"
   Chapter 3: "The Selective Serotonin Reuptake Inhibitors (SSRIs): Prozac, Zoloft, Paxil, and Luvox"
2. Markway, B. G., C. N. Carmin, C. A. Pollard, T. Flynn. *Dying of Embarrassment—Help for Social Anxiety & Phobia.*
   Chapter 17: "How Do I Find Professional Help?"

The Antidepressants

Pluses: No abuse potential for addicts and alcoholics, easier to stop, usually taken only once a day.
Minuses: Must be taken every day for months or years, often produce side effects (which are bothersome but not dangerous).

Trade Names (Generic)	Usual Maximum Dose/Day (mg)
Tofranil (imipramine)	200
Norpramin (desipramine)	200
Pamelor (nortriptyline)	150
*Prozac (fluoxetine)	40 (100 for OCD)
*Zoloft (sertraline)	200
*Paxil (paroxetine)	40
*Luvox (fluvoxamine)	300
Effexor (venlafaxine)	225
*Anafranil (clomipramine)	250

All these medicines are used to treat depression as well as the anxiety disorders, except specific phobia and OCD.

*Used to treat obsessive-compulsive disorder as well as panic, GAD, and depression.

The Benzodiazepines

Pluses: Rapid onset of benefit, few side effects, can be used either as needed or several times a day.

Minuses: Abused by some alcoholics and people addicted to drugs, can be more difficult to stop after months of everyday use, usually taken several times a day if used every day.

Trade Names (Generic)	Usual Maximum Dose/Day (mg)
Xanax (alprazolam)	4
Valium (diazepam)	40
Ativan (lorazepam)	10
Serax (oxazepam)	120
Tranxene (clorazepate)	60
Librium (chlordiazepoxide)	100
Klonopin (clonazepam)	4

All these medicines are commonly used in the daytime for anxiety.

Four Tips to Help Time Pass

1. Tell yourself you will go one more block before you take a break from practice.
2. Guess how many seconds it will take to go through a tunnel or up an escalator. Count it out, or use your watch, and see if you were close.
3. Look at the seconds tick away on your watch.
4. Knit or crochet.

CHAPTER 18

Step 7

Structure Your Life without Anxiety

We have found that the lives of many anxious people lack structure. Thinking of your life as having a "structure" may be unfamiliar. Everyone, rich and poor, young and old, on every part of the planet, has exactly the same twenty-four hours each and every day. What distinguishes us is how we use those hours. The uses we make of our time is what we call the "structure" of our lives; it is how we organize our lives. If you make no effort to control your life, your life still has a structure. It may be similar from one day to the next, or it may change every day. Whatever you do, your life has a unique structure, one that you can understand by thinking about how you use your time and recording those uses in your journal.

In this step, the structure of your life refers to the routine, everyday activities of your life, or how you normally spend your time. As we will explain in this step, a chaotic pattern is both caused by anxiety symptoms and contributes to worsening of anxiety. This chicken-and-egg balance of panic and structured living is important to understand, since often people who have become very focused on panicky feelings and who have lost a functional structure in their lives believe it is impossible for them to have structure again. This step will help you think through the role of structure in your life and, with the aid of your support person, rethink areas that have become problems for you.

Structured living is often lost when anxiety hits because your feelings of panic are so overwhelming. They demand attention when they surface and take precedence over any other plans that had been made. This giving in to feeling-driven scheduling means that it is very hard to stick to any plans. Almost all people who suffer from panicky feelings recognize the dominant role of panic in making daily plans. For some people, this takes an extreme form and leads to avoidance of almost all activities. For others, it means that they are never sure if they will be able to execute a plan when the time comes. Once the anxious feelings become the focus of how you react to life, it is hard to live by any routine without being swayed by how you feel from moment to moment. When this happens the dragon is running your life, not you.

This feeling-based reaction to life is terribly harmful. It leads to instability and to being able to count on nothing—not your feelings, not your actions, not your schedule. Everything in your life is chaotic. All people, but especially people with anxiety problems, need structure to their living. The chaos that is caused by impulsive, feeling-driven planning undermines all structure and exacerbates the feeling of being out of control that characterizes anxiety disorders. We have found that the more choices you are able to exercise over how to spend your time—for example, if you are retired, work in your home, or are a homemaker—the more difficult it is to impose structure on your life. Employment and other obligations that are structured by external forces help keep you from focusing too much attention on your feelings. See Part Six, Chapter 25, for more thoughts about retirement and anxiety.

Take Charge of Your Actions

By focusing on the areas in your life that are troublesome because they lack structure, you are taking charge of your actions. You are once again affirming that, although your feelings are powerful, they are not your master. As you have seen in Part Two, The Basics of Anxiety, and in earlier steps, it is vital to move away from allowing your feelings to govern your actions. You can get a wonderful boost of self-confidence as you live your life according to your personal plans, not your panicked emotions. Try adopting our suggestions to add thoughtfully planned, positive activities to your daily routine. Many anxious people find that these principles make an enormous difference in reducing their symptoms of panic and anxiety, and as the symptoms diminish, so does the role of anxiety in shaping how you spend your time.

When people who have lost huge parts of their lives to chronic anxiety have gained relief, either through medication and/or behavioral approaches, they often are left not knowing how to use their newly created time. In this case as well, try using these suggestions to further enhance your new-found abilities to live a more satisfying life.

Answer the questions on the test below to help focus on the parts of your life that trouble you. Record the answers in your journal, or make a copy of the test before you fill it out and have your support person fill it out for you as well. This is important because when it comes to these feeling-driven, automatic behaviors, we are all likely to deny important facts to ourselves because we are afraid to change. There are six areas of behavior in which your life may lack structure:

- Eating
- Sleeping
- Exercising
- Working
- Relating to other people
- Having fun.

There are several questions to be answered under each of these sub-headings. Answer *T* for true and *F* for false for each question, and then evaluate each of the six areas as being one of no problem, possible problem, minor problem, or serious problem.

The Structure of Your Life

Area One: Eating

_____ I spend too much time thinking about eating.
_____ I weigh too much or too little by more than fifteen pounds.
_____ I do not have a stable pattern of eating.
_____ I eat in binges and then starve myself.
_____ I almost always eat alone.
_____ I am distressed in some way about my eating. Describe:

My structure of eating is:

_____ No Problem　　　　_____ Minor Problem
_____ Possible Problem　　_____ Serious Problem

Area Two: Sleeping

_____ I do not have a regular bedtime.
_____ I do not have a regular time to awaken.
_____ I do not have a bedtime routine.
_____ I am often sleepy during the day.
_____ I often nap during the day.
_____ I do not get enough sleep.
_____ I am distressed in some way by my sleeping. Describe:

_____

_____

_____

My structure of sleeping is:

_____ No Problem   _____ Minor Problem
_____ Possible Problem   _____ Serious Problem

Area Three: Exercising

_____ I do not exercise for a minimum of twenty minutes at least three times a week.
_____ I often feel out of breath climbing a flight of stairs.
_____ I have frequent aches and pains in my muscles.
_____ I am distressed in some way by my exercising. Describe:

_____

_____

_____

My structure of exercising is:

_____ No Problem   _____ Minor Problem
_____ Possible Problem   _____ Serious Problem

Area Four: Working

_____ I do not like my work.
_____ I am not fulfilled by my work.
_____ My hours are too long or not long enough.
_____ I am not able to learn and grow in my work.
_____ I am not proud of my work.
_____ I am distressed in some way about my work. Describe:

_____

_____

_____

My structure of working is:

_____ No Problem   _____ Minor Problem
_____ Possible Problem   _____ Serious Problem

Area Five: Relating to Other People

_____ I do not have relationships with people who care about me.
_____ I do not have people I enjoy spending time with.
_____ I do not talk with and listen to other people on a regular basis.
_____ I do not have at least three people I can share good and bad news with.
_____ I am distressed in some way by my relationships with other people. Describe:

_____

_____

_____

My structure of relating to others is:

_____ No Problem   _____ Minor Problem
_____ Possible Problem   _____ Serious Problem

Area Six: Having Fun

_____ I do not have a routine for relaxation and having fun.
_____ I do not have activities that give me pleasure.
_____ I do not have fun regularly.
_____ I wish I had more fun.
_____ I am distressed in some way about having fun. Describe:

_____

_____

_____

My structure of having fun is:

_____ No Problem   _____ Minor Problem
_____ Possible Problem   _____ Serious Problem

Make Healthy Changes

Most people—with or without anxiety—have problems with at least some
of these areas of their lives. These six areas encompass the most fundamental of human behaviors. Now that you have focused on the areas that
you could improve, you will use once again the same techniques you have
already been using to overcome your anxious thoughts. There are three

principles that will enable you to make healthy changes in these behaviors:

1. Plan for change.
2. Implement new behaviors.
3. Make yourself accountable to your support person.

Like the earlier work you have done that has used this progression to
overcome your anxiety problems, you can make small changes in behaviors over time, and if you do this work systematically and consistently, you
will see a great improvement in your quality of life.

Using the test as a guide, take each area that distresses you and break it
into small component parts. Try to find out more information about an
area of distress from your physician, self-help groups, or books and other
published material. Look at Parts Five and Six of this book for more about
some of these topics. Many people who have long-term anxiety problems
will need help with this stage of making changes because they have lost all
sense of "normal" behavior that is not driven by feelings. If you believe
this applies to you, we urge you to seek professional assistance in making
plans for change. A therapist can be helpful, but so can your support person, a friend, or an organized program such as Weight Watchers or
Overeaters Anonymous for improving eating habits. Tell the person with
whom you are working that you need assistance in establishing healthy
routines in your life. You need them to help you decide what is healthy,
since you have no idea! Like anxiety problems in general, some therapists
and friends will understand this and some will not. Remember, you are the
coach of the team of people helping you with your anxiety problem. If you
feel a person or a program is not helpful, find another one.

Another helpful way to add structure to your life, particularly if you are
retired, a homemaker, or work from home, is to set up a basic schedule for
each week. Once you have the basic schedule in place, you will be surprised
to find how much less anxious you are once you do not constantly have to
decide what to do next every minute of every day. Of course, the basic schedule can be changed if necessary, for example, for vacations or holidays. Having regular routines, a basic structure to your twenty-four-hour day, is calming and helps signal your body that you are in charge of what you do and
when, which reduces the need to constantly ask yourself what you *feel* like
doing. As you have seen, feeling-driven choices are not always beneficial!

Try filling out daily schedules like the prototypes at the end of this step, and add them to your journal. Fill out one schedule with how you spend your time now. Then make a new schedule to reflect how you would like to spend your time. How different are the two? For the second schedule, don't be limited by your present level of anxiety. For example, if you now take an hour to leave the house in the morning due to OCD rituals, don't put this into your ideal schedule. Seeing how much more time you could have without the limitations of an anxiety disorder is a great motivation to keep working toward your goals. Remember to schedule "down" time— time to take it easy. If you really like to watch daytime TV, assess whether it is realistic to eliminate that completely from your schedule. First, you may try modifying what you do. For example, instead of the average four hours of daytime TV you now watch in your unstructured time, you may choose to watch one or two hours in your new plan. The point of this new schedule is not to overwork yourself but to provide a comfortable routine within which to function, so you can live your life the way you want to live it. Letting anxiety or guilt shape your life is a bad idea.

Be realistic as you begin to move toward implementing your new schedule. For example, if you now get up at 8:30 A.M. and you would like to get up at 6:00 A.M., don't be discouraged if you have some setbacks. Simply try again the next day.

Remember, set small steps. Achieve these steps and then think about taking new small steps. Long journeys are made up of small steps.

The work in this step is exactly like the work that you have already done in earlier steps. This new focus on a healthy lifestyle, rather than on disturbing feelings, takes you a step further in your cure, moving you closer and closer to taking control of the behaviors that make up your life.

Good Pleasures and Bad Pleasures

Healthy pleasures last and lead to increased self-esteem and closer, more positive links with other people. Unhealthy pleasures are brief and lead to lowered self-esteem. They are not suitable for open, honest sharing. Try this approach with any pleasure, from cookies to cocaine, from walking to TV watching. You do not have to be a rocket scientist to use this approach, you just have to notice what you are doing and think it through for a few hours. Making behavior changes, of course, takes longer, but the first step is clearly identifying the troublesome patterns you have in your life and committing yourself to more healthy living.

Tips for Friends and Family

This step offers another good opportunity, like Step 5, for you to evaluate your own life as your anxious person evaluates his or hers. Then you can help each other make changes. This can be rewarding to do together and can allow you to gain some benefit from the hard work you, too, have been doing as your anxious person recovers. Remember that pleasurable, relaxing activities are important parts of a healthy life. Overscheduling yourself or your anxious person is not an improvement.

It is important, however, to be honest about what is pleasurable. Is that bowl of ice cream before bed a pleasure or a self-destructive habit? Is spending Sunday morning reading the paper a pleasure or an avoidance of finding something more useful or active to do? Only you, with the help of another caring person, can evaluate your particular situation. We urge you to be kind to yourself and your anxious person. If you make a change and then after a month or so miss the old way of doing things, try changing back. The structure of your life is yours to choose each day, and each day you again decide what is truly in your best interest.

Homework for Step 7

1. Read Step 7.
2. Select and record a goal for this week's practice.
3. Practice in your discomfort zone daily and record this practice on your Weekly Practice Worksheet.
4. Meet once to practice with your support person and to review your journal.
5. Complete the test The Structure of Your Life.
6. Complete the How My Time Is Spent forms, one for your current schedule and one for your desired schedule.

Readings for Step 7

1. Bolles, R. N. *What Color Is Your Parachute?—A Practical Manual for Job-Hunters & Career-Changers.*
   Part I: The Parachute Workbook—"The Quick Job-Hunting Map"
2. Burns, D. D. *The Feeling Good Handbook.*
   Chapter 10: "A Prescription for Procrastinators"

How My Time Is Spent—Now
(List Usual Activities)

Time	Monday	Tuesday	Wednesday	Thursday	Friday	Saturday	Sunday
6 A.M.							
7 A.M.							
8 A.M.							
9 A.M.							
10 A.M.							
11 A.M.							
12 noon							
1 P.M.							
2 P.M.							
3 P.M.							
4 P.M.							
5 P.M.							
6 P.M.							
7 P.M.							
8 P.M.							
9 P.M.							
10 P.M.							
11 P.M.							
12 mid.							
1 A.M.							
2 A.M.							
3 A.M.							
4 A.M.							
5 A.M.							

How My Time Is Spent—Goal
(List Ideal Activities)

Time	Monday	Tuesday	Wednesday	Thursday	Friday	Saturday	Sunday
6 A.M.							
7 A.M.							
8 A.M.							
9 A.M.							
10 A.M.							
11 A.M.							
12 noon							
1 P.M.							
2 P.M.							
3 P.M.							
4 P.M.							
5 P.M.							
6 P.M.							
7 P.M.							
8 P.M.							
9 P.M.							
10 P.M.							
11 P.M.							
12 mid.							
1 A.M.							
2 A.M.							
3 A.M.							
4 A.M.							
5 A.M.							

Three Tips to Help Ignore Unwanted Thoughts

1. Sweep your fingers over your forehead to vacuum unwanted thoughts from your mind.
2. Look around at others. Notice that they are not paying any attention to you.
3. Look at yourself in a mirror and see that the panic does not show on your face.

CHAPTER 19

Step 8

Plan for Lifelong Recovery

Expect and allow the panic and the other symptoms of anxiety to reappear. Take away the power of the dragon by facing him and practicing acceptance of the distressing feelings and worries that are his weapons. Certainly the panic and anxiety may continue, and certainly they may come back even if they have been gone for a long time. But each time the dragon shows up, is the same, even as he attempts to fool you with ever-new disguises. These disguises may masquerade as mysterious, life-threatening physical illnesses, and it is important to consider this as you work on your anxiety cure.

Setbacks and Springboards

As you will see in Part Seven, Chapter 26, identifying a setback and turning it into a springboard for coping successfully in the future with an anxiety problem is a crucial part of being cured of anxiety. If you are living your life now with little interference from anxiety, you may be tempted to assume that anxious thoughts and feelings will never bother you again. We urge you not to take this stand. Rather, keep the techniques you have learned for dealing with anxiety accessible to you, and keep up the life changes you have made to prevent the dragon from encroaching on your hard-won freedom.

Setbacks are sometimes triggered by unexpected changes, like the promotion that set off Sue's anxiety in Chapter 14. Sometimes setbacks are triggered by not having been exposed to an event or an activity for a period of time, such as occasionally occurs with fear of flying. It is often hard to separate lack of opportunity to fly in a plane from avoidance of flying, and if you do not seek out opportunities to practice in areas that once caused anxiety or panic, the dragon can easily take back parts of your life. Sometimes setbacks occur in a different form from the expected, so that someone who was phobic of driving now has a fear of walking across a footbridge. Phobias do not commonly transfer themselves, but it does happen. Often there is no explanation for why a setback occurs. It is as likely to come after good news as bad news, and it is as likely to come for no reason as for an apparently good reason.

However a setback occurs, it is never as bad as the first episodes of anxiety because, after you have done your work in the Anxiety Cure, you know that fear of the fear is an anxiety disorder, and you know you can get over this fear of the fear. You know what you need to do to get better. This knowledge takes much of the fear of the fear out of having an anxiety problem, but even so, when you are amid a setback, it is sometimes hard to gain enough perspective to know what to do first. If possible, plan ahead, and during a time when you are doing well, answer the following questions in your journal so you will have the answers on hand when a setback occurs.

Questions to Help Me Plan for When I Have a Setback

1. What support people will I talk to?
2. What chapters in *The Anxiety Cure* or other books will I reread?
3. What new life habits have I found to be helpful?
4. What external sources of anxiety will I watch for?
5. What techniques have I found helpful in the past in dealing with anxiety?
6. What medicines will I use?

Answering these questions now in writing in your journal will also help you keep the surprise of a setback from overwhelming you, since you acknowledge to yourself that it is possible that your anxiety will increase sometime in the future. You may want to put a paper clip on the page of your journal that lists your plan in the event of a setback, because you may want help fast in the future.

If you are reading this amid a setback, it may not be possible for you to make a plan ahead of time. Rather, answer the following questions to help you get back on track with your anxiety cure. Be sure to date this entry because you want to keep close track of setbacks as you evaluate your progress into the future.

Evaluating a Setback—Gaining Perspective

1. On a 0–10 scale, what is my anxiety level right now?
2. Who can help me evaluate this setback?
3. Is this setback a surprise?
4. When did I first notice increased anxiety?
5. What have I tried so far to help with this setback?
6. What dose and type of antianxiety medicine am I using, and when did I last evaluate my use of the medicine?
7. How have I been sleeping recently?
8. Have I been exercising/stretching regularly?
9. What might have contributed to this setback? Am I using any over-the-counter or prescription medicines or street drugs? Am I drinking alcohol or beverages with caffeine?
10. When did I last eat/how have I been eating recently?
11. Have I been avoiding situations because of anxiety (or for OCD, have I resumed compulsive behaviors) that I had stopped while I was doing well?
12. Is there any unusual stress in my life right now?

The next step is to figure out what to do about the setback and how to move forward with your anxiety cure. Answering the above questions has put you on track already, as it will help you sort out the individual pieces that may have contributed to this setback. Now you can put your past experience with the Anxiety Cure to work for you as you answer the following questions in your journal.

Treating a Setback—Turning It into a Springboard

1. When I was using the Anxiety Cure in the past, what techniques helped me to keep myself in the here and now?
2. When can I get in touch with my support person?
3. Do I need to take medicine for this attack now?
4. Do I need to call my doctor today/tomorrow to review my use of medicine?
5. How could I improve the quality/quantity of my sleep tonight?
6. Could I find time to exercise/stretch today or tomorrow?

7. Do I need to evaluate any medicines I am taking for possible anxiety side effects? Should I call the pharmacist? My doctor?

8. Do I need to cut back/cut out use of alcohol, caffeine, or street drugs?

9. Do I need to eat? What is my plan for eating during the next twenty-four hours?

10. Do I need to begin practicing my automatic anxiety techniques systematically?

11. What can I do about the stressful things in my life? Do I need to talk this over with my support person? An anxiety group? My doctor? A therapist?

12. What can I learn from this attack to help lessen anxiety in the future?

It is important during an upsurge of anxiety to stay in the present when working to make your life better. There is a tendency to generalize this painful but predictable experience into a catastrophe that proves you will never be well. Answering these questions can help avoid that trap, a trap that may lead to your feeling out of control and result in a worsening of your anxiety.

Remember that the only food the dragon can eat is your fear of him. Try to step back from this setback and counsel yourself as you would want a good friend to counsel you if you could talk to someone immediately. Say calm things to yourself: "It is going to be okay." "This will pass." "I have been here before, and I know I can handle it."

During a setback and in the days that follow, you will be glad that you kept your hard-learned lessons documented in the pages of your journal. You are your own best teacher because the anxiety is your own and no one else's.

Work in Progress

Every setback is a springboard for you to make further progress, to increase your understanding of your anxiety disorder, and to increase your self-esteem by rolling up your sleeves and getting on with the work needed to solve your anxiety problem. You need to have your support systems in place for a lifetime. That means keeping track of your books and information about anxiety so you can understand the problem, even when the dragon comes at you in an entirely new disguise. It means keeping your support person educated and informed. *If you lose one support person, recruit and train another one.* It means finding therapists and doctors who understand anxiety disorders and who can help you, whatever the problems are that you are facing at any point in your life.

Evaluate Medical Problems

Medical problems can confound even people who have been free of anxiety for many years. Facing a new medical problem that may or may not be

---

Gut Dilemma

Cheryl, a twenty-four-year-old woman, offers us an example of the complexity of a person with anxiety having even a relatively simple medical problem. For two years Cheryl had been living her life fully, without constraint from the GAD and depression that had brought her to seek help.

Without warning, she developed diarrhea, and after three weeks of being afraid to eat away from home because the food went through her too quickly for her to get to a public bathroom, she sought help from a family doctor. The doctor wisely suggested over-the-counter remedies and a bland diet for a week and told Cheryl to call him at the end of the week to report how she was doing.

Cheryl had been horribly frightened that the doctor was going to tell her there was something seriously wrong with her, and when the doctor was so calm about a problem that had been terribly worrisome to her, she thought to get out Evaluating a Setback—Gaining Perspective the checklist from this chapter of *The Anxiety Cure*.

In her evaluation of her anxiety, she realized that the anxiety increase had predated the onset of the diarrhea and that her sleeping had been disrupted because of the increased anxiety and diarrhea. She had stopped her daily walks when she began to feel sick. Her stress, she now noticed, was also quite high from an external cause. She was planning to move into her boyfriend's apartment in a month and was having second thoughts about the relationship.

Once Cheryl recognized that the diarrhea was in all likelihood a new anxiety symptom, she was quick to use Treating a Setback—Turning It into a Springboard from this chapter and to call her therapist to talk over her ambivalence about her relationship with her boyfriend. After a week Cheryl felt so much better that she forgot to call her family doctor to report her progress. She was surprised when her doctor called to check on her. She was happy to report that the diarrhea was gone.

related to the anxiety disorder is confusing and frightening. We hesitate to list the medical problems or symptoms that may be rooted in anxiety for two reasons. One reason is a fear of giving anxious people more bodily symptoms to watch for anxiously. The other reason is that sometimes a symptom is not caused by anxiety and needs medical intervention.

With any medical problem that may or may not be anxiety, it is important to seek reasonable medical advice, but it is also important to try to gauge the impact that anxiety may be having in either causing or continuing the medical problem. Not all doctors are as sensitive to the role of anxiety as was Cheryl's.

A Cautionary Tale

Tony, a sixty-five-year-old retiree, only learned of the likely impact of anxiety on his backaches after he had had a surgical procedure to help with back pain. But the surgery caused such severe chronic pain that he was bedridden for six months. Only when his physical therapist told him that his anxiety was too high for physical therapy to make any improvement in his pain did Tony seek help for his anxiety. By that point, he had so many physical complications from the surgery and the subsequent bed rest that the treatment of his anxiety was both complicated and prolonged.

We urge you to draft a letter to your doctors, alerting them to your anxiety and any medicines you take to help deal with the problem. The letter can help if you are in need of emergency dental work, for example. As was described in Step 6, novocaine is usually formulated with epinephrine. Epinephrine, however, can cause paniclike symptoms in susceptible people. If a dentist or doctor is aware of your susceptibility to anxiety, it is easy to avoid the epinephrine formulation, and a great deal of unnecessary distress can be avoided.

This letter can also be a help if you need surgery and in the hospital will be in contact with a number of nurses and doctors who may not be aware of your anxiety disorder. Such a letter documenting your specific worries can help you deal with recovery rooms with no windows or support your request to follow closely your medicine schedule. Use your anxiety history from Step 1 to write this general Dear Doctor letter. Be sure your family is aware of this letter so they can help to get this information to the medical personnel who need it in the event of an emergency.

We are indebted to a longtime patient of ours for sharing a copy of the letter she wrote when she was expecting her second child. She found this letter helpful in dealing with her obstetrician, pediatrician, and the nurses and doctors in the hospital when her healthy daughter was born. Because she is a nurse herself, she had a clear idea of how to draft this letter. You may wish to have your letter follow her format. If you are on medicine for an anxiety disorder, it is a good idea to include your prescribing doctor's name and telephone number should any questions arise.

Example of Dear Doctor Letter

Dear Doctor:

Our family is expecting a baby in the spring. We are very excited about the new arrival. We have a few questions for you and a few things to tell you about this pregnancy. I have an appointment to see you next week to discuss these questions.

The pregnancy has been going well—both mother and baby appear to be in good health. However, I have a familial anxiety disorder for which I take diazepam daily in small dosages. The diazepam eliminates the physical symptoms associated with the anxiety disorder and greatly reduces the anxious thoughts and ideas. Understanding the risks and benefits, I have continued to take the diazepam during the pregnancy.

My obstetrician is not comfortable with my taking the diazepam until the due date arrives. She is concerned that the baby may go through withdrawal.

I have received genetic counseling and discussed the possible dangers of taking medicine during pregnancy with my psychiatrist at length. My psychiatrist is comfortable with my taking the diazepam throughout the entire pregnancy. He has followed other pregnant women in similar situations; from his experience, he does not expect any withdrawal symptoms to occur at such a low dosage. However, he recommended that I share the obstetrician's concerns with you.

At our appointment next week, I would like to get your thoughts on the following:

1. A plan of action should the baby experience withdrawal symptoms such as irritability.
2. A recommendation about formula for the baby. (Nursing and diazepam consumption appear to be contraindicated.)

I appreciate your taking the time to answer my questions. Thank you for helping me to continue to do what is best for both me and my baby.

Sincerely,

[Your Name]

Anxiety and Cancer

Confronting an anxiety disorder and regaining control of your life can be terribly hard, but it also can be a terrifically valuable lesson in life. We have a friend whom we admire greatly who became an expert at using these antianxiety techniques. She was diagnosed with malignant melanoma, a form of cancer for which there was no effective treatment. Her primary cancer was removed from her back, but six months later she had a recurrence of the cancer in a lymph node under her arm and the diagnosis of metastatic malignant cancer. This woman asked her oncologist what the treatment was for the recurrence. Her doctor said that radiation and chemotherapy could not help. The diseased lymph node could be removed, but that was all that could be done. The potentially fatal cancer might or might not have spread beyond that node.

Imagine her terror. She said later that she used her antianxiety techniques of staying in the present: "I just reminded myself that once that malignant lymph node was gone, I didn't have a recurrence of the cancer until the doctor told me I did. My anxious mind kept running ahead to the horrible 'what if,' but I kept pulling my thinking back to the 'what is' of the situation. I used my anxiety disorder techniques every day. The oncologist told me that the five-year survival rate for melanoma with the factors I had was only 20 percent. That meant that one person in five who had what I did lived for five years and that 80 percent were dead before five years. Those were not good odds, but they were my odds. I reminded myself often that until I got a diagnosis of the spread of cancer beyond that lymph node, I was still in the 20 percent who were making it one day at a time."

Twenty years have passed since that event, and this brave woman has had no recurrence of that cancer. We do not claim that her use of these antianxiety techniques, which she had learned when facing her own phobia, has kept her from having a recurrence of cancer. Her use of these antipanic techniques helped her to live a far more normal and happy life during that time than she would have if those "what ifs" had gripped her, as they threatened to when she had her second operation.

Find a Support Group

Another strategy for getting and staying well from an anxiety disorder means getting in touch with local support groups that can help you. See the Resources in the back of this book.

The founder of a local anxiety support group noticed that although she had made efforts to build a core group of participants, most group meetings were made up of newcomers, people who had been diagnosed with anxiety relatively recently. This may happen because, as people get better, they no longer need to go to support group meetings. Friends and family may also find these groups helpful in seeing how common the experiences are that their anxious person is reporting. Some self-help support groups are specifically targeted to OCD, social phobia, or panic, while others are for people with mental health problems in general. There are many types of groups throughout the country. Support groups can help you feel less alone and help you connect with local doctors and therapists who have been successful in treating others with anxiety. Every support group is different. If you find a group that does not address your needs, simply try another group. Often, if you talk informally to people after the meeting, you can learn of similar groups that may fit your needs more closely.

Think about your answers to the following questions prior to going to a group. Bring your journal to the group so you can write down ideas and phone numbers you learn at the meeting.

Seeking an Anxiety Support Group

1. What do I hope to find at an anxiety support group meeting?
2. What questions do I want to ask at or after the meeting?
3. What referrals to support groups do I have so far? (See the Resources for a place to start).
4. What information did I gather at the group meeting?
5. Are there other resources I want to explore?

Connect with a Higher Power

There is a final dimension to finding a cure for anxiety disorders that we write about with more hesitancy, since it is more personal and more subject to misinterpretation: finding help in a spiritual connection with a Higher Power. This means turning over personal problems to a Higher Power, or as one patient phrased it, "let go and trust your body." For most people, the most reliable beacon to lasting serenity is to be found in our relationship with God as we know him. From this perspective, the prescription is "let go and let God."

This is not an argument for any specific religion, although most of us find God in highly individual, often religious ways. *It is a simple fact that one of the best ways to gain control of your life and to find serenity is to find a spiritual base for your new growth.* All of the great religious traditions share the sense that you can find the strength to live by submerging one's personal will into the will of God. All religions deal with fear directly and often. This means thinking about what is good in a larger sense than can be found in one individual and instead turning to a force of good or a world good.

Not every reader will find this advice useful or even acceptable. But before rejecting this idea, talk it over with your support person. Remember that to relate to one's Higher Power, it is not necessary to become involved with a formal, religious organization. This spiritual dimension to your continued self-growth may take many forms. Some people find their Higher Power in nature and regularly seek to spend quiet time in a beautiful spot as a way to make a connection to a larger meaning of life. Others find that being involved with art leads them to their Higher Power. For some people, an organized religion can be both a wonderful way to benefit from structured time focusing on one's Higher Power as well as a powerful source of community.

Tips for Friends and Family

Accept the unknown. It is important to learn to live with the uncertainty of anxiety. Know that your anxious person has an anxiety disorder and allow the dragon to do what he wants to do. Keep track of what has and has not worked for you in relating to your anxious person so that you will not need to start from scratch in the future. If the dragon comes, he comes. If he does not come now, he may come in the future. Either way, you have learned how to live your life and let your anxious person live his or her life not only with the anxiety disorder but also with whatever other challenges you each find on your paths. Each problem in your life is a growth opportunity waiting to be utilized, including having a family member or friend with an anxiety disorder.

Homework for Step 8

1. Read Step 8.
2. Select and record a goal for this week's practice.
3. Practice in your discomfort zone daily and record this practice on your Weekly Practice Worksheet.
4. Meet once to practice with your support person and to review your journal.
5. Fill in your Personal Progress Log.
6. Review your need for an ongoing support group or religious organization.

Readings for Step 8

1. Ross, J. *Triumph over Fear—A Book of Help and Hope for People with Anxiety, Panic Attacks, and Phobias.*
    Chapter 23: "Becoming Acquainted with the New You"
2. Young, J. E., and J. S. Klosko. *Reinventing Your Life—How to Break Free from Negative Life Patterns and Feel Good Again.*
    Chapter 5: "How Lifetraps Change"
    Chapter 17: "A Philosophy of Change"

Three Tips to Occupy Your Mind

1. Count backward from a hundred by threes or by sevens.
2. Say the alphabet backward.
3. Do crossword puzzles.

PART FIVE

Anxiety and Your Daily Life

CHAPTER 20

Anxiety and Your Work Life

Anxiety has a profound impact on work life. In the past you may have limited your choice of jobs or chances for promotion to appease your anxiety dragon. Perhaps you chose a job based on its proximity to your home, a subway, or a familiar street. Once you have begun to recover from an anxiety disorder, you may find that the job that you tolerated because it allowed you to avoid anxious situations no longer fits your needs. Prior to the Anxiety Cure, you may have tried to reduce stress by having a job that was easy for you. This strategy almost always ends up actually increasing anxiety symptoms, as you find that you have too much time to worry while at work.

Or in contrast, perhaps to reduce your anxiety, you may work more than you would like to. Some anxious people find that the time they are on the job is mostly anxiety free, as concentration clearly must be on work, not on anxious thoughts. This helps block anxious thoughts and keeps the hours at work relatively clear of anxiety. Worry about work when away from your job coupled with reduced anxiety while at work can make work the major focus of your life to the exclusion of friends and family as well as leisure activities. If your work has been affected by your anxiety disorder, chances are you have had a problem balancing work and play in your life. You may want to review Part Four, Chapter 18, Step 7, Structure Your Life without Anxiety, to think about what parts of your life could use development as you fit your job into your life.

Avoid Avoidance

Whether you work too little or too much or you are in a job that does not challenge you to grow, if you are in a job that does not allow you to be exposed regularly to your anxious situations, then you are missing a daily chance to practice your anxiety cure at work.

Fear of Driving

Amanda was a twenty-nine-year-old teacher with a driving phobia. She chose to teach at a school that was on her husband's way to work so he could drop her off and pick her up every day on his way to and from his office. This meant that Amanda had to stay at work from 7:30 A.M. until 7:00 P.M., even though her job ended at 3:00 P.M. The school was locked at 5:00 P.M., so Amanda had to walk to a local public library and wait there for her husband. Occasionally, however, her husband had to travel out of town or the library was closed for various reasons. This created a crisis for Amanda, who worried about how she would get to and from work.

As she used the eight steps of the Anxiety Cure, Amanda gradually began to drive herself to work. She found, however, that when she had setbacks, she would again rely on the old pattern of having her husband drive her and pick her up.

Amanda had hoped to return to graduate school one day, so in order to see how she would like a particular course of study, she decided to take classes while she was still teaching. This positive choice forced Amanda to drive herself to work, since she needed to get from her teaching job to the university campus. Amanda found that her anxiety went down once she knew that falling back on relying on her husband to drive her back and forth to work was no longer an option. She knew she would drive herself, and even if she had some anxiety, she used the techniques she had learned to move forward with her day. She was surprised to see that she had previously put a lot of energy into choosing whether or not to have her husband drive her. Once it was not a choice, she simply drove herself and felt a lot less anxious.

Additionally, Amanda found that she had spent time during the day, especially after the school day ended as she waited for her husband to pick her up, thinking of excuses not to drive places with friends or figuring out how to get places when her usual avoidance strategies broke down. Once she was back in graduate school driving herself, she had no time for this type of worrying. She felt less anxious during the day, even though she was much busier.

Evaluate Options

Once you stop making anxiety-driven decisions and instead seek to make choices based on what is best for you, you will find that there are more options for employment than you had imagined. This does not mean you have to be busy with paid employment or be in a terribly hard job. Everyone has different priorities. You may want to volunteer at a museum or spend time fishing or playing volleyball in a league. To overcome the dragon, you need to choose how much you work, what work you do, and where you work. You are then in charge of your life.

Low self-esteem is a common problem with people suffering from anxiety problems. This in itself can cause you to avoid work for which you are well suited. Be sure not to sell yourself short. Talk with your friends and family about your skills and interests, and consider doing the work in a book like *What Color Is Your Parachute?* (See Suggested Additional Reading.) Or taking a career-development class at your community college. *You may be so accustomed to limiting your choices about work because of anxious avoidance that you are unfamiliar with thinking of all the choices that you have.*

Urge for Perfection

Maria was a forty-five-year-old homemaker with GAD. Her two sons were in high school, a time when she had always planned to return to paid employment to begin saving for their college tuitions. Maria had put all of her attention into her husband's career, moving when he needed the family to move for a better job and caring for their children while he worked long hours. Without realizing what was happening, she spent more and more time worrying. Her efforts to eliminate her worries led to her attempts to become the perfect homemaker. For example, she packed her sons' bags for camp a week ahead of time to be sure they had all the clean clothes they needed. She cooked elaborate meals for religious holidays, and she spent hours studying the family's ethnic heritage to bring more traditions into her sons' lives.

This drive for perfection, however, did not make the dragon happy. Instead, Maria felt she had no self-esteem because she did not have a college education and a paying job. She found, however, that eighteen years of being out of the workforce had left her feeling that she had nothing to offer an employer. On the one hand, she wanted to return to school or to find a job. On the other, her inner worry machine undermined her self-confidence so thoroughly that she was afraid to make a start.

For Maria, as for many people with anxiety disorders stuck in work that does not suit them economically, socially, or intellectually, it is important to upgrade work skills with the Anxiety Cure by looking nonanxiously at the alternatives open to you. Maria used the Anxiety

Cure program to make tentative progress toward preventing worries from dominating her life.

She prioritized finding a job and spent two hours a day learning about job options and practicing her office skills. She began to assign household chores to her family and tolerated their less-than-perfect results. Maria managed the anxiety that these changes caused her, noticing that overall her anxiety was actually lessened by reducing her perfectionistic tendencies. She went on a job interview. In preparation, she role-played the interview with a friend. Her friend had encouraged her to act as though she were confident of her abilities.

To her amazement, Maria landed a job at a large corporation. Within a matter of months, her efficiency and hard work had won the approval of her bosses, earning her a promotion. Maria's self-confidence soared as she found that the busier she was with the new opportunities that she had chosen, the less her anxiety bothered her.

How to Relate to Bosses and Coworkers

Throughout the Anxiety Cure we recommend that you be honest about your anxiety with friends and family. These people who care about you can be enormously helpful as you work to get free of your anxiety. We have stressed, however, that honesty about anxiety does not always extend to bosses and coworkers. Think of the difference between the relationships you have with your friends and family and those with your bosses and coworkers as being like having a private face versus having a public mask. In ways everyone differentiates between private and public relationships. For example, we dress differently around our friends and family from the way we do at work. We may talk differently and say different things about our personal experiences. A man whose wife has left him, for example, may remove her picture from his desk and simply ask the human resources department to take her name off of his insurance policy. While his boss and coworkers know there is trouble at home because the wife no longer calls him and her photograph is gone, most people at work respect the husband's privacy and do not ask him the details about this personal problem.

Often people with anxiety do not think through what they want to say (or not say) to employers or coworkers. The long-term employment implications of a panic attack can seem insignificant while you are having one. At a less anxious time, think through how you want to handle anxiety at work. If your anxious symptoms are noticeable, like sweating or shaking, people may ask questions out of concern for you. How do you want to answer? Right or wrong, remember that there is still a stigma about mental health problems. What you say to one well-meaning colleague can easily become gossip. While we never recommend lying, a careful choice of words may be necessary to maintain the professional, public mask that you have chosen. If physical symptoms like sweating or shaking are a noticeable problem, for example, it may be necessary to say something like, "I have a little trouble with that now and then. My doctor is trying to help me with it. Thanks for caring, but I am really all right." This reassures your concerned coworker, and while it is not a lie, it does not specifically explain the anxiety that is the cause of your physical symptoms.

Think about what to tell people on a need-to-know basis. Keep in mind that no one is as focused on you as you are. No one is going to notice your lack of concentration and physical symptoms as much as you are.

In general, anxious people are far more critical of themselves than other people are. No matter how much you sweat or shake, for example, it is unlikely that anyone at work will notice because they are too busy thinking about themselves to think about you (as you are too busy thinking about yourself to think much about them!). Assume that they do not notice your anxiety unless someone says something. If they do, the most important thing you can say is that you know about the problem but that it is not as serious as heart disease or other major medical problems.

Some people are always open about having an anxiety problem and tell us that they have not had difficulty at work even with this self-disclosure. We also have found that some people who disclose too much information about having an anxiety problem end up with limited job responsibilities. This may happen out of the employer's fear of overwhelming the anxious person or not wanting the job to be mishandled because of anxiety. Either way, the anxious person can end up being deprived of opportunities to advance. Prior to the Anxiety Cure this may have been an acceptable trade-off for you: if you tell people at work about having anxiety then you will have more escapes if anxiety strikes, even if it means limiting your future.

Remember that outs are always available even if people around you do not know you have anxiety. They just take a little more planning and creativity than escaping does. Using outs also means that you will have to come back to the situation that has been a problem in the past. This is helpful for your anxiety recovery. In general, then, your public face will help you decrease your anxiety and increase your self-confidence as you see that you can function even though the people around you do not know about, or cater to, your anxiety problem. In this way, your anxiety problem is similar to most other health problems: it is mostly a private matter.

If your anxiety gets in the way of your work, consider talking with your Employee Assistance Program (EAP) counselor about the problem if your employer has an EAP. Do not use your anxiety problem as an excuse to get special benefits that everyone else wants. We were asked to consult on a case of a woman who said she had claustrophobia and therefore needed an office with a window. Her position and seniority did not qualify her for a window office. When we offered her help with her claustrophobia so she could get along without a window, she refused. She did not want to get well; she wanted a window office.

In another situation, a man claimed he failed an oral test because of social phobia. His employer let him take the test three times, twice with his therapist present. He used medicines as needed. He functioned well in many social settings at work, including making presentations. Passing this oral exam was a requirement for his job. When his employer rejected his claim that he be excused from the exam, he sued for discrimination because of his anxiety. He lost the case, as we believe he should have. His problem was not social phobia but not knowing the material.

Assess Whether to Work Alone

Different jobs can be especially good or bad fits for people with anxiety problems. Working alone presents a unique set of problems and opportunities, and with the growth in telecommuting, it is important to pay special attention to this possibility. Parents who choose to stay at home with their children face the dilemma of working alone or working with adults. The line between avoidance as phobic response and avoidance for personal preference can be blurry when it comes to working alone. Are you choosing this type of work so you do not have to confront your anxiety of public speaking or because the opportunity is a good one for you?

Open Your Mind

Work, like most other areas of your life, is not a one-time decision. Thankfully, most of us get many opportunities to do different types of work. Open your mind to different possibilities and even try different

Peter

Peter, a thirty-one-year-old with social phobia and spontaneous panic attacks, had a difficult time with this choice in his chronic anxiety. In the ten years after he graduated from college, Peter had seven different jobs and was fired from three of them. He left two jobs because he had panic at work and could not face going back into that situation. Two other jobs he left because he had conflicts with coworkers and did not want to work with them anymore.

Peter recently faced the fact that he was an alcoholic. He sought help in a crisis, having been fired from a job because his drinking was out of control. He was afraid he was going to be evicted from his rented room because he had been unable to pay the rent.

Peter began intensive work on his addiction, attending Alcoholics Anonymous meetings daily, working toward ninety meetings in ninety days, a standard path to recovery. With so much energy focused on his recovery from alcoholism, he needed a way to make money to pay the rent before he could work on his anxiety problems. He found a job as a legal transcriber, which he could do from home. He began working long hours to earn the money to pay his overdue bills. For Peter, this ability to work alone solved a short-term problem of needing a steady job that would not be threatened by his anxiety problems. But this job did not help him recover from anxiety; it merely marked time until he could do the work he needed to get well. This type of interim bargain with the dragon can be fine if a short time is needed to prioritize other areas. In Peter's case, he decided to begin working on his anxiety after he had been clean and sober for ninety days.

At that time he reevaluated his anxiety and realized that without even being aware of it, he had been doing practice for his social phobia daily— at AA meetings. He built on that success by continuing to do legal transcriptions from home in the evenings to pay his bills and volunteering at his church office part-time during the day, where he wrote grant proposals for a program to assist needy children. This volunteer work helped him feel more confident about his ability to work with others. He felt appreciated for his writing skills. He felt good that he was helping others through his work. Instead of seeking a different job, he chose to continue this combination of working from home and volunteer work, which he found to be a good balance. It is not necessary to challenge yourself in every arena of your life to live your life fully. If working alone allows you to do other things you would not be able to do with regular office work, then it may actually help you regain control of your life.

Laura

Laura was a forty-five-year-old woman with OCD who worked from home assisting her husband with his business. She used this home-based business as an opportunity to avoid driving. She went out only when her husband drove. She did not socialize with other people other than eating an occasional meal at her parents' home. Her husband initially supported her choice to leave her office job to help him full-time as his business grew, but he found that more and more of their time was taken over by Laura's rituals and avoidance. He sought help because she did not recognize that this was a problem.

Working from home had allowed Laura to stop ignoring her obsessions and instead to devote more and more time to them. Maintaining her public mask in her office job had prevented her from completely submitting to anxiety. Working at home, she could let her husband see all the anxiety she had. He worked with her to give the anxiety what it wanted. The result, sadly but predictably, was that anxiety increasingly dominated the lives of both Laura and her husband when she worked at home.

---

work options and environments and different levels of private faces versus public masks. Above all, keep a record in your journal of how each change affects your anxiety level. This will enable you to decide whether the changes you make have any overall benefit or not and will give you ideas about which direction to go next.

CHAPTER 21

Anxiety and Depression

Depression is part of the general class of mood disorders, which, like the anxiety disorders, is a group of related brain disorders. Moods are feeling states. People with mood disorders feel extremely down or, more rarely, extremely up; they feel abnormally depressed or abnormally elated. To be diagnosed as a mood disorder, these mood extremes are not just minor and not just for a brief period of time but to an extent and for a time that seriously erodes the sufferer's quality of life, causing major deficits in important areas of life functioning, such as family life and work. Mood disorders cause significant distress and mental pain.

Depression is worry about the past and about your failures and inadequacies. Depression—a sense of hopelessness that the future will be no better than the past—is linked to a feeling of helplessness about being able to make the future any better than the past. As with anxiety disorders, there is a characteristic distortion of thinking with depression. When you are depressed, you feel so hopeless and helpless that no amount of talking and no amount of realistic assessment of the past, present, and future can shake the conviction, born of your depression, that misery is your deserved lot in life. Also like anxiety disorders, depression comes in grades, from relatively minor to hugely disruptive. Again, like anxiety disorders, depression tends to wax and wane over time. Unlike anxiety disorders, however, it is common for depressed people to have periods, which can often last for many years, when they have no depressive symptoms at all and then to have another depression, called a "depressive episode."

Elation, or mania, is the reverse of depression. A manic person believes he or she can do anything and that the outcome of every event will be positive. The manic person buys a lottery ticket knowing it will be the winning number. The manic person thinks his or her words and ideas are the cleverest in the world. Depression is associated with lowered energy, while mania is associated with excessive energy. The manic person needs little or no sleep and seldom feels tired. Mania is an unrealistic optimism that is usually short-lived. But then the person heads for an inevitable crash in mood and the crushing burden of the bad judgments made in the manic state (for example, reckless spending and promiscuous sexual behavior).

When depression is part of a disorder of mood swings, over days or more often months and years, with extremes of both depression and mania, it is called bipolar disorder or what used to be called manic-depressive disorder. When the person suffers from depression, without manic episodes, the depression is called unipolar, meaning there are episodes of depression without mania. Depressions can be single episodes in a person's life or they can be recurrent. They can also be more or less continuous, or they can be episodes separated by longer or shorter periods of normal moods, called euthymia (a normal mood state in which the swings between high and low are not extreme and usually related to changes in your life circumstances). When not depressed and not elated, a normal person feels a bit down when something unpleasant happens and a bit elated when something good happens, but all these mood changes are in a normal range of moods.

When you have relatively mild but more or less continuous depression without depressive or manic episodes, it is called dysthymic disorder, meaning you feel mildly but chronically depressed. The mood disorders include major depressive disorder (either single episode or recurrent episodes), and dysthymic disorder. Bipolar disorder is more complex, including a single episode, which can be primarily depressed or manic, or a relatively mild manic episode called hypomania. Bipolar II is a less common form of bipolar disorder and is characterized by serious depressive episodes mixed with relatively mild manic episodes. Cyclothymia is a relatively minor form of bipolar disorder, with both minor mania and minor depression alternating. Cyclothymia is similar to dysthymia.

Anxiety Contrasted with Depression

In Part Two of this book, The Basics of Anxiety, you became familiar with the various anxiety disorders; for example, you know that agoraphobia is different from obsessive-compulsive disorder even though both are anxiety disorders. The anxiety disorders share a common core: excessive worry, tension, and irritability. In contrast to mood disorders, the anxiety disorders typically are disorders of future thinking, of what will happen. They are malignant diseases of the "what-ifs." Recall that for a person to be identified as having a diagnosable anxiety disorder, the problems must be serious and prolonged.

About one-third of people with depression are comorbid for anxiety—that is, they have both disorders—and about one-third of people with anxiety have depressions at the same time. These numbers also make clear that many people have one disorder and not the other. Although there are differences in the thought patterns of depressed and anxious people, many of the symptoms of depression are similar to the symptoms of anxiety disorders, including sleep disturbance, excessive worry, and low self-esteem.

There are four ways that depression and anxiety are linked:

1. The two disorders are often confused, so some people who are depressed mislabel themselves, or they are mislabeled by their therapists or physicians, as suffering from anxiety disorders.
2. Both anxiety and depression are commonly seen in the same people because the groups of disorders share similar brain mechanisms and similar genetic backgrounds. It is common to find histories of depression in families of people with anxiety disorders, as it is common to find histories of anxiety disorders in families of people with depression.
3. One disorder can lead to the other in the sense that you can have an anxiety disorder and get so demoralized that you have a secondary depression, or you can be so anxious in a serious depression that you develop a secondary anxiety disorder.
4. You can have both disorders, and even though they are not related, they can be coexistent. This can happen just the way you can have an anxiety disorder and diabetes mellitus at the same time even though they are unrelated disorders.

Depression or Anxiety?

Depression is secondary to an anxiety disorder when the anxiety disorder came first in time and when the anxiety disorder dominates your problems. On the other hand, the depression is primary when it came first and when it dominates your life (and your symptoms of anxiety). Usually it is possible to discern which came first and which is dominant, anxiety or depression, but sometimes they are both primary disorders in the sense that they either occurred at the same time or they are about equally disabling. If both are primary disorders, then your anxiety did not make you depressed and your depression did not make you anxious.

Though not ideal, the reality is that some therapists are expert in dealing with anxiety but not so expert in dealing with depression, and vice versa. Health care professionals who have an orientation that is clearly toward one or the other of these two classes of disorders tend to see in their patients the problems with which they are most familiar. It may be useful to talk over with your therapists and your doctors what they think about this distinction between anxiety and depression as it relates to your symptoms and to your treatment.

Treatment for Depression and Anxiety

Some of the medicines used to treat anxiety disorders also treat depression. These medicines are the antidepressants, including the selective serotonin reuptake inhibitors (SSRIs), such as Prozac (fluoxetine), Zoloft (sertraline), Paxil (paroxetine), and Luvox (fluvoxamine), as well as the older tricyclic antidepressants (TCAs), such as Tofranil (imipramine), Norpramin (desipramine), Pamelor (nortriptyline), Sinequan (doxepin), and Elavil (amitriptyline). There are a group of new antidepressants that are not SSRIs. This group includes Wellbutrin (bupropion), Serzone (nefazodone), Effexor (venlafaxine), and Remeron (mirtazapine). Because of the success of these medicines in the marketplace (which reflects their good results with many patients), new antidepressants are being introduced every year. By the time this book is published, several new antidepressants are likely to have been marketed. All of these antidepressant medicines take several weeks to produce their full effects (for both depression and anxiety), and they all are effective against both depression and anxiety.

Another class of antianxiety medicines, the benzodiazepines, are powerful antipanic and antianxiety medicines, but they are not effective antidepressants. If you are using a benzodiazepine for anxiety and you also have depression, you will want to discuss this with your prescribing doctor, since you may need a medicine that has antidepressant properties. Because many people with anxiety disorders have secondary depression, when their anxious symptoms are reduced by using a benzodiazepine, their hope returns and their depression lifts. If the depression is primary, and if it persists despite resolution of the anxiety symptoms, than using an antidepressant is an option you need to discuss with your physician.

Just as many of the medicines that are used to treat anxiety are also effective against depression and vice versa, so it is with nonpharmacological treatments. Therapy for depression also reduces anxiety, while therapy for anxiety often reduces depression. Books written about the mood disorders often have major sections discussing the anxiety disorders, since they are closely related problems. When a person has both depression and anxiety, it usually means the disability is greater and the challenge of treatment is also greater, than if the person has only one disorder. Comorbidity does not mean the prognosis is any better or any worse for people with one disorder or the other, as opposed to people who have both disorders. Both depression and anxiety are biopsychosocial disorders, meaning that they have biological, psychological, and social dimensions to their causes and their treatments.

Mood disorders and the anxiety disorders are usually long-term, if not lifelong, problems that require substantial efforts over prolonged periods of time to overcome. We want you to understand your problems. We do not want you to be discouraged or overwhelmed by them. A step-by-step approach will help you with mood disorders, as it does with anxiety disorders. We encourage you to learn more about mood disorders, to join with others who have them, to read about them, and to talk openly about them with people who can help you overcome whatever disability and distress they are causing you.

Depression is a serious, biologically based, real, and treatable disorder. But like the anxiety disorders, it can be treated with medicines or with nonmedicine therapies. We urge you to identify depression when it exists and be sure that you get good care, whether it exists alone or along with an anxiety disorder. Most of the treatments for depression are also effective against anxiety, and most of the treatments for anxiety are effective for depression. But in come cases, highly specific treatments are needed. Your therapist or doctor can help you sort out your personal needs.

CHAPTER 22

Anxiety and Insomnia

Insomnia is having difficulty sleeping that causes distress or disability. Insomnia, like pain, is a symptom, rather than a disease, that can be caused by many illnesses, from arthritis to depression. It also can be caused by serious sleep-related illnesses, such as sleep apnea and narcolepsy. If you have had anxiety for a long time, and only recently have developed insomnia, that suggests your insomnia may not be part of your anxiety disorder. If insomnia is a major problem for you, we suggest that you talk it over with your doctor to see if you need a specialized sleep study to identify the cause of your insomnia. Many times when the underlying disorder is treated, insomnia is reduced or disappears. For example, when arthritis pain is reduced, the patient's sleep is more normal. When depression is well treated, insomnia usually disappears.

Having said that, however, it is also true that many clinically anxious people suffer from sleep disorders that have no other cause. These people have insomnia as part of their anxiety disorder, which means it has waxed and waned with other anxiety symptoms from the onset of the anxiety disorder itself.

Sleeping Like a Cat

To understand how anxiety and insomnia are related, think about a pet—a dog or a cat. Now think of the pet having insomnia. You will quickly conclude that even though the animal may have many maladies, it does not have insomnia, as do many anxious people. The dog may sleep soundly through the night (uncommon for a dog), or it may wake several times (more likely). It may sleep in the day. It may sleep a lot or a little. But one thing you can be sure about is that no matter how solicitous the dog's owner, the dog will never be taken to the veterinarian for "insomnia," because the owner will never identify that as a problem for the dog (or a cat or any other nonhuman animal).

The reason pets do not have insomnia is that most insomnia is sleep worry. Without the worry, there is no insomnia. Animals (including unworried humans) may sleep a lot or a little, but they do not have sleep worry, or insomnia. Studies of human insomniacs show that they sleep an average of twenty minutes less each night than do age- and sex-matched control noninsomniac subjects. That twenty minutes is not much difference in total sleep. In both the insomniac and the normal-sleep groups, there is a huge variation in sleep, from less than six hours to more than nine hours. Babies sleep about twelve to fifteen hours, while elder adults sleep about six or seven hours. In other words, the need for sleep normally decreases as we age. The sleep of older people often gets lighter than the sleep of younger people. That is normal, and it is not something to be worried or upset about. Sleep is similar to sexual responsiveness in that it cannot be willed. The harder you try to make yourself sleep, the harder it is to sleep. You have to "let" yourself fall asleep, you cannot "make" yourself fall asleep. Worry, tension, and irritability keep the anxious insomniac awake. The content of these typical nighttime worries is varied. The worry may relate to the activities of the day. The worries may be focused on chronic problems that the particular person has both day and night without respect to the events of the particular day. Most insomniacs worry about insomnia. They worry that sleep will not come. "Oh, no, another night when I cannot fall asleep, which will surely lead to another day when I am tired." This fear of insomnia is heightened by the fact that when sleep is poor, the anxiety dragon has an easier target—lack of sleep usually adds to daytime anxiety and panic. You can easily see the vicious cycle: the more worry, the less sleep; the less sleep, the more worry. Fear of insomnia is the nighttime equivalent of daytime fear of fear.

Nonmedication Treatment of Insomnia

Nonpharmacological approaches to insomnia work just the way nonpharmacological approaches to daytime worry work. To get well you need to learn to let go of your worry. You need to accept your worry and not to add to it with your "what-if" anxious thoughts. Acceptance is the one-word antidote for anxiety, whether it occurs in the day or in the night. Stop fighting your anxiety, and it will fade away from neglect.

When it comes to insomnia, use your antianxiety techniques, which means accepting that you (like your cat or dog) may sleep a lot or a little on any particular night, but that your body will get the sleep it needs, if not tonight, then tomorrow night or the night after. *Let go and give up the fight for sleep. Let sleep find you.*

Get a Sleep Window

You need to set up a sleep window of not more than seven to eight hours. If you try to sleep longer, you are sure to spend time awake in bed, since it is unlikely your body can sleep more than seven or eight hours. Many insomniacs have wide-open sleep windows, going to bed early because they are tired from sleeping poorly the night before, and staying in bed late because they sleep so poorly each night. Going to bed at 9 or 10 P.M. is common for insomniacs, and getting up at 9 or 10 A.M. is also common. If you understand that your body cannot sleep more than about seven hours, you realize that this big sleep window ensures that the worried person will have four hours or more of awake time each night. The simple next step to get well is to close that window to a maximum of six or seven hours.

Pick times to go to bed and to get up that work for you, for example 11 P.M. to 6 A.M. Use that as your sleep window. Make sure that your sleep window is not more than seven hours. Once you set the time, do not go to bed before 11 P.M., no matter how tired you are. Do not stay in bed past 6 A.M., no matter how poorly you sleep. You need to train your brain to sleep the way you would train an animal, with consistency. You should be out of bed except for the seven-hour period of your sleep window.

If you are not sleepy during your sleep window, you can get out of bed and read or do anything else that you like to do until you are tired and ready to go sleep. Do not get back in bed until you are sleepy. *If you wake up but are in a mental twilight or half asleep, stay in bed and figure that your body is resting.* You are probably sleeping more than you think at these times. Count this twilight time as sleep in your mental accounting of your sleep. Only get out of bed during your sleep window if you are wide awake.

Bed is for sleep and sex, period. No food, no reading (except for a few minutes to fall asleep). No conversations or TV. Just use your bed for sleep as you train your body that when you get in bed, you sleep.

Use a Sleep Routine

A routine before bed will help signal to your brain that it is time to quiet down for the night. A routine is anything that promotes a smooth transition from being awake to being asleep. For most people this routine will include using the bathroom, brushing teeth, changing into night clothes, and getting into bed. If you currently have a routine, be sure it is simple, brief, and comfortable, and then work to perform your routine consistently at the time you have chosen to begin your sleep window. For example, if your sleep routine takes you ten minutes and you have decided that your sleep window starts at 11 P.M., then you will start your sleep ritual at about 10:50 P.M. every night. This will help you with your transition to sleep in another way, in that it will alert you that this is not the time for phone calls, TV, or any other distraction that can stimulate you and keep you from feeling tired just before bed.

If you do not already have a routine before bed, consider what to include. While some people enjoy reading or watching TV right before sleep, remember that it is not a good idea to do these things in bed if you are having trouble with insomnia. Your sleep routine may include your pets, children, spouse, or others who live with you. For example Kim, a twenty-five-year-old with agoraphobia who developed a terrible fear of falling asleep, found it soothing to get ready for bed and then sit in a chair by her bed while she held her dog on her lap. She stroked the dog and reminded herself about all of the good things that had happened during the day, and then in her mind she rehearsed getting into bed and turning off the light. Initially this increased her panic, but as she let time pass while stroking her dog, Kim found that she could calm down enough to finally put the dog in his bed and go to sleep herself.

In Step 5 you learned several techniques that may be useful as you deal with insomnia. Relaxation, yoga or tai chi, and exercise are all areas to explore as you try to improve your sleep. Relaxation exercises like those in Step 5 may be useful to quiet your mind from the anxiety of the day. Remember to do these exercises before you get into bed. Then when you do get into bed, try to re-create the feeling of peace and relaxation that you found while listening to your tape.

Though these quiet exercises may be helpful to get sleepy, be sure not to schedule *aerobic* exercise into your day too close to your bedtime. Exercising vigorously within two hours of going to bed may make you too energized to go sleep. It is important, though, to get aerobic exercise during the day so that your body is truly tired and ready for sleep.

Do not let your bedtime ritual become a compulsion. It is a simple structure that can be varied as circumstances and your needs change, even day to day. If the rituals last more than ten to fifteen minutes, or if you feel compelled to do them just right, or at exactly the same time—fearing dreadful outcomes if you don't do it just right—consider being more flexible so you are not trapped by an obsessional routine.

Bedtime Rituals

Gloria was a thirty-five-year-old professional woman. She had struggled for many years with the symptoms of OCD. She had a complex bedtime ritual that could take several hours to complete. If the ritual was not done "properly," she would get very anxious and often would be unable to sleep. Her ritual involved checking many things several times. For example, the stove, the front and back doors, and the windows. Anything that interrupted her ritual would force her to start again. Unfortunately, the person who most frequently interrupted her ritual was her husband. She could not start her bedtime ritual until he came home, or she would worry that he had not properly checked all of the things that she already had checked, such as the lock on the door. After her bedtime process had started, he was not allowed to go out of the house, or even into the kitchen.

Her husband was her support person in her work to overcome her OCD. The two of them spent several hours reviewing her baseline ritual and discussing what a new ritual should involve. For example, they agreed that the process should not take longer than one hour and should not involve him. At first it was difficult for Gloria to make these changes, but with diligent practice, and the support and encouragement of her husband, she was able to reduce drastically the time it took her to get to sleep, resulting in marked improvements in the quality of her sleep and in her relationship with her husband.

It will take a while to retrain your insomnia-dominated brain to this new approach. If you are firm with yourself, as you would be if you were training a child or an animal, you will succeed. If you are unwilling to adopt a restricted sleep window, that is okay, too, but remember that you have chosen to sleep this way. Stop complaining and fighting about your chaotic sleep pattern and just figure that this is how you chose to spend those hours. If you have something better to do with that time than lying in bed awake, use some of those hours for better purposes. If not, be happy that at least you have the extra time to use in this way.

Be Consistent

Remember, as you learned with other aspects of the Anxiety Cure, you need to let go of worry to regain control or your anxiety-driven life. Trust your body to get the sleep it needs. Your job is to set up and maintain a healthy sleep window with enough hours in it. Give your body a chance to adapt to that sleep window.

Try to be consistent weekdays and weekends. When you shift your sleep window from day to day, especially when you shift your sleep time every weekend, you are doing the equivalent of flying over several time zones each weekend. It is like flying across the country or even to Europe for the weekend. Is it surprising that your body has trouble adapting to that time zone shift each week?

Sleep

Sleep is normal, natural, and unavoidable, like breathing and eating. Sleep is also subject to being disturbed by anxiety, again like breathing and eating. In the Anxiety Cure, we encourage you to let go of your anxiety-driven abnormal sleeping (as well as abnormal breathing and eating) so that you can slip into more healthy patterns that you can maintain over long periods of time. If you worry less about insomnia and daytime sleepiness, you will have fewer of these problems. Your worry machine drives your insomnia.

Medicines to Treat Insomnia

Some people with anxiety benefit from the occasional use of sleep medication. As with medication use for anxiety that is not related to sleep problems, we encourage you to think of medication as a tool to help you live a full life, not as a mark of failure. Whether or not you choose to go talk to your doctor about the possibility of using sleeping medications, we suggest that you also use the nonmedication suggestions in this chapter. Medication on its own will not solve your sleep worry if you are expecting to have eight hours of unbroken, anxiety-free sleep every night. It is important to help the medication work by setting up realistic expectations. Ask your doctor how often you may use any sleep medication you are prescribed, as different doctors take different approaches to short- and long-term use of sleep aids. Similarly, if you want to take an over-the-counter sleep medication, be sure your doctor is aware of that, too. Some people do well with occasional use of over-the-counter sleep medications, but it is important not to use them without a doctor's knowledge and approval while you are on other medications.

The medicines used to treat insomnia are the same medicines used to treat daytime anxiety. This is a surprise to many people, who assume that sleeping pills are "knockout" pills. The pharmaceutical companies recognize this public perception, so they market different medicines for daytime anxiety and insomnia. For example, Valium (diazepam) is used in the daytime and Dalmane (flurazepam) at night, even though both are long-acting benzodiazepines that could be used in reversed roles with no problem (i.e., Dalmane [flurazepam] could be taken in the daytime and Valium [diazepam] at night for insomnia). Similarly, Xanax (alprazolam) and Halcion (triazolam) are two short-acting benzodiazepines, the first marketed for daytime use and the second for nighttime use. Those medications could also be reversed, except Halcion is so short-acting that it is not practical for daytime use.

These same antianxiety medicines used for daytime anxiety also work to reduce insomnia, not because they knock you out but because they reduce your worry. They are "antiworry" pills. When your worry is reduced, your previously worried brain lets your tired body go to sleep. This is how sleeping pills work. That is why Valium, Xanax, and Klonopin are good sleeping pills.

Medication for insomnia can be particularly useful if you have nocturnal panic attacks. Panic attacks can occur during sleep, with or without dreaming. Sleep panic is often especially troubling and may occur with little or no mental content, meaning you feel panic but have no specific worried thoughts. Nighttime panic can cause or complicate insomnia because the anxious person fears panic and comes to fear sleep because it may lead to panic during sleep. Knowing you have medication available to help you in this situation is particularly comforting as you work to reduce your fear of sleep.

Using medicines to reduce insomnia is fine, if that helps you sleep better. There is nothing wrong with using antianxiety medicines every single night for insomnia anymore than there is anything wrong with using these medicines every single day. Anxious people do not escalate their doses of antianxiety medicines over months or even years of everyday use, and similarly neither do anxious people who use antianxiety medicines to sleep better. If you find that your use of antianxiety medicines at bedtime escalates beyond the usual therapeutic dose (which you will find in the medicine package's insert, the *Physicians' Desk Reference* [PDR], or from talking with your pharmacist or doctor) and/or if you use the techniques that we have taught you and nevertheless you continue to have troubled sleep, it is wise to consult with your doctor.

We want you to rethink your suffering from anxiety. That includes rethinking daytime and nighttime worry. We want you to be less afraid of your anxious symptoms and to be more confident that they will pass if you do not fight them and if you do not add your fearful thoughts. Stop feeding the dragon, and he will drift away from you.

CHAPTER 23

Anxiety and Addiction

Addiction, like depression, is commonly coexistent with anxiety. About one-third of people with addiction also have an anxiety disorder, while about one-sixth of people with an anxiety disorder also have an addiction to alcohol or another drug. Far more common than actual addiction among anxious people who take medication, however, is the mistaken belief that they are addicted to their medicines when they are not addicted at all. This distinction between actual addiction and fear of addiction is crucial, since treatment for the two problems is completely different.

Fear of Addiction to Antianxiety Medication

Anxious people are often afraid that they will use a medicine, it will work, and then they will be "hooked" on the medicine. Depressed people who find Prozac (fluoxetine) or Zoloft (sertraline) helpful sometimes fear that they are hooked or addicted when they cut down or stop and then find that their symptoms of depression return. Even more commonly, anxious people who find benefit in medicines, especially the benzodiazepines such as Xanax (alprazolam) or Valium (diazepam), fear they are addicted, because when they stop the medicine, they feel more anxious or have more insomnia. Feeling addicted when you are not addicted is one more blow to your already damaged self-esteem.

It is important to understand clearly that needing medication to function well is not the same as addiction. Imagine a person with myopia (nearsightedness) who relies on eyeglasses to see. The nearsighted person could be described as "glasses dependent," since if the glasses are removed, the person would do almost anything to get the glasses back. But this person has not lost control over his use of eyeglasses. Neither of the following hallmarks of addiction are present: he does not continue to wear glasses despite problems caused to himself or others by his use of glasses, and there is no dishonesty.

Now think about the agoraphobic person taking Prozac (fluoxetine) or Xanax (alprazolam). Does the medicine help the person live a better life the way the glasses help the myopic person? Is the agoraphobic person honest with his or her doctor and others who have a reason to know about his or her medicine use? Clearly, the typical anxious person taking medicines, including the benzodiazepines, is similar to the person using eyeglasses in that there are terrific benefits and no problems for each in using the respective medicines or eyeglasses.

Withdrawal Symptoms

The fact that the anxious person using a medicine may have withdrawal symptoms on rapid discontinuation is not a factor in making the distinction between addiction and nonaddictive medicine use. Many medicines produce withdrawal symptoms on abrupt discontinuation (such as high blood pressure medicines, antiepilepsy medicines, and antidepressants), even though they are neither addictive nor abused by alcoholics or people addicted to drugs.

We recommend that you use medicines for your anxiety disorder if the medicines improve the quality of your life. If you can function fully without medicines and not have too much distress, so much the better. If you find that without medicines your functioning is limited and/or you have significant distress because of your anxiety disorder, than you should at least try using medicines. Do not let inappropriate fear of addiction scare you away from medicines that can make a big difference in your life the way glasses can help the nearsighted person.

Addiction to Antianxiety Medications

Some people who are alcoholics or drug addicts do abuse antianxiety medicines. They use these medicines at high doses and right along with their usual quantity of alcohol and other drugs. They often get medicines from many doctors and lie about their medicine, alcohol, and other drug use. For such people, these medicines do not help much because their anxiety problems are substantially worsened by their continuing use of alcohol and other drugs. Alcoholics and drug addicts use high and usually unstable doses of antianxiety medicines along with alcohol and other drugs, and they do not get good responses. Anxious patients who are not addicted to alcohol and other drugs usually use these medicines in low and stable doses (i.e., they do not use above the level normally prescribed by doctors), and their doctors are fully informed about their use of medicines (as well as about their use of alcohol and other drugs). Nonaddicted anxious people typically have good responses to these medicines at low doses. We have never seen anyone who was not previously an addict to alcohol and other drugs who became addicted to these drugs as a result of using them as directed by their physicians. The only people we have seen who have had addiction to these medicines had prior personal and family histories of addiction to alcohol and other drugs.

Dealing with Addiction

Having dealt with the inappropriate fear of addiction to antianxiety medicines, let us focus on what to do if you have an addiction problem. If your use of alcohol is excessive or if you use illegal drugs, you have a problem that needs attention. If you use more medicines than your doctor prescribes, if you are dishonest with your doctor about your use of medicines, if you steal or forge prescriptions, or get medicines from multiple doctors without telling each and every one of them what medicines you are using, then you are an addict. If you use more alcohol than makes sense for you, if you have good reason to stop drinking but find it hard to do, if you have negative consequences in your life from alcohol or other drug use, then you need help in overcoming your alcoholism.

If you have a problem with alcohol or other drugs, there are many experts in the field of addiction who can help you. One way to find expert assistance is to ask for help from a friend or relative who has a problem of alcoholism or drug addiction. You can also go to free Alcoholics Anonymous (AA) or Narcotics Anonymous (NA, the 12-step program for drug addiction) meetings and ask for referrals to good therapists in your area. The people at these meetings are experts in using the local providers of health care services. Ask their advice. Another good way to get help is to call the American Society of Addiction Medicine (ASAM) at 301-656-3920 to find the names of physicians in your area with expertise in addiction.

Addiction is a real disease, and like anxiety disorders, it can be overcome. We want you to be able to recognize addiction in yourself and others (including family members) and to know what to do when you see it. If you are concerned about another person's addiction to alcohol and other drugs, we suggest you go to some local Al-Anon meetings. This is the 12-step program for family members and friends of addicted people. As with AA and NA, phone numbers for Al-Anon are listed in your local telephone directory that you can call for information about the times and locations of nearby meetings. Like the anxiety disorders, substance-use disorders—addiction to alcohol and other drugs—does not cure itself like the common cold. On its own, addiction just gets worse. If addiction is your problem, you need to clearly identify the problem of addiction to alcohol and other drugs and take positive action to regain control of your life.

Although we have seen some recovering alcoholics and drug addicts who have used these medicines in nonaddictive ways over long periods of time with no relapses, because the benzodiazepines are subject to abuse by alcoholics and drug addicts, we do not recommend using them in the treatment of either recovering alcoholics or drug addicts. Today there are many good medicines to treat anxiety with no abuse potential for active and recovering alcoholics and drug addicts. The antidepressants are the best place to start, as they offer a wide range of choices with broad antipanic, antianxiety, and anti-OCD benefits. For insomnia, Desyrel (trazodone) is a sedating antidepressant that can usually be used in relatively modest doses (25 or 50 mg before bed). BuSpar is a good alternative to the benzodiazepines for daytime anxiety. When thinking about the treatment of anxiety in people comorbid for addiction, recall that these people can participate fully in the nonpharmacological treatments for anxiety, which have shown great success in recent years.

12-Step Programs

One clear benefit alcoholics and drug addicts have, compared to nonaddicted people with anxiety, is that they can use the full power of the 12-step programs, working the program by using a sponsor and the 12 steps. This reduces the anxiety and panic because of the support these resources offer. In itself, stopping drinking and drug use reduces anxiety, panic, and depression. Sobriety, when prolonged, helps the addicted, anxious brain heal.

The 12-step programs are a modern miracle. One of our goals is to encourage people with addictions to use these programs. We also want non-addicted people to learn how to help addicted people (whether they have anxiety or not) find their ways to, and then fully use, these programs. We ask nonaddicted readers, whether they have an anxiety disorder or not, to call their local AA or NA telephone number to learn the times and locations of a few convenient open meetings. Go to one so you can understand how these wonderful programs work. Open meetings are open to all those interested in learning about alcoholism, whether or not they have a drinking problem. Plan to arrive at the meeting fifteen minutes early, introduce yourself by your first name, and let your hosts know you have come to learn about addiction and recovery. Sit next to someone who can explain what is going on. You can learn about these programs from reading not only *The Selfish Brain— Learning from Addiction*, but also *A Bridge to Recovery—An Introduction to 12-Step Programs*, both written by Robert DuPont, the latter coauthored with his colleague John P. McGovern, M.D. *A Bridge to Recovery* is written for nonaddicts who work in all major American disciplines, such as education, health care, religion, and the criminal justice system, so they can learn how they can use the 12-step programs in their everyday dealings with alcoholics and drug addicts, and their families.

At the age of fifty a psychiatrist who is also our patient lost her beloved husband to cancer. This woman did not have a problem with alcohol or other drugs. She joined a grief program and also began therapy to help her cope with her feelings of loss. She also turned to a friend who was a longtime member of Alcoholics Anonymous. She said that she sought out this friend "because I have learned that people in AA live on a higher, more spiritual level than other people, and I felt that then, after my husband's death, I especially needed this level of support to carry on my life." If you understand that woman's thinking, then you understand how we think about 12-step programs and the potential for spiritual rebirth that is part of the recovery from alcoholism and drug addiction.

Imagine a doctor going into two wards in a busy hospital. One is the cancer ward, the other the ward for people addicted to alcohol and other drugs. The doctor first goes to the cancer ward, telling all the patients "I have good news. Although your disease will kill you if we leave it untreated, you can be cured. If you will go to a meeting once a day for about an hour, and if you will follow the few steps the program recommends, including quitting drinking and the use of drugs, your disease can be arrested so that you will live a full, normal life." Then the doctor takes the same message to the addiction ward.

Think how those two groups of patients would react. The cancer patients would react as if the doctor were a saint offering deliverance. Gladly and eagerly they would do what the doctor said. Now think what the reaction would be in the addiction ward. Most addicted people pooh-pooh such advice, returning to their addictive substance use as soon as they are released from the hospital. Like people returning to abusive lovers, they convince themselves "this time it will be different."

Why is there such a difference when both diseases are painful and frequently fatal? The addicted people suffer from a little voice in their heads, which we call their addictive disease. This voice whispers to them, "It's okay to use alcohol and drugs. Other people don't understand you. This time you can use just a little. This time you can control your use. This time there won't be any bad consequences when you use. This time no one will find out. This time your body won't be hurt. This time listen to me, not to them!"

Whether addicts are weak-willed or strong-willed, whether they have good or bad characters, they are subject to this subversive inner voice. It is terribly hard for them to say no to that voice, to admit that they suffer from the disease of addiction, and that the only way they can regain sanity is to give up their abusive lover, go to meetings, and work the 12-step program. We have tremendous respect for the difficult time addicted people have getting well. We know just how hard it is and how often addicted people succumb to the tempting voice of their disease. We know just how easy it is to go back to that abusive lover. For many addicts, the disease of addiction ends only when their addiction claims their lives.

On the other hand, we have seen many addicted people get well. That usually means not only no more alcohol and drug use, but also regular participation in NA and AA. We have sympathy for addicted people because we respect the power of their disease. We are hopeful for every addicted person, since we have seen lasting recoveries of addicts at all stages of this dreadful disease. It is never too early and never too late to get well from addiction, whether the addiction occurs with or without a comorbid anxiety disorder. We also want to be sure that worried anxious people do not mislabel themselves as addicted and because of this mislabeling deprive themselves of the benefits medicine can bring to them.

PART SIX

Anxiety over the Life Span

CHAPTER 24

Anxiety in Children

All children have times when they are anxious and fearful. Sometimes kids are fearful because of inexperience or uncertainty, for example, many children are afraid of putting their heads under the water when they are learning to swim. At other times the fearfulness is a part of normal development. For example, it is common to see a ten-month-old child crying desperately when a mother leaves him or her with a baby-sitter. These times of fearfulness in the child can be upsetting and frustrating for parents, but they do not represent an anxiety disorder. Many of the techniques described in the Anxiety Cure can be used to help children and parents cope with normal anxiety.

Normal Fear versus an Anxiety Disorder

One little girl, Sarah, was afraid of putting her head underwater at the swimming pool. This was particularly upsetting to her because she was an active child who wanted to be able to play with the bigger children in the pool. Sarah's mother was working to overcome her own problem with a phobia of flying. To assist her daughter, she used some of the ideas that she had found helpful in overcoming her flying phobia. First, they talked about what frightened Sarah. Sarah said that she was afraid her head would go under and she would not be able to get it back above water. Her mother helped her think about what Sarah could do to get her head back up. For example, she could stand up. Another option was to dog-paddle, which Sarah had learned to do. She also reminded Sarah that she was always there with her when Sarah was playing in the pool, and she could pull her out in a second. That night Sarah practiced holding her breath and putting her head underwater in the bath. The next day she practiced this new skill with her mother in the pool. After a few practice sessions, she was able to put her head under the water without fear.

When Sarah made putting her head underwater a familiar activity, her brain's alarm signal for danger was no longer activated. Sarah could not have talked herself into this position and neither could her well-meaning mother. She had to do the thing that she was afraid of, over and over, to stop the alarm from sounding in her head. Talking helped and support helped, but in the end Sarah had to do the very thing that frightened her to stop feeling afraid. The same principles in the Anxiety Cure work for normal fear like Sarah's and for pathological fear seen in anxiety disorders. The main difference is in the magnitude and duration of the problem. Sarah was able to get right to work with her mother to conquer her fear. If she had a phobia of water, the process would have been the same, but it would have taken much longer and required more gradual exposure. Talking about water might have been a beginning, for example, instead of Sarah's ability to get into the water right away.

Normal childhood fears are age appropriate and more common than phobic fears. Children can have normal fear and anxiety or pathological fear and anxiety the same way adults can. Look back to Part Two, Chapter 4, The Vocabulary of Anxiety, to review the difference between normal and pathological fear and anxiety. Talking about anxiety can be difficult for children, so they will often express their distress by crying, freezing up, clinging, and having tantrums. Sometimes parents mistake anxiety for bad behavior. The difference is clear when you see how much a child who is anxious is suffering from the anxiety. The tantrums are the outgrowth of terror, not the result of willful disobedience. Punishment will not help a child overcome fear; it will only lower the already low self-esteem of the fearful child.

The Seven Anxiety Disorders in Children

Children can have the same types of anxiety problems that are seen in adults. Many adults with anxiety disorders realize that their problems began when they were very young. Often adults say, "I have *always* been a nervous person." This is why it is so important to begin to help a child learn how to cure anxiety *now* and not wait for the problem to become a part of his or her identity. The main anxiety diagnoses in children are: *separation anxiety disorder (SAD); agoraphobia/panic disorder (PD); generalized anxiety disorder (GAD); specific phobias; social phobia; obsessive-compulsive disorder (OCD);* and *posttraumatic stress disorder (PTSD).* These are the same as the list of anxiety disorders for adults in Chapter 6, The Six Anxiety Disorders, with the addition of separation anxiety disorder.

Separation Anxiety Disorder (SAD)

Unlike the developmentally normal anxiety of the ten-month-old child being left with the baby-sitter, children with SAD have a persistent pattern of becoming severely anxious and upset when separated from a trusted adult or situation. There are many ways that the children may demonstrate their distress, for example, crying, whining, having nightmares, or reporting physical symptoms like nausea or stomachaches. Children with SAD not only worry about their own safety but also about the safety of the people they care about. They may be afraid to leave their family, even for a short time, because they worry that they will never see them alive again. This can lead to fears of everyday activities like going to school. The anxiety can start long before the actual separation, simply in anticipation of being apart in the future.

Fear of Separation

Roger was a seven-year-old boy whose mother brought him to see his pediatrician because she was at her wit's end. She had been unable to leave Roger with a baby-sitter, or even his grandparents, for a year. Before an evening out, she would carefully plan ahead by arranging for all of Roger's favorite foods and activities. She tried several techniques. She tried telling him a few days in advance, hoping he would be calmer if he knew what to expect. At other times, she tried to slip out quietly while he was busy. Either way was a disaster. If she told him in advance, he would beg and plead for her to cancel her plans. He would cry and say he was afraid she would die and never come back. If she persisted in her plan to leave, he would complain of a stomachache, and one time he even vomited. If she tried the technique of slipping out unnoticed, he would scream and cry, causing the baby-sitter great distress. On several occasions, the baby-sitter called the restaurant and told the parents she could not console Roger and they had to come home. Whenever Roger's mother did try to leave him, she had a miserable time because of her own feelings of guilt and anxiety.

Panic Disorder/Agoraphobia (PD)

Panic disorder results in recurring panic attacks (see Chapter 5, The Six Anxiety Disorders), which lead to worry about having future panic attacks and the worry that a panic attack may cause the anxious person to die, go crazy, or lose control. Panic attacks are periods of intense fear that may be associated with a number of different physical symptoms. Agoraphobia is the fear of being helpless and alone while perceiving great inner danger. This leads to avoidance of situations in which the person is outside of his or her familiar territories or away from a trusted person.

Panic Strikes

Ron was an eighteen-year-old boy who was brought to see a therapist by his mother. He'd had a panic attack for the first time six weeks before. It was a terrible and frightening experience. His mother had taken him to his pediatrician, who did an electrocardiogram (EKG) to check Ron's heart and laboratory tests to check his blood. The results of all of the tests were normal, and the doctor assured them that nothing was wrong. Ron had several more panic attacks and had started skipping school. He spent most of his time in his room because he was afraid that he was going to die.

Specific Phobia

A specific phobia involves an extreme, unrealistic fear that is not logical and not shared by most people. People with a specific phobia will go to great lengths to avoid the situation that they fear. Children with specific phobias worry in anticipation of encountering the situation or object, and they may express their fear in nonverbal ways. These tantrums or outbursts have an intensity that is often frightening to the adults around them. The magnitude of the distress is clearly out of proportion to the danger—a signal that the dragon is at work. Many adults trace the origins of their specific phobia to childhood.

There are five categories or types of specific phobias:

Animal: fear and avoidance of a type of animal
Natural/environmental: fear and avoidance of environmental processes like thunder, storms, or heights
Blood/injection/injury: fear and avoidance of seeing blood or having an injury or having an invasive medical procedure

Situational: fear and avoidance of a specific situation, like flying, tunnels, or enclosed places
Other: fear and avoidance of another stimuli

Dog Terror

Suzie was an outgoing five-year-old girl who had not had a lot of exposure to dogs. She became terrified of dogs after being bitten by a dog at her best friend's house. At first she was just frightened of going to the same house in which she was bitten. This was a big enough problem, since she refused to go back to her best friend's house.

Several weeks later she refused to go to her aunt's house for dinner because her aunt had a dog. This was unusual because she had never been bothered by the aunt's dog before and had visited her house many times. She then began refusing to go to other people's houses because "there might be a dog there." Her mother also noticed that Suzie was playing inside the house more than before, and Suzie mentioned that several of the neighbors had dogs. Her mother reminded Suzie that the neighborhood dogs were kept on leashes or in fenced yards, but Suzie said, "They might escape," and refused to go outside. When Suzie's mother tried to force her to go to the aunt's house several times, she cried and threw terrible tantrums, an unusual occurrence for her. After they arrived at the aunt's house, Suzie clung to her mother and refused to go and play with her cousins.

Social Phobia

The child with social phobia suffers from pathological fears and avoidance of a social situation or situations. The anxious child fears he or she will do something that will be embarrassing or humiliating. This leads to the person limiting his or her social experiences. An important distinction between social phobia and other types of problems is that children with social phobia are able to have normal, appropriate social relationships with familiar people. School, however, can be very difficult, as the socially phobic child fears being called upon in class, or being teased in the cafeteria or playground.

Sick at School

Tom was a thirteen-year-old boy who was just starting ninth grade at the public high school. He had gone to small elementary and junior high schools where most of the kids were from his neighborhood. He became exceedingly anxious about going to school after he learned that his best friend would not be in his class with him. On the first day of class, the new teacher asked each student to give his or her name and tell which school he or she had attended the previous year. Tom's heart was in his throat as the other kids began to follow this direction. As it got closer to his turn, he thought his chest would burst. He was afraid that he would miss his turn because he could hardly hear over the rushing noise in his ears. When it was his turn, he choked out his name, but his voice cracked when he said the name of his school. Tom heard somebody giggle as he sank into his seat in humiliation.

The next day he told his mother he was sick and stayed home from school. By the afternoon he was bored and went outside to ride his bike. His mom figured he was better and said she was glad he would not have to miss another day. He went back to school, but his grades slipped. He spent so much time worrying about what would happen if the teacher called on him that he often did not listen to her talk. Tom was also afraid that other kids had heard about his humiliation on the first day, so he was slow to make friends and did not join any extracurricular activities.

Generalized Anxiety Disorder (GAD)

GAD is a general pathological anxiety that causes excessive worry and tension. This chronic worry prevents a child from really being able to enjoy his or her life. Almost every aspect of life is subject to "what-if" worries for the child with GAD. GAD is *not* accompanied by panic attacks, phobic avoidance, pathological shyness, or obsessions and compulsions.

Worried All the Time

Ian was a bright seven-year-old boy who was a chronic worrier. He was particularly nervous about making mistakes at school and had a difficult time completing assignments because he was afraid his work was not good enough. He worried not only that he would mess up but about his classmates' success as well. On one occasion his class performed a play before the entire school. For weeks before the play he could talk about nothing except the many concerns he had about the play, his role, and the performance of his classmates. He was so tense and irritable that his parents asked the teacher to excuse him from the play. The teacher refused because she felt Ian needed to be more self-confident. One of the girls made a mistake in the dress rehearsal, and Ian stayed awake that night, worrying that she would make the same mistake the next day. He was very critical of his own performance, and on the way home from the play he told his father that he had ruined the play because he had said his line too quickly.

Obsessive-Compulsive Disorder (OCD)

Obsessions are unwanted and intrusive thoughts, often of a violent nature. Compulsions are repetitive behaviors or thoughts that one feels driven to complete to reduce the anxiety associated with the obsession. The obsessions and compulsions are unreasonable, although younger children may not realize this.

"Just Right"

Lee was a nine-year-old boy who was brought to see a child psychiatrist by his parents. They said that Lee was having severe "behavior problems at bedtime." They explained that it took two hours to get Lee to sleep on most nights. Lee needed all of the elements of his complicated bedtime ritual to be "just right" before he could go to sleep. One or both of the parents were involved in the time-consuming process. He needed the bedtime story read in a particular way, he needed the closet to be opened and checked for intruders and then firmly closed, he needed the bed to be made tightly so it had no wrinkles and his arm or leg could not be outside of the covers, he needed a glass of water (with ice), he needed the door to be left open at a certain angle, and at least one parent must remain upstairs with him while he went to sleep.

If any element of the ritual was not "just right," they would have to start all over again. He would become anxious and increasingly angry at his parents if he felt they had done something wrong. Nighttime became a battleground, with Lee and his parents often deteriorating into yelling and the other siblings into whining about the disturbance.

Posttraumatic Stress Disorder (PTSD)

This anxiety disorder can occur in people of any age who have been exposed to a traumatic situation in which they were in serious danger, or they saw somebody else in serious danger. The trauma is reexperienced in recurrent memories, dreams, or behavior. For example, some children reenact the trauma in play. The person develops phobic avoidance of thoughts, people, or places that are associated with the trauma and may have an increased startle response. Many people with PTSD have difficulty sleeping or concentrating.

Aftermath of the Crash

Sam was a five-year-old who lived with his mother until she was killed in a car crash. He had been in the car with her during the accident but was not injured. He went to live with his grandmother after the accident. Sam had frequent nightmares in which he would wake up, calling "Mommy," but at other times he would not talk about her. He played with toy cars, by himself, for hours. He ran the cars into one another and would say, "Call an ambulance!" His grandmother became very worried about him and brought him to see a social worker when he refused to ride in the car pool to school.

Can You "Give" Your Child an Anxiety Disorder?

Some parents with anxiety disorders worry that they will "give" their child anxiety, either through genetics or by teaching the child to be anxious. It is true that anxiety disorders do run in families. There are many reasons for this, with genetics playing a big role. You cannot choose to give your child the gene for your eye color and you cannot choose *not* to give them your gene for an anxiety disorder. You have a lot of responsibilities as a parent, but this is not one of them! The things you can affect are how you treat anxiety in your life (kids learn from watching their parents) and how you help then understand anxiety in their lives. Most children of chronically anxious parents never develop an anxiety disorder.

Helping Your Anxious Child

You are already helping your child simply by educating yourself about anxiety disorders. This is the case whether you, your child, or both of you suffer from clinically significant anxiety. You can help your child whether he or she has an anxiety disorder or normal anxiety. Sarah's mom helped Sarah overcome her normal fear of going underwater, and in doing so, she helped her not only get one step closer to swimming but also taught her skills to overcome the many fears Sarah will encounter in the future. It may be helpful for your child to hear some stories about other children who have had anxiety problems. You might want to read to your child Chapter 1 of this book, Caroline's Story: Anxiety Is My Companion, or some of the case histories from this section.

Dragon!

If your child is having significant difficulties with anxiety, you can teach him or her about the dragon (see Chapter 8, Understanding the Anxiety Dragon). The concept of the dragon was first developed by a child, although many adults have found it a useful way of thinking about their fear. Most kids can easily imagine their fear as a dragon. Working with children who have panic attacks helps us understand the dragon because kids are so much more open in expressing their feelings and describing their experiences than are most adults.

One eleven-year-old boy named his dragon Antwerp. The boy's best friend was named Antoine, which was part of the reason he gave the dragon the name Antwerp. He told us, "The other reason I picked that name was to let the dragon know that I was not afraid of him. I did not want to call him a 'twerp' because he might think I did not respect him. So I called him 'Antwerp,' a name that showed him a mixture of friendship and respect, but which also put him in his place." You might want to help your child pick a name. Just naming the dragon can be the first step in getting control.

False Alarm

Another idea that can be helpful is that of a false alarm. Most children have had fire drills at school, which can be used to help them understand their feelings of anxiety and panic. If the fire alarm goes off at school, everybody has to behave as if it is a real emergency. Children file outside in lines, the classroom door is closed, the teacher takes roll call, and sometimes the firefighters have to check the school before anyone is let back inside. All that activity even though there was no emergency! Anxiety and panic are like a false alarm in the body. Help your child understand what the body's normal response to fear is. You could ask him or her, "How do you feel when something really scares you? For example, how would you feel if somebody jumped out at you in the dark? Would your heart beat fast? Would your hands sweat? Would your breathing become irregular and your chest feel tight?" Explain that these physical sensations are the body's way of sending out the signal that there is an emergency. When the dragon pulls the alarm, your child's body responds as if it really were a real emergency. His or her heart will beat faster, and he or she will feel frightened, but there is no real emergency. You can reassure your child that the alarm does not go off for very long and the frightening feelings cannot hurt him or her. Once your child understands false alarms, the dragon has lost a lot of his punch and a lot of his ability to cage your child with fear.

The Worry Machine

The worry machine was discussed in Chapter 8, Understanding the Anxiety Dragon. This is another concept that is understandable for children as well as for adults. Anxiety is like having a big worry machine in your head. It cranks out worry, after worry, after worry! Sometimes the worries are things that a nonanxious child would worry about, but at other times the worry machine gets your child worrying about things that normally would not concern him or her.

Ian, the seven-year-old in the "Worried All the Time" example of GAD, spent weeks worrying about the class play. Several weeks after the play was over he told his mother he was sad they were not going to perform another play that year. Surprised, his mother said, "You did nothing but worry about the play." Now it was Ian's turn to be surprised. "Yeah, but I liked acting!" Ian's worry machine had been so busy, it had tried to turn a fun activity into a miserable one.

Does an Anxious Child Become an Anxious Adult?

There is a lot of interest in this topic, but not a lot is known yet. Many anxious adults report that their anxiety began in childhood, but many anxious children do not have anxiety disorders as adults. There is no way to look into the future to see what will become of your child's anxiety. The old adage "Expect the best, but prepare for the worst" can be useful.

If you give your child the skills and confidence to cope with his or her anxiety in the present, then you have done a great deal to help him or her in the future, even if the anxiety disorder remains or returns. These skills are useful even if your child "outgrows" anxiety. Remember that the goal is a cure from the anxiety disorders, and that means a life that is full and free from anxiety-induced restrictions.

A Word to Other Concerned Adults
(Teachers, Coaches, etc.)

This section has been directed toward parents, but it applies to you, also. If you notice anxiety problems in a child you care about, you can help. Imagine how Tom's situation (the boy in the example of social phobia) might have been different if his teacher had noticed his fear of talking in class. The teacher may have been able to intervene early to help Tom manage his fear. Help can take many forms. It might be just a few extra sessions with an anxious student, or it might be a call to his or her parents. You can refer the family to *The Anxiety Cure* or one of the other good books now available to help them understand anxiety disorders. Treatment with a therapist or psychiatrist is another good option.

The Anxiety Cure Works for Kids, Too

The same principles and lessons explained in this book that work for adults, work for kids, too. You may need to modify the lessons for young children. A parent is usually the most obvious and appropriate support person. However, if a parent is not able to be the support person, then a teacher, neighbor, or other relative may be appropriate. Refer to Chapter 11, How to Be a Support Person, for more help in making this decision. You also need to be sure that you break the practice steps into manageable steps for your anxious child. What seems easy for you may be overwhelming to your child. Do not hesitate to get help from a therapist or doctor if you are uncertain, if you are not making progress, or if the problem is placing the child in any danger (including the danger of failing school). A professional can assess the situation with you and help guide you. He or she may recommend medicines. The same medicines that are discussed in Chapter 7, Medicines and Anxiety, can be used safely and effectively by children.

While smaller children may require lower doses of most medicines than adults require, younger livers are more effective at metabolizing medicines, so children often require the same doses of antianxiety medication that adults use. The decision about dose, as well as the choice of medicine, is best made by your child's doctor.

CHAPTER 25

Anxiety and Aging

Although anxiety disorders affect people of all ages from early childhood until death, the older anxious person faces several specific problems. We use the term "older" because these problems may be encountered at any age from midlife on and are not just a concern for the elderly. An anxious person who has a disability from a car accident at age thirty faces some of the same dilemmas as a much older retiree. The dilemmas of aging and anxiety revolve around the realities of human mortality. For the anxious person, any sign of physical decline is an opportunity for the worry machine to spin out of control, predicting terrible problems in the immediate future. This process of fear of bodily decline makes aging a time fraught with the potential for upsurges in anxiety. Additionally, friends and family can be hard-pressed to cope, as there is often some basis to the worry at this stage of life. Most families marshal resources of time and money to solve the presenting medical and/or social problems of aging without realizing that in many cases it is worry, not declining health, that cripples the aging anxious person.

Unfortunately, focusing on the anxious person's physical health is like reassuring him or her that nothing is wrong. It leads the anxious person to try harder to convince those around him or her that something *is* wrong, since he or she feels so bad emotionally. This leads friends and family to feel exhausted by the endless expressions of worry that know no end and that fail to respond to reasonable reassurances.

For example, Charles was a fifty-two-year-old executive at a major corporation. He earned a good salary, his social life was based on business acquaintances, and he looked forward to retiring at sixty with a nice pension. Charles had been a worried person all his life. His worry was helpful at work as it made him detail oriented, punctual, and determined to produce a good result. Without warning, his corporation was purchased in a hostile takeover, and he lost his job with no severance package and no prospect of a pension for many years. His wife had worked part-time, but when Charles lost his job, she quickly picked up more hours and was gone from home all day during the workweek. Charles found himself alone at home and overwhelmed with his unleashed worry. He could not find a job in his field. He realized that being hired as a middle-aged executive was unlikely. A year after he was fired, Charles began to deliver pizzas in the evening to earn some extra money and to leave his days free for developing his own consulting business. The consulting business was slow to develop, so he spent most of his time sitting alone at his desk at home, worrying and obsessively sorting bills and papers.

Charles's wife sought help for him, as she found his anxiety and depression to be unbearable. Finally seeking help for problems he no longer thought he could handle on his own, Charles used the Anxiety Cure techniques along with medicine to reduce his anxiety and depression. After several months of treatment, he developed a new way of looking at his life. It was not the happy life he had dreamed of—a life leading to retirement, playing golf, and a second home in a retirement community. That dream was gone. Charles saw that he now had years of freedom that he had never expected. He began to plan how to use the time to his best advantage and to see this crisis as an opportunity for a new, good life. He accepted what had happened to him and looked for the real opportunities this unchosen life had for him and his wife. When he did that, he was able to help more at home (a role reversal that pleased both him and his wife), and he enjoyed the new experiences his fledgling consulting business brought to him. He spent more time with his children and grandchildren.

Retirement

Retirement is imagined by most people to be a golden time—the light at the end of the tunnel of work. Freedom from financial worries, child-rearing tasks, the drudgery of work, and all the time in the world to pursue leisure activities. The tanned, fit senior playing golf on a beautiful green with a group of healthy friends is a common fantasy. Yet for most anxious people, the reality of retirement is a world away from this idyllic picture. The jobs and responsibilities of work life, as well as responsibilities for children, that were imagined to be the causes of anxiety suddenly are gone.

Many anxious retirees are devastated when, with the increased open time, their anxiety levels soar. External responsibilities helped contain their anxiety. With those responsibilities gone, anxiety has free rein to dominate your whole life. You have more time to feed the dragon with your worries.

As you can see from other parts of this chapter, suddenly new sources of anxiety are present in your life as you age. They join the familiar stable of worries that have been with you throughout your life. The added worries of retirement are a shock to most people, causing embarrassment as friends and family who are still working enviously assume you are having the time of your life. And what explanations for this unhappiness can you offer? No one seems to listen or to take your worries seriously, even though they feel so real to you.

Some people who have never had significant trouble with anxiety find retirement triggers the onset of their anxiety disorder. Some people immediately return to the workforce to once again blame anxious feelings on job stress and to contain anxiety with ever-present responsibilities. Others give in to the anxiety and lose precious years to worry and the demands of the voracious dragon. We suggest that retirement be viewed as an opportunity for practicing your antianxiety techniques on many fronts. Especially use the ideas in Part Four, Chapter 18, Step 7, Structure Your Life without Anxiety, and work to build your own dragon armor specifically tailored for this part of your life.

This is your life, not the dragon's. Do not let him convince you that there is a reason he must have your life now. Whatever is going on in your life—whatever sadness, physical problems, or financial concerns—the worry machine will make it worse if you let it. Do not be ashamed of the troubles retirement causes for you, and do not hide them from people who care about you. This does you and them no good. Simply talking about your fear of fear can help you sort out the real worries from the exaggerated worries and can reduce your anxiety tremendously.

What is the difference between "real" worries and "exaggerated" worries? Real worries are ones that a nonanxious person in the same situation would have. Real worries are solvable problems that respond to practical solutions. Exaggerated worries are worries that nonanxious people would not have in similar settings. Exaggerated worries are not solvable in practical ways. They flourish regardless of practical steps to reduce them. You can work on your anxiety and bring your retirement closer to the idyllic experience you had hoped for if you build working on your anxiety into your retirement plans. Use your anxiety as a springboard.

The Elderly and Medicines

As with other types of medicines, there are special considerations for people age sixty-five and over using medicines for anxiety. *Usually, the same medicines that are useful for younger people with anxiety will be useful for older people as well, but elderly people may need lower doses.* See the table on page 224 for typical dosages of antianxiety medicines for older people. You will need to be monitored more closely by your prescribing doctor than a younger person because side effects can be more serious. For example, the drowsiness that can accompany using a benzodiazepine can lead to a fall, which could have devastating consequences for an older person (such as a fractured hip).

Be sure to talk to your doctor about any special concerns that you have before you begin taking medicine, and report side effects promptly so adjustments in dosages can be made. Also be sure to tell all your doctors what medicines you are taking to avoid problems of drug interactions. If you are taking any medicine, whether a prescription or an over-the-counter medicine, check with your doctor before taking any other medicine, even if you have used the medicine previously.

On the other hand, it is important not to shy away from using medicines if that is what you and your doctor decide would be best for you. There is no reason to try to tough out the anxiety problem. You will not get extra credit for not using a medicine. The goal of the Anxiety Cure is for you to live a full life without restriction because of anxiety. If you can do that without a medicine, great. If you cannot do that, then you are probably unwise to forgo using the medicine simply because you are older or because you do not want to use a medicine. Even worse, if you are morbidly afraid of taking a medicine, you are giving in to the dragon. Review the risks and benefits of medicine in Part Four, Chapter 17, Step 6, Evaluate Your Need for Medicines and Therapy in Your Anxiety Cure, with your friends and family prior to assuming that medicine is not for you. If you are having troubles that are related to anxiety, such as difficulty concentrating, medicines may significantly improve your problems.

Fear of Death

Worry about death is a problem for many anxious people of all ages. This problem is especially likely to strike later in life as you begin to have more people close to you die, and as your own inevitable death approaches. Death, which felt almost impossibly remote as a young adult, can feel frighteningly close as you age. Death is the ultimate loss of control. Death feels lonely—you are alone in death. The prospect of being in a coffin, even in death, may seem terribly claustrophobic. These typically anxious fears are all the more troubling to many anxious people because they are so obviously unreasonable.

You may worry that your physical symptoms of anxiety mean that there is something wrong with you that your doctors cannot find. One patient who had this type of worry said that she had a "cardiac neurosis." Yet having a severe case of this fear of anxious symptoms can make you feel as if you are almost dead already because you are so constrained by what you can and cannot do because of anxiety. People with OCD commonly have terrible images of death and feel that if they do not do their rituals, then horrible things will happen to them or their loved ones. These fixations on death are all the more horrible because you fear death so terribly. It is clearly one more example of how the dragon can scare you better than any horror movie because the terror is made by your own brain to control you with your own worst fears.

You will die. All living things will die. Accept death—your death—to free yourself from the fear of death, so you can live whatever life you are fortunate enough to have.

If you spend all of your time worrying about your anxiety, there is no room to enjoy being alive. What, then, is there really to fear in death if you are hardly living your life now because of anxiety? You will be dead a long time, and worrying about death will simply diminish the possibility of enjoying the life that is left to you.

We have seen over and over the delight a person who has suffered from anxiety problems can feel when the anxiety is under control. Mark, a sixty-year-old lifelong agoraphobic, said he felt reborn as a nonanxious person when he worked with the Anxiety Cure. He felt sad about the years of his life he had spent trapped by his fears, but mostly he felt awed by the chance to spend the remainder of his life without those terrible fears.

Mark was like a kid in a candy store—life offered so many wonderful possibilities he could hardly decide where to start.

Tips for Friends and Family

If an older friend or relative has anxiety symptoms, you may have struggled to know how to approach the problem or how to seek help. Perhaps you knew that anxiety was a problem for years, but now it seems worse than ever. This may be simply an unmasking of an old problem. If, as sometimes happens, this is a brand-new problem in an elderly person, there may be a physical cause of anxiety. In this case, it is important to point out your concern to the anxious person's doctor so medical evaluations can be made.

Many people who are past midlife will resist acknowledging the problem that they have with anxiety. Often it is such a long-standing problem that it seems not only unchangeable but also to be an intrinsic part of the person. The anxiety problem may have some medical basis (like a heart condition) that makes the anxious person believe the problem warrants the amount of worry and attention that is devoted to it.

You as a supportive friend can be of great assistance in gently helping your anxious person see that he or she does not need to feel so bad. Try to help your anxious person see that the potential gains justify the effort needed to make a change. If using the Anxiety Cure, or seeing a therapist, or trying a medicine do not help, what has possibly been lost by trying? And there is much to gain when it succeeds. A new perspective can reveal just how wonderful life is again, or in some cases, for the first time. Sympathize with your anxious person about the terrible feelings anxiety produces. Physical ailments are difficult, and aging can be painful and distressing. But there is nothing so bad that worry will not make it worse.

Typical Doses of Medications Used to Treat Anxiety in Adults (Ages 65 and Older)

Antidepressants	Dosage
fluoxetine (Prozac)	5–10 mg/day
imipramine (Tofranil)	25–100 mg/day
fluvoxamine (Luvox)	50–150 mg/day
nefazodone (Serzone)	100–300 mg/day
paroxetine (Paxil)	5–20 mg/day
sertraline (Zoloft)	25–100 mg/day
venlafaxine (Effexor)	75–150 mg/day

Benzodiazepines	Dosage
alprazolam (Xanax)	0.25 mg 1 to 3 times/day
clonazepam (Klonopin)	0.25 mg 1 to 3 times/day
clorazepate (Tranxene)	3.75–7.5 mg 1 to 3 times/day
diazepam (Valium)	2 mg 1 to 3 times/day
lorazepam (Ativan)	0.5 mg 1 to 3 times/day
oxazepam (Serax)	10–15 mg 1 to 3 times/day

PART SEVEN

Maintenance

CHAPTER 26

Setbacks and Springboards

Panic and anxiety tend to wax and wane over time, with some periods of the sufferer's life being characterized by minor or even nonexistent anxiety problems and other periods being characterized by severe or even crippling symptoms of anxiety. Big upsurges of anxious symptoms often lead to setbacks, times when things that had once seemed easy become terribly difficult. Every one of these distressing experiences of relapse leading to heightened symptoms of anxiety is an opportunity for new growth. That is why we call them springboards, because these setbacks are opportunities for dramatic movement forward. Seeing a difficult experience as a challenge and a chance to grow comes in many forms.

Expect Anxiety to Return

Sue's experience offers a wonderful chance to examine in detail the way a setback in anxiety can turn into a springboard for further learning. Sue is thirty-six years old and has had anxiety problems for most of her life. She has suffered from GAD and has had several bad flare-ups of phobias. She was a diligent follower of the Anxiety Cure method, and after a period of hard work, she had regained control of her life. Then for about a year she had spent only brief periods of time working at reducing her anxiety.

One evening Sue was in the passenger seat as her husband drove to the grocery store. Suddenly Sue banged on the dashboard, yelling, "I am not cured!" She told her husband that her panic and anxiety had returned with a vengeance, and she was angry at the arrogance of any therapist who would tell her that this was a normal way to feel. Sue's husband was understandably concerned at this sudden outburst. He asked her to breathe deeply so he could concentrate on his driving until they reached the grocery store parking lot. They sat in the parking lot and reviewed what had provoked Sue's outburst and her increased anxiety.

Notice how Sue, even when she was completely frustrated by her painful feelings of anxiety, was able to reach out to her husband for help. Notice also the sign of a loving, trained support person in the way her husband refocused the experience on the here and now and the short term, asking her to be quiet for safety's sake and to work on breathing only until the parking lot was reached, a few minutes away. In this brief interaction, you can see the calming effect of the outreach and response even before their more formal reevaluation occurred.

In the Anxiety Cure we ask you to rate your anxiety level from 0 (no anxiety) to 10 (the worst anxiety you ever had). This interlude allowed Sue to reduce her anxiety from a level 8 to a level 5 prior to the time they reached the parking lot.

Once Sue and her husband began to review the problem, they quickly assessed Sue's anxiety level and agreed that, at a level 5, they could continue to talk without stopping to calm the anxiety before they began to figure out the problem and the solution. Sue's husband noted that there were a number of different reasons for her anxiety to be more active and intense at this time. This seemed to be a reasonable time for the panic dragon to be more aggressive, given how much was going on in Sue's life. Sue's husband listed the following reasons for her increased anxiety:

1. Sue had arrived home from work late and had not yet eaten dinner, which they knew from past experience always made it harder for her to deal with anxiety.

2. It was the night before her final day of work prior to a promotion into a new department. Even good changes were always hard for Sue, as her worry machine pumped out every possible problem she might encounter in the new, unfamiliar situation.

3. In her present department, it was traditional for each employee who was departing because of a promotion to bake and bring in a fancy cake on the final day of work as a farewell gesture. People in the department competed about bringing in fancy "farewell" cakes. Sue had talked all week about her worry that her offering would not measure up to the lavish work of others.

4. Sue and her husband usually enjoyed biking together three or four times a week for exercise, but they had not managed to find time for

biking during the last week. Not having a physical outlet for her tension had made it hard for Sue to sleep at night and added to her anxiety.

5. Sue had not slept well for two nights, complaining when she woke in the morning that she did not feel refreshed. She also had nightmares. Not sleeping well made her feel tired and slower at work, and that meant she had worked longer hours to compensate for feeling groggy during the day.

You can see from her husband's summary of this setback how, in hindsight, it was almost inevitable. Each contributing factor laid the groundwork for another part of the anxiety problem. Sue's carefully worked out anxiety reducers had been put aside the previous week without thought of the likely consequences.

Sue agreed with her husband's assessment. However, she was unable to sort out all those factors herself when she was in the middle of a setback. This was normal, even for someone who has been "cured" of his or her anxiety. Remember, when your anxiety is over about a level 6, it is hard to get any perspective on yourself. What is needed is exactly what Sue did—reach out to your support person, family member, friend, or therapist. The two of you together can more quickly reactivate the techniques you have learned from all of your hard work.

Remember at a time like this that your hard work has not been useless. Notice how, within minutes of her peak anxiety, Sue was once again in control because she knew the cause of her anxiety and the solutions to the problem. This was enormous progress for Sue and her husband.

For most people who suffer from anxiety without the Anxiety Cure method, this outburst of Sue's would have resulted in increased anxiety for her, and her husband would have been frightened and unsure of what to do. They would not have come up with good solutions to a problem they did not understand. In fact, they could easily have reached several erroneous conclusions that would have made all of the five problems listed above even worse. For example, they could have gone right home without getting any food at the grocery store, and instead of eating, they could have sat up far into the night worrying together about why Sue was so upset. Sue's husband could have become angry at her as well as scared, and that would have further upset them both and driven them further apart, worsening both of their problems.

Specific Solutions to a Specific Anxiety Problem

Here were the good solutions to these problems that Sue and her husband came up with together:

Solution 1. Instead of buying food that needed to be prepared, Sue and her husband got take-out sandwiches and sodas from the deli counter. They also got a quick-to-fix dinner for the following night so they would not again arrive home to find nothing to eat.

Solution 2. Sue spent a few minutes over dinner focusing on the sadness she felt about leaving her old job and her former coworkers and the fear she felt at facing a new, more challenging job. She had been afraid to share these feelings before, but she knew that talking about something frightening helped her not to have nightmares.

Solution 3. Sue bought a prepared cake at the store, and she did not stay up late baking, as she had planned to do. She had been worried about how her store-bought cake would be viewed by her coworkers, but the type of cake actually received less attention than she had recalled from previous parties, and it was eaten quickly. No one commented on the fact that she had not spent time baking it.

Solution 4. Sue and her husband, with their purchased sandwiches and sodas, went on a short bike ride to a local park and had a picnic. They promised each other that they would take a longer ride on the weekend and set a day and time so they would not forget.

Solution 5. Lack of sleep had been an ongoing problem that Sue felt she had not fully resolved prior to this flare-up in her anxiety. She had recently bought a yoga videotape and resolved to try yoga prior to going to bed on nights she felt anxious to see if that would help her get a more restful night's sleep. She planned to leave on time from work the following day instead of staying late to do final wrap-ups on work-related projects, which she knew she probably would have done without this setback.

By reaching out for help when anxiety reappeared and by sticking with the lessons she had learned from her work with the Anxiety Cure, Sue was able to turn an anxious moment into a pleasant evening. She was not anxiety free, but anxiety at level 3 or 4 seemed reasonable and manageable to her, given that she was going through an understandably stressful time. Handling this stress well, and even adding the future plan of yoga to her regular routine, turned this setback into a springboard of increased self-confidence for more future success for Sue and into an improved relationship with her husband.

Most people with anxiety and the family and friends who care about an anxious person will see that this example of a setback is common in terms of how it grew from a positive event—Sue's promotion. Many anxious people do almost anything to avoid change, even to the point of turning down promotions or awards for excellence. Anxiety is too often the driving force in an anxious person's life. The Anxiety Cure turns this around by looking not at the feelings of anxiety, but at the contributing factors and at the practical and positive solutions to lowering anxiety. In Sue's case, it is clear how this normalization of her feelings combined with some creative problem solving moved her quickly from anxious to able to enjoy her life. See Chapter 19, Step 8, of the Anxiety Cure for an outline to follow when you have a setback.

Sue's husband felt good after this setback. He had learned what to do to help Sue. He did it, and it worked for Sue and for him. Both Sue and her husband remembered the Anxiety Cure's definition of "cure"—knowing what is wrong and what to do about it. They concluded, with pride in their hard work and their achievements, that in just that sense not only was Sue cured, but so was her husband.

Last Words

Thank you for reading *The Anxiety Cure*. We hope you have found it helpful as you work on finding your own cure from anxiety disorders. Wherever you are with your care, at the frightening beginning, in the midst of a long difficult patch, or in the discouragement of a setback, there is hope for you. Keep your notebook ever ready so you can always learn from your past. Keep your eye on the goals you have so you know in what direction to move to make progress. Keep your worst moments in your memory so you can appreciate how far you have come. Above all, remember that by facing anxiety honestly and by practicing systematically you will know what is wrong and what to do about it—that is your cure. Good luck.

GLOSSARY

acceptance The one-word antidote to anxiety disorders. Accept the painful feelings and worried thoughts but do not accept avoidance as part of your life. Acceptance is active and difficult, it is not a passive or weak response to anxiety.

addiction Loss of control (initiated by continued use despite problems) and dishonesty (denial).

agoraphobia/panic disorder (PD) Spontaneous panic attacks coupled with situational panic as well as pathological anxiety, with or without significant avoidance. The fear of being alone when perceiving great inner danger.

anticipatory anxiety A type of pathological anxiety. The fear of panic feelings. Anticipatory anxiety often leads to avoidance (or phobia) of situations that are associated with panic.

anxiety The body's signal of possible future danger, an emotional early warning message.

avoidance The phobic response to stay away from panic-producing situations, even though you would do these things if you did not have anxiety.

cure Knowing what is wrong and knowing what to do about it. When anxiety no longer impedes your life.

depression A mental disorder characterized by feeling hopeless, helpless, and blue or despondent. May be a single episode, a chronic condition, or recurrent over many years.

desensitization Practice in a fear-generating situation so that the second fear is progressively reduced.

discomfort zone Anxiety is measured on a scale of 0 (no anxiety) to 10 (the worst anxiety possible). The discomfort zone represents midlevel anxiety of 4 to 7.

dragon The anxiety dragon personifies the fear of the fear, the second fear. This is a mythical creature. Dragons do not exist outside of thinking, and neither do anxiety disorders.

false alarm The brain-based first fear that causes the flood of anxious symptoms. These are normal bodily responses at an incorrect time.

first fear Biological surge in adrenaline that causes the physical symptoms of anxiety.

generalized anxiety disorder (GAD) General pathological anxiety without

233

panic attacks, phobic avoidance, or pathological shyness, as well as without obsessions and compulsions.

obsessive-compulsive disorder (OCD) Obsessions that are repugnant, unwanted, and intrusive thoughts leading to efforts to reduce this discomfort with compulsions, or ritual senseless behaviors, like checking or repeating a word or number over and over.

pathological anxiety Normal anxiety that occurs when there is no generally understandable danger.

posttraumatic stress disorder (PTSD) Intense fear after a traumatic event. Characterized by flashbacks to the event.

practice Voluntary, repeated exposure to the fear-generating situation.

quality people People who care about others and their feelings. Usually characteristic of people with anxiety disorders.

recovery The process of getting well from an anxiety disorder.

second fear Fear of the first fear, the biological flash of anxiety symptoms. Fear of the fear.

separation anxiety Fear of being apart from a safe person. A diagnosis of childhood anxiety disorders. Agoraphobia in adults is sometimes called adult separation anxiety, as the anxious person fears being away from a safe person if anxiety strikes.

setback A recurrence of panic and severe anxiety after a period of relatively mild, or even nonexistent, anxiety problems. A setback can be demoralizing if it is not expected. Accept and allow the panic to return. A setback can be a springboard to new growth and new learning.

situational panic A linked response of a specific situation to panic feelings. A biologically based brain response. A first fear that triggers further anxious thoughts and, usually, avoidance.

social phobia Fear, panic, and anxiety of embarrassment. May be limited to public speaking or may be part of a global shynes

specific phobia Fear and anxiety of panic in a specific situation, such as fear of heights, medical procedures, claustrophobia, or insects or snakes.

spontaneous panic A biologically based brain response. A first fear that triggers anxious thoughts that are not linked to any specific situation. "Out of the blue" panic.

stress Any change is stressful because it means a new mental and physical adaptation. Stress can be painful, but it also can lead to growth.

support person Any person who is chosen by a person with an anxiety disorder to help with practice sessions. A support person supports the process of recovery.

worry machine The characteristic of anxious people to focus on "what-if" problems in thinking about the future. The worry machine imagines only bad outcomes.

SUGGESTED ADDITIONAL
READING

Anxiety Disorders

Markway, B. G., C. N. Carmin, C. A. Pollard, T. Flynn. *Dying of Embarrassment—Help for Social Anxiety & Phobia*. Oakland, Calif.: New Harbinger Publications, Inc., 1995.

Ross, J. *Triumph over Fear—A Book of Help and Hope for People with Anxiety, Panic Attacks, and Phobias*. New York: Bantam Books, 1994.

Weekes, C. *Hope and Help for Your Nerves*. New York: Hawthorne Books, 1969.

_____. *Peace from Nervous Suffering*. New York: Hawthorne Books, 1972.

Wilson, R. R. *Don't Panic—Taking Control of Anxiety Attacks*, rev. ed. New York: Harper Perennial, 1996.

Zane, M. D., and H. Milt. *Your Phobia: Understanding Your Fears through Contextual Therapy*. Washington, D.C.: American Psychiatric Press, 1984.

Obsessive-Compulsive Disorder

Foa, E. B., and R. R. Wilson. *Stop Obsessing! How to Overcome Your Obsessions and Compulsions*. New York: Bantam Books, 1991.

Rapoport, J. L. *The Boy Who Couldn't Stop Washing—The Experience and Treatment of Obsessive-Compulsive Disorder*. New York: New American Library, 1989.

Schwartz, J. M., with B. Beyette. *Brain Lock—Free Yourself from Obsessive-Compulsive Behavior*. New York: HarperCollins Publishers, Inc., 1996.

Addiction/Problems with Alcohol and Other Drugs of Abuse

Cermak, T. L. *A Primer on Adult Children of Alcoholics*, 2d ed. Deerfield Beach, Fla.: Health Communications, Inc., 1989.

DuPont, R. L. *Getting Tough on Gateway Drugs: A Guide for the Family*. Washington, D.C.: American Psychiatric Press, 1984.

_____. *Getting Unhooked: A Guide to the Twelve-Step Programs*. Rockville, Md.: DuPont Associates, P.A., 1989.

_____. *The Selfish Brain: Learning from Addiction*. Washington, D.C.: American Psychiatric Press, 1997.

DuPont, R. L., J. P. McGovern. *A Bridge to Recovery—An Introduction to 12-Step Programs.* Washington, D.C.: American Psychiatric Press, 1994.

Ford, B., with C. Chase. *Betty—A Glad Awakening.* Garden City, N.Y.: Doubleday & Company, Inc., 1987.

Depression

Burns, D. D. *The Feeling Good Handbook.* New York: Penguin Books, 1989.

Family Relationships

Wolin, S. J., and S. Wolin. *The Resilient Self—How Survivors of Troubled Families Rise above Adversity.* New York: Villard Books, 1993.

Career Planning/Financial Planning/Money Problems

Bolles, R. N. *The 1997 What Color Is Your Parachute?* Berkeley, Calif.: Ten Speed Press, 1996.

Quinn, J. B. *Making the Most of Your Money: A Comprehensive Guide to Financial Planning.* New York: Simon & Schuster, 1991.

Medicines/Diagnoses

American Psychiatric Association. *Diagnostic and Statistical Manual of Mental Disorders (DSM-IV),* 4th ed. Washington, D.C.: American Psychiatric Association, 1994.

Appleton, W. S. *Prozac and the New Antidepressants.* New York: Plume (Penguin Books USA Inc.), 1997.

Medical Economics Data Production Company. *Physicians' Desk Reference (PDR).* Montvale, N.J.: Author, 1997.

Norden, M. J. *Beyond Prozac—Brain-Toxic Lifestyles, Natural Antidotes & New Generation Antidepressants.* New York: HarperCollins Publishers, Inc., 1995.

Religion/Spirituality and Getting Well

Adams, J. R. *So You Think You're Not Religious? A Thinking Person's Guide to the Church.* Cambridge, Mass.: Cowley Publications, 1989.

Kurtz, E., and K. Ketcham. *The Spirituality of Imperfection.* New York: Bantam, 1992.

Young, J. E., and J. S. Klosko. *Reinventing Your Life—How to Break Free from Negative Life Patterns and Feel Good Again.* New York: Plume (Penguin Books USA Inc.), 1994.

SELF-HELP PROGRAMS

We recommend comprehensive self-help programs to deal with anxiety disorders. Two excellent programs by Jerilyn Ross and R. Reid Wilson are listed below.

Ross, J. *Freedom from Anxiety: A Self-Help Program* (cassettes, a workbook, and a video). Washington, D.C.: The Ross Center for Anxiety and Related Disorders, 4545 Forty-second Street, N.W., Suite 311, Washington, D.C. 20016. Telephone 202-363-1010.

Wilson, R. R. *The Don't Panic Self-Help Kit—The Homework Guide to Conquering Your Fears.* Chapel Hill, N.C.: Pathway Systems, 1997. Telephone 800-394-2299.

RESOURCES

Many of the following organizations offer a wide variety of material on anxiety disorders, including general information, books, articles, and pamphlets. Write or call for further information and, where appropriate, local meeting times and locations of support groups. Support groups may also be available on-line at some Internet sites.

Anxiety and Phobia Treatment Center
The P.M. Newsletter
White Plains Hospital Center
Davis Avenue at East Post Road
White Plains, NY 10601
914-681-1038

Anxiety Disorders Association of America (ADAA)
6000 Executive Boulevard
Rockville, MD 20852
301-231-9350
http://www.ADAA.org

National Institute of Mental Health
Anxiety Disorders Education Program
http://www.nimh.nih.gov/anxiety

Emotions Anonymous (EA) International Services
P.O. Box 4245
St. Paul, MN 55104
612-647-9712

National Alliance for the Mentally Ill (NAMI)
200 North Glebe Road #1015
Arlington, VA 22203
703-524-7600

National Anxiety Foundation
3135 Custer Drive
Lexington, KY 40517-4001
606-272-7166
http://lexington-on-line.com/naf.html

National Panic/Anxiety Disorder (NPAD) Newsletter
Editorial Offices
NPAD, Inc.
1718 Burgundy Place, Suite B
Santa Rosa, CA 95403
707-527-5738

National Self-Help Clearinghouse
25 West Forty-third Street, Room 620
New York, NY 10036
212-642-2944

Obsessive-Compulsive Anonymous
P.O. Box 215
New Hyde Park, NY 11040
516-741-4901

Obsessive-Compulsive Disorder Foundation, Inc.
P.O. Box 70
Milford, CT 06460
203-878-5669

Recovery, Inc.
802 N. Dearborn Street
Chicago, IL 60610
312-337-5661

INDEX

ABOUT THE AUTHORS

Robert L. DuPont, M.D., has practiced psychiatry since he began his residency in 1964. He was the founding president of the Phobia Society of America, the organization that later became the Anxiety Disorders Association of America (ADAA). ADAA is the leading national advocacy group for the interests of people suffering from anxiety disorders. From 1973 to 1978 Dr. DuPont was the first director of the National Institute on Drug Abuse (NIDA), the federal government's principal treatment, research, and prevention agency dealing with drug abuse. He has been a leader in the fields of anxiety disorders and addiction for more than twenty-five years. Dr. DuPont graduated from the Harvard Medical School in 1963 and did his psychiatric training at Harvard. He is board certified in psychiatry and addiction medicine. He is clinical professor of psychiatry at Georgetown University School of Medicine.

Elizabeth DuPont Spencer, M.S.W., L.C.S.W.-C., graduated from the University of Maryland School of Social Work in 1992. Since that time she has worked in private practice and on clinical research with people who suffer from anxiety disorders.

Caroline McDonald DuPont, M.D., is a 1994 graduate of the University of Texas Medical School at Houston and completed her training in psychiatry at the Johns Hopkins University School of Medicine in Baltimore. Her special areas of interest are the anxiety disorders and depression.